EASTERN TIDES

ALSO BY FRANK DAIGNAULT

Twenty Years on the Cape: My Time as a Surfcaster

Striper Surf

Striper Hot Spots: The 100 Top Surfcasting Locations from New Jersey to Maine

The Trophy Striper

EASTERN TIDES

Frank Daignault

BURFORD BOOKS

Printed in the United States of America.

10   9   8   7   6   5   4   3   2   1

Library of Congress Cataloging-in-Publication Data
Daignault, Frank, 1936–
     Eastern tides / Frank Daignault.
          p.   cm.
     ISBN 1-58080-104-8 (hardcover)
     1. Striped bass fishing—Northeastern States—Anecdotes.
     2. Surf fishing—Northeastern States—Anecdotes.
     3. Daignault, Frank, 1936–   I. Title.
     SH691.S7 D34 2002
     799.1'7732'0974—dc21
                                        2002009222

Paperback   ISBN: 1-58080-123-4

CONTENTS

INTRODUCTION

OF FOUR PREVIOUS books I've written on the striper surf, among the most popular subjects is the better surf fishing of the past. It was made up of a number of factors: There were more fish; there was more access; and there were fewer sport fishers. Commercial fishing thirty or so years ago was a noble venture both inspired and heightened by our poverty. The law allowed it, while the ethics of carting fish in huge numbers to market were still in transition. Access to New England beaches, while threatened, was less restrictive. For the early years in the period, striper fishing was good enough to be profitable. However, the greatest motivation lay in the "sport" of seeking out this great gamefish, which added the forces of enigma to the mix. As rod-and-reel commercials, we were never able to separate fishing for the market—and its resultant remuneration—and the inspiration of sport that beckoned us. Lastly, never forget the influence of time in the formulation of *Eastern Tides*. We did our best fishing, made our most noble efforts, while we were both young enough to do it and hungry enough to dedicate ourselves to the mission.

One purpose of this book is to document the stormy period of striper management during a less enlightened moment in history. Indeed, the rise, fall, and subsequent recovery of the species plays out through its entire range twice, which shows how conditional are our planet's animals. Nevertheless, the most profound, most entertaining aspect of our fishing here is the stripers themselves, and how their presence and absence pulled the strings of surfcasting's puppets while still stoking the fires of an adventuresome spirit. Though oblivious to it all the while, just about everything we did was done to accommodate fishing the high surf.

Life is a continuous ribbon of frames that shape our movements, decisions, results, and end. These images spring from those around us, who inspire, advise, cajole, trick, delude, and misinform us to influence our passage. What is life and its experiences but an endless line of accidents? These misadventures, while providing some entertainment, are told here because they testify to the universal flaws in all of us.

In order to spare those described in this book, I have changed names and events to protect them. Literary license, some of the tools of fiction, and composite characters are in full play here for the same reasons. I've changed some names and places without—I hope—hurting the story. Time is compressed in places while stretched out in others. Keep in mind that life does not dole out adventures evenly spaced, nor does memory do them all justice. Everything is all still true.

Above all this is a fishing book about a difficult and demanding activity—surfcasting. Indeed, I hasten to distinguish fishing from boats and fishing from the shore, especially for money. Understand that if you want to catch a lot of fish, you should seek your quarry from boats. If you're serious in the pursuit of such fish, be wise enough to imitate biblical Peter, the fisherman, and use nets. Those people about whom you will read largely did neither. Rather, they juggled the demands of marriage, family, education, monetary survival, and fishing; but they forgot about time, our most overlooked resource.

After striped bass, the most influential character in this play is the family. Note the interplay between the children, their career choices, and the consequences of their chosen directions playing out while their parents stand by—almost powerless, it seems, to do much about it.

Read this in oilskins and waders, because these are the memoirs of a rod-and-reel commercial, the life-and-times book that I always wanted to write. If you don't occasionally want to stop to gaze into the pastels fading from an evening sun, I will have failed. And if after loaning this book to another surfcaster, you never see it again, it is a clear sign that I have succeeded; it has happened before.

ACKNOWLEDGMENTS

IN MY LIFE on the Striper Coast, I can now look back and clearly see how each person with whom I was acquainted influenced me in ways that I could never have anticipated. Life on the beach exerted some force upon my directions; striper numbers and the resultant fishing I experienced moved me from one beach to another, but the lead characters here are love and the striper surf.

Among those with true identities who must be acknowledged are: John Ashcroft for his advice; surfcasters "Muff" Briere, Red Hudson, Butch Calkins, George Carlezon, the late "Moose" Dobwado, Joe Croteau, and Nel Marquis for priceless surfcasting camaraderie, which was a joy to experience. The LaForest brothers, Joe, Richie, and Bob, for teaching me about surf cod. In P-Town Kenny at Seafood Packers for the accommodations he provided. Race Point Charley, USCG (Retired), who knew how to dance a runabout in the waves there. Evelyn Talvy for her sensitive remembrances of life in a buggy when I am sure we passed like ships in the night.

For his emergence twenty years after we had long forgotten him, Arno Groot with his moving and prayerful address to Union Congregational Church. We are fundamentally related, aren't we, Arno? Rear Admiral James P. Stewart, Commander First Coast Guard District, for his inspiring comments. The mid-1970s Coast Guard command of Woods Hole Group with the staff of Race Point Station. Coast Guard enlisted men David Kelley, Ned Rogean, and William Beard—all of whom, through their heroics, fortified our faith in humanity. My daughter, Commander Susan Daignault, USCG (Reserve), for her poignant insights on life as a swab at the academy and the CG cadet adventures at the Pensacola Naval Air Station "dunk tank." *Semper paratus.*

Please acknowledge, and I hope you can identify him, Rhode Island's Ray Jobin as the most profoundly gifted striperman on our coast. We hardly knew you, Ray. My brother, the late Norman Daignault, is remembered each and every day over a joke, a drink, or an errant cast. You bet.

I had to change the names of those who are now "Squid" Beaumont, PWB, Buck Henderson, Joe Crow, and "Disco" Danny. It breaks my heart to deny them their true identities but that is the world in which we live. Similarly, all the attorneys were given made-up names. I couldn't remember them anyway. But don't for a minute think that there were not such people in Joyce's and my lives. Your existence has cheated you if you have never known a "Squid" Beaumont or a PWB.

For his insight and experience with the torturous route a wounded soldier must wend from faraway and forgotten Vietnam, I am indebted to B. M. Geiger. Welcome home, Mr. Geiger—better late than never. For her guidance and dedication to language, usage, and literary skills, I am indebted to my wife of forty-five years, Joyce. That is a long time to hunt, fish, and slurp raw oysters together.

Lastly, I want to snitch a line from my late mentor, Frank Woolner, who is often quoted in this book and who was then editor of *Salt Water Sportsman* magazine, overheard when he held court before a clutch of admiring outdoor writers at a convention. Because he was a fine writer and entertaining speaker, we hung on his every word while still under the gun of social intimidation that had somehow preceded him. It was one of those times when someone important had others there straining to hear what would come out of him. While this was happening, a young man stood at the door, tenderly clutching a book against his chest and looking like a trespasser, apparently hesitant to come into the room. He had perhaps evaded enough security and ignored enough signs to find Woolner and feared most that he would be ejected before locating him. Pausing to make eye contact across the room, and clearly recognizing the book's jacket, Frank beckoned the nervous young fellow forward. Without missing a word in his story, Woolner autographed it and mumbled something about good pointing dogs to the young man, more than likely in an effort to put him at ease. After a sigh of relief that he had at long last gotten the master's autograph for the grouse book, he uttered, "I read it over and over, sir. It is my favorite."

"Thank you, son. It was written for you."

—FRANK DAIGNAULT
Massachusetts Striper Coast
February 2002

THE STRIPER COAST

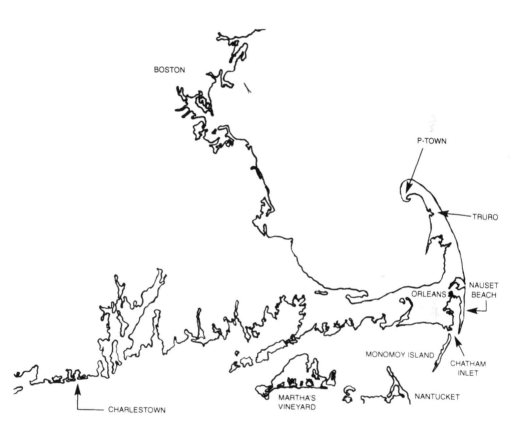

BOSTON

P-TOWN

TRURO

NAUSET
BEACH

ORLEANS

MONOMOY ISLAND

CHATHAM
INLET

CHARLESTOWN

MARTHA'S
VINEYARD

NANTUCKET

1

THE FORMATIVE YEARS

EARLY SUMMER 2001   These were the survivors. Born from what had been fisheries management's last chance to save the Atlantic striped bass, the 1977 year-class was down to a comparative handful—but they were now the stuff of a striper fisher's dreams. First, their mother had safely lunged from a nocturnal otter the night they were spawned on the Choptank River. Later they survived the nets of Chesapeake watermen for two seasons, after which they ran an annual gauntlet of efforts to kill them first at Cape May, then at Sandy Hook, then at Montauk. Now they disregarded the scent of menhaden from Narragansett Bay sliding east toward the Elizabethan Chain, a course set by a millennium of past generations. A few hundred dream bass glistening in the mix of blue and sunlight, their lateral lines acted as a natural cover for their movement. What distinguished these from the countless other linesides that could be found anywhere on the Striper Coast was their size. Because they were the desired fish of a moratorium-starved fishery whose anglers had never been allowed to take, they were now fair game—fair game in the sense that now a generation of stripermen had been tossing back fish that took two hands to hold. Within two days the first of the big fish slid through the cut at Chatham unnoticed in the low light of a setting sun. And the schoolies were already all over Maine.

In Harpswell for Joyce and I—together for forty-five years—it would be another night of motions, another night of sitting on the shore; make casts and fight fish, remove hooks, watch them pump off. Although we had promised one another many times not to reminisce about the old days, it was a certainty that something would happen that would stir an association in our memory, and we would scroll back to our youth, to our babies, to a sweet life we had once lived. We had a life on the Striper Coast where we never wanted for love, where we lived night to night for one thing: to fish for striped bass. Each summer we would pack four small kids in a truck camper that never started easily and head east to the adventure of the New England high surf. Now, a lifetime later, again prodded by the beach that had been a part of my life, I could not think of anything else but the time when we had been simple enough to be good.

LONG BAR, NAUSET BEACH, ORLEANS, CAPE COD, MASSACHUSETTS, 1964   Water had started south again on the outside, a clear sign that the tide had changed. Darkness closed, and you could see the occasional flicker of a surfcaster's light for baiting up or taking a fish off. Cautioning me to watch his rods, Eddie slid down the back of the bar to slosh across the ankle-deep shallows to his van for a new bag of pipe tobacco. He had probably been gone five minutes when I noticed that the line of his nearest stick had fallen slack—something had moved the sinker. It could have been a small cod: From May to early July these cod, never more than fourteen inches long, created havoc stealing baits from worm fishers who were out after stripers. Walking over to examine it, I saw the mono tighten, causing the rod first to bounce gently, then bow hard over from a good take. "Eddie," I called, positioning myself in front of the stick. Having seen this many times, I knew that the sand spike could be pulled over easily in the wet sand. Once that happened, it was common for a surf rod—which cost easily a day's pay— to slide out of the tube in which it was cradled and then disappear in the dark sea, never to be seen again. Bad enough that you could lose that kind of folding green in tackle; the shame of having lost the kind of fish that could do that was one thing, and wondering just how big it was another.

Those were the thoughts that flashed through my mind as Eddie walked up. Putting on my best pidgin French, I greeted him: "The pole, she go over pretty good, Eddie, hey?" Finding the weight of the sinker, he hauled back on the ten-foot stick. Whatever was on the other end got awfully mad, taking a whole lot of line as it pulled for the Gulf of Maine. Half expecting that there might be more, I checked the remaining rods, all motionless, then went looking in the darkened surf for Ed. Nearly to the top of his waders, he had followed the big striper seaward, line snapping off the spool. Eddie was breathing deeply and staring out into the night, trying to fathom what he had on, trying to figure what kind of striped bass could fight like this. This was not like anything that he had ever encountered before. Line given, more line taken, the fight had gone for maybe ten minutes when Eddie began to lament a standoff. Thumb and forefinger around his line to find my way out, I waded into the surf, some foamers breaking where I stood, others lifting me momentarily off my feet. Then, in the fore, I saw the dark form of a monster bass finning softly, its dorsal breaking the surface. Trying not to think too much about what had to be done, I slid the rubber tube cover off the small hand gaff that was under my belt, then came up sharply at the fish's forward end from below. Struggling only slightly, the two of us rode the next good foamer into the beach.

Eddie gasped when I wrestled his dream fish to the dry sand. Out of our heads with excitement, we weighed Eddie's striped bass that night and found it to be fifty-five pounds. He swears that his trophy striper ate a cod that had eaten his sea worms. It could have. Ed was one of probably twenty people who had beached a fifty-pounder on the Striper Coast that season. Still, no doubt ten times that number of fish of comparable size were taken from boats. It was then that I decided that fishing stripers in the surf was something I wanted to do seriously. Neither of us was ever going to be the same.

Here is what striper fishing from the Cape shore was like in the mid-1960s: Nauset Beach was an eleven-mile spit of sand that stretched south from Orleans into Chatham. A natural peninsula, it was bounded on the west by Pleasant Bay and on the east and south by the formidable Atlantic. At the extreme south end, the currents of the bay and the warm waters of Vineyard Sound west of Monomoy collided at Chatham Inlet. Here you could look south and see foamers sliding toward the inlet, bucking white at each place where a little sand bulged up off the bottom, resembling mare's tails streaming where the waves broke. It was an oceanic garland of color by day; green and blue melded and changed at the whim of an ever-changing sea. By night, moonlight depending, shades of black and gray betrayed the presence of a changing bottom. On the beach the sand curved in a hook before dropping off deep. It was possible to stand on this extreme end of Nauset, water flying this way or that, and see Morris Island to the west, Monomoy to the south, and a boundless horizon on the east. But most importantly, here at the inlet you could stand at the threshold of the most important striper surf on the planet.

Bass love moving water for any number of reasons. First, moving water is nearly always deep, providing close cover—a place to which they can escape. Linesides can also lay in wait and ambush baitfish. And, of course, water moves to where it can go. Thus, as long as a striper is in the current, it's safe from the danger of shallows. A by-product of all this current is the varied bottom structure that it creates. Where current erodes the beach away, a bar forms; we called that one Long Bar. Wherever there was a bar, there was usually deep water behind it. Also, where cuts developed by water flowing to behind a bar, stripers would swim into the shallows behind. Spawned out of the currents at Chatham Inlet was a delicious mix of bars, holes, and sloughs—all natural striper water.

Nonetheless, eleven miles of sand is no easy obstacle for striper fishers to overcome. Even if you were willing, there was no walking it. Cape sand was formed by millennia of a sea tossing everything in its way, moving the smaller grains first and throwing them the highest to form Nauset Beach. This is sand so amorphous that a boot leaves an indentation, not a track, and a tire leaves an impression in the shape of a V. Driving is the only way, but it has to be done right. Four-wheel drive helps, but an assist is needed from both weight distribution and the better traction of a tire that makes greater contact with the ground. Amateurs seek more contact with a bigger tire; professionals do it with less air in the tire. These two factors—weight and tire pressure—actually conspire to produce a better result than four-wheel drive. Then, when few could afford what infrequent "four-wheelers" were around, many of us resorted to two-wheel walk-in vans, discarded milk or bread trucks. These could be rigged with all the creature comforts for a family. It was, after all, no place that you wanted to travel the length of every day. Because the rigs were homemade, layouts were highly customized. But in general these one-room campers had bunks stacked along both sides of an aisle that led aft to a small kitchen area with a sink and countertop stove. More ostentatious buggies had gas refrigerators instead of iceboxes. Toilets were also a great source of one-upmanship that could cost as much as all the other appliances combined. Did I say family somewhere here?

I was twenty-seven and Joyce, my high school sweetheart, was twenty-four. Dick was seven and just learning how to cast. Carol was four and, about the time we believed that birth could be controlled, we were proven wrong about both timing and numbers with twins, Susan and Sandra, then aged three. Those were scary times for us. It was a case of providing for a family by holding down a job while knowing enough about your work to be in demand. There were the usual fears, including having healthy babies and retaining a marriage while those of friends around us failed. We also made mortgage payments—in our case two mortgages. With six of us and only one working, there wasn't a whole lot that a family could do but pack a cooler and go on a picnic. An obvious extension of that was to have enough sleepable quarters to make the picnic last around the clock—and anytime you're on a picnic, you might as well go fishing. For all our natural fears, life on the Striper Coast had begun to take on the flavor of adventure.

Having grown up fishing with my father and older brother, I knew about stripers. We had chummed for them in Narragansett Bay, drifted sea worms for them on the Warren River, and I had walked the beach for them in Charlestown, Rhode Island, not long after high school, while Joyce had stayed home with our new baby. I had watched the snow accumulate outside the window of a Rhode Island tavern, the scent of stale beer wafting in with the cigarette smoke, while Johnny Koback, a local surfcaster, sang the praises of the high adventure available anywhere linesides could be found. The thing is that I knew what stripers were about. I knew that you could eat them. What I didn't know, however, and would find out that summer on Nauset Beach, was that many people so liked to eat stripers that they were willing to pay bigger money than was ever paid for other fish.

No one ever starts out wanting to be a rod-and-reel commercial fisherman. The ones whom we knew sort of fell into it. Invariably, you had a good hit of fish one night, where you ended up wondering what to do with them all. One of the first nights for me was with "Muff" Briere, an old-time regular, fishing Long Bar.

Muff happened to be beside me that first night when I was scurrying around to gather my gear from the sand while a rising tide sought to sweep everything away. My worm bucket sliding and bounding dizzily, foam splashing on my reels, he scolded me softly for not knowing that I was fishing a rising tide. I didn't. Once I realized that the water could rise so fast, I couldn't get out of there fast enough. It was Muff who cautioned me that I was leaving at the best time, that—if I wanted to catch stripers—I should stick around a bit. And it was Muff who taught me where to sell them. Once I had tasted the money paid to play, I was hooked big time. It was so easy.

My first sale was roughly a hundred pounds, for which I was paid twenty bucks. At that time I was working for a hundred dollars per week. It seemed to me that a day's pay for a night of having fun fishing was a pretty nice setup. The babies were rarely ever more than a shout away playing in the soft sand or splashing around in sun-heated shallows behind the bar. Of primary importance, Joyce was always beside me. It doesn't take a mathematician to figure out that a day's pay for fishing on a night that nobody was talking about was nothing to compare with a really good night of fishing, a blitzy night—a night like the one I had that first year.

You could learn the drill on how to fish the end of the beach by watching how the buggies moved. At low tide the regulars fished sea worms from Long Bar. The farther out on the bar you were, the sooner you ran into the fish—but the outside also drove us off first. If you were lucky or gutsy enough, you could grab a spot that somebody close to shore had left ahead of you. Naturally, he'd left because the water had begun pushing him around. You took his spot because you were willing to risk a little of that push. Moreover, you needed the water to float your fish off, because they were too heavy on the clothesline stringer to be carried and no fun to drag.

Not far from where the bar hooked up with the beach, I buried my sand spikes in a foot of surf slosh, each wave pulling on fifteen or so schoolies that were washing into the deep water behind the bar. Muff was still fishing, but a lot of the regulars had gone ashore. By the time surf was washing into my parka and waders, I had added another half a dozen small fish to the rope. Total weight from both stops was around 140 pounds.

Up top I put the fish under the buggy, and around midnight ate a hastily prepared dinner. When I came out to smoke, I heard a pop in the surf. Then, while tying a plug to a spinning outfit, another fish broke near shore. Enough water had risen behind Long Bar to provide cover for bass that had slid over it—and it was now too deep for the bait fishers. It was then a simple matter to cast small swimmers in the foam in order to continue taking the same fish I had been catching while worm fishing earlier. I'd lost track of the numbers, but there had to have been another dozen schoolies under my truck when I realized that a few campers had passed heading sou'west toward Chatham Inlet—one of them, I was later to know, Red Hudson. It seemed to me that if many of the regulars were moving away from what seemed to be good fishing, it might be better where they were going. Rocket science.

The inlet was easy to find because all the trucks were parked there in a gaggle so thick they blocked out the light from our headlights. A few were fishing, but it didn't seem to be any big deal—only strays. Let's put a couple more in the fish box so as not to surprise you too much later. Soon all the casters were gone, a missing guy here, a light on in the buggy; another guy climbing out of his waders, then a light on in another buggy. Tired surfcasters were going to bed. Exhausted, Mom and the kids were sound asleep.

Having dozed for about an hour, I could have sworn that I heard the *thump* of a billy club coming down on something. I sat up in my bunk. Then, as I peered through an opening in the curtain up front near the controls, one dark form stood in the foggy gray of the inlet's surf. A nagging concern came over me—somebody might be doing it without me.

My manic walk to the shore was a carefully disguised, casual approach that was trying to say, *Ho-hum, nice night for fishing.* Yet inside I knew that this person was fishing as if there was a good reason, and I wanted to be part of it. I was watching him haul back when a striper took my plug, and I could tell that he could see me but nothing was said. This guy was all business. Besides, this was no time for idle chitchat: Linesides were taking on every cast. Both at the top of our waders, we were roughly fifty feet from the dry beach, but he, not wanting to lose the time I was losing, was stringing his up. I, my rope still through the gills of Long Bar fish half a night earlier, had to walk each six-pounder to shore.

At that point the tide had been coming, rushing around the horn at the end of the beach. Now the water was slacking, the action off a little, and we met on the beach as he bent over a fish. I learned that he was "Red" Hudson; he recognized me as the guy with all the kids.

We chatted about the fishing some. I took a few minutes to retrieve my stringer to keep up with the action. I could see him clearly out there in deep water, his rod bent.

"You think they were out there before," Red said, with a grunt. "I got hit three times on that cast."

This went on for another hour, taking schoolies on every cast. I had so many fish on my clothesline that I was wondering how long it would be before I would have to go in. Each time I brought a fish to the fore, I would turn my back on the sea on the chance that if I did use my light, I wouldn't spook the fish. Red's light was used only rarely—he easily fought three fish before I saw the dull glow of it through the fog.

I had just strung one up when I turned my head, wondering which way to go. The fog had enveloped me so thoroughly that I sensed vertigo, a loss of relationship between up and down, in or out, here or there. Until then Red had been on my right, and I had learned that I could walk to shore if Red was off my left shoulder— but I couldn't find him. If I didn't know which direction to cast to, I certainly didn't know which direction to find shore. There was no surf behind me, no sudsy sound in front. I might have thought that deep water was where the fish were, but they had been all around me. Nothing to go by, I was lost and very scared. "Red," I called, trying to hide the panic now tugging on my insides. *"Red?"*

Splashing out to the top of his waders, he again positioned himself on my right and started to fish. I could not ever remember having been that scared before, but having him come back and resume his position put my orientation back into place. Once relieved from my fears of being lost at sea on foot, I went ashore with my full stringer, unloaded everything under the buggy, and returned to my position on Red's left. Suicidal stripers were still at it, and we both tonged until the dull fire glowed in the east. At daybreak we could see birds wheeling all over Chatham Inlet, the tide now falling, sweeping over the shallow bars, linesides darting in all directions, mostly small fish. Still, it was only memorable in the sense that it was the first time I'd experienced a blitz, seen so many fish for so many hundreds of acres. Otherwise, that was life on the Striper Coast. I would experience it many more times.

I tell this story because it was the first time that I was involved in a serious take of sellable stripers. At dawn, when fishing ended, there were about four hundred pounds either in or under our buggy. A week later, when I picked up my check at the Old Harbor Fish Company, there was more money than I was making for working all week after taxes. The revelation that a person could fish his brains out and make as much in one night as from working all week began to take a positive hold upon my mind.

I worked for a manufacturer in Pawtucket, Rhode Island, as a gofer for the engineering department; there were three people working for me in the shop. As a journeyman machinist, I was considered skilled enough to estimate costs, supervise and give out metal fabricating jobs, hire machinists when we could find them, and farm out work to job shops that overcharged us. It was a pressure-cooker job where one mistake could cost the company a ton of money, where I begged off from overtime, where the chief engineer stalled my wage reviews. It was the most awful—*Frankie this, Frankie that*—place you could imagine. Ten people with neckties in air-conditioned offices picked my brain, allowing me a chance to think only during the time when *they* were on their extended lunch hours. Fridays, or before a holiday, the brass were always gone for lunch early and they never came back; even the guy who was supposed to be minding the place screwed around once he knew that *his* supervisors were gone. The situation was so predictable that the factory virtually closed down on the basis of whose Lincoln had left the reserved parking. We had guys who used to put an oily chunk of bar stock in a lathe in a slow turn to make it smoke. That was one thing about the industrial world that I knew: Nobody was smart enough to care about productivity or profits. It was a case of making smoke. If you could fill the shop with smoke, the high command was happy. *Incentive management*—buzzwords from a pep-rally book of the same title—was a source of contempt.

Along with all the standard industrial jokes about how you could sweep the floor on the way to somewhere in the shop, a gnawing reality had taken hold of me. It was that the guys with parking places with their names on them were drum beaters in a vessel where the galley slaves rowed until their creaking oarlocks were well enough lubricated with our sweat and blood. I just plain hated the place and was distracted by a sense that I was too good for that life. Still, when you have a house full of kids who rely on you, there isn't much you can do.

CHATHAM, ONE WEEK LATER   The check for my last
drop of rod-and-reel-caught stripers, the ones that had blitzed
small fish at Chatham Inlet, was $122.15. Having never seen that
much money with *anyone's* name on it, I ran across the parking lot
of the Old Harbor Fish Company. Slack jawed, Joyce was stunned
at the amount and asked me if it was a mistake. Dick shoveled ice
into the coolers and I walked back to look at the fish in the display case. There were cod, haddock, and "Boston blue," but no
striped bass.

The two-wheel-drive walk-in van labored into the sou'west under
the heat of the afternoon sun. She was going badly, and I knew
that the tires had heated enough to raise pressures. Checking them
with the gauge, I found that they had picked up another five pounds,
so I dropped the rears by that amount. A mile later, near the Second
Coast Guard Station, we had a flat. Not wanting to live without a
spare—the idea would have kept me awake the entire trip—we
turned back to get it patched. Now driving north toward Orleans,
the wind blew behind us, starving the radiator, and the seventeen-
year-old truck boiled over.

Having turned the International into the wind, we all bathed in
the fifty-five-degree Nauset surf. Then I slept fitfully long enough for
the radiator to cool.

In town at Bill's Sunoco, where the beach-buggy jockeys all pro-
cured gas, air, water, motor jobs in winter, weekday parking in
summer, I begged Bill, who had just finished washing his grimy,
grease-covered hands for the day, to fix my flat. Perhaps he saw the
anxiety in my eyes or the urgency in the faces of the children. Just
before sunset we were again southbound on Nauset.

The pain of an ending vacation and return to the factory in
Pawtucket had never been more overwhelming than this season. It
was the first time that I had ever felt the oppression of having a bigger family than I could care for properly. When I got back to the
plant, my workbench-desk combination was piled high with blue-
prints with notes attached: *"Frank, what are your thoughts on running
100 of these on an experimental basis? Can we hold sizes on an O-ring
groove designed around such a small shaft?"* On and on.

John Ashcroft was practically the only person in the place who
could relate to both hunting and fishing. He was my frequent confi-
dant in this factory that I had grown to despise. Whenever he

stopped by to palaver, I felt a break in the monotony. It was the Wednesday before Thanksgiving.

"So, Frank, what's on tap for tomorrow?"

"Black ducks in the bay, maybe teal," I answered.

"Got Friday off," he boasted, grinning with the idea that he was one up on me for the weekend. "The guys I'm huntin' with are all teachers. They're even huntin' this afternoon. We're in the wrong racket, Frankie. They got every holiday, a week at Christmas, summers off. With your background you'd have it knocked," John continued. "And they're beggin' for machinists. Carpenters they got. Jeezus, anybody can build a birdhouse, but machinists . . ."

I thought about four days of hunting only long enough to get to the notion of summers off and asked John, "Tell me, if it's such a racket, why are they short of people?"

"Because the money stinks for anybody who has gone to college, but that's changin' real fast. Besides, *you* don't have to go to college because you're a tradesman. You take the exam, get into a program—equivalent to half a year of college—and you're off fishing every summer and out-o-here."

"Just like that," I said, not taking him seriously.

"Just like that. Dumber people than you are doing it. You could live there, stay on the beach all summer."

I couldn't shake the back-of-the-mind feeling that becoming a teacher was doable. Imagining myself teaching the rudiments of machine shop to youngsters was nowhere near as distracting as the notion of fishing the beach for ten weeks every summer.

APRIL 1965   I'd sent an inquiry to the Massachusetts Department of Vocational Education weeks before, and that spring a packet of materials explaining teacher certification procedures arrived. After a written exam, there was a manual test to determine my shop proficiency before entry into the teacher-training program. The written test was laced with routine trade questions and a trig problem—all industry standards. I then went to a high school on a Saturday for the performance part. Roughly fifteen men all started making a shoulder screw at the same time, bringing the piece as far as we could in an hour. All looking for the same tools, making the same item, the things I needed to complete the project melted away quickly. A proctor told me to do my best. Finishing at about the same point as the others, I got into line at the proctor's desk when the buzzer went off. There I watched a fellow who had been beside me on the milling machine, slightly behind, turn in a *completed* shoulder screw. Realizing the method behind this miraculous accomplishment, I assessed the projects of all those around me. At least half the teacher candidates had substituted their test piece with one they had completed elsewhere long before the actual examination. They had known what they were going to have to do. On the way out to the parking lot, I struck up a conversation with one of the guys, asking if the testing for teacher candidates was always like that. Smiling awkwardly, he nodded as though his failure to actually say so could exonerate him from exposing one more outrage of the time. In other words, he knew what had to be done to pass the test and he was not going to admit it unless he was asked. Anyone who thinks that teaching is a noble profession should think about how a system had somehow evolved where only those who cheated could be trusted to teach children and where those of conscience would be denied. When I'd served my apprenticeship at Pratt and Whitney Aircraft, I was told that not 1 percent of the tradesmen in my field had a comparable background. Read on to see how the Commonwealth of Massachusetts acknowledged it.

Dear Vocational Teacher Applicant:

We regret to inform you that your recent test in the performance portion of the teacher candidate qualifying examination failed to qualify you as a candidate for teacher of Vocational Machine Shop. You will be notified when the examination is again given.

Dr. D. B. Causewell, Director
Massachusetts Department of Vocational Teacher Certification

When I told Ashcroft about my experience and then showed him the letter, good old John needed ten seconds to find a solution. "Go to Rhode Island," he said.

After an interview with the Rhode Island director of vocational education, I was enrolled in courses at Rhode Island College. Within two months I was given the name of a town looking for someone with my aspirations and skills and began teaching immediately on an emergency certificate, all the while continuing as an undergraduate. After completion of my bachelor's degree, I would have six years to complete my master's in education—a journey that would take a total of twelve years. For a life in the striper surf, fishing all summer every summer, it seemed worth it.

2

FISHING AT NAUSET

ONE OF THE THINGS about life on Cape Cod for the summer was that you never seemed to be able to keep the days straight. About the only way that time asserted itself was Fridays, when those poor working buggers would come for the weekend, when my friend Eddie would arrive in his walk-in with his family. My wife visited with his wife, our girls played with his girls, and Dickie, nearly ten, would stand between us to walk the way that we walked, talk the way that we did, fish with the big men.

One Saturday afternoon, a sunny summer day, the sou'west was blowing over Monomoy against the late rise in tide and the birds had shaped up over Long Bar, which was covered with water. We didn't feel at the time that there was any way we could get out there, but once the sea began to burst with the breaks of stripers cruising in a scant three feet of water, I wanted to try the four-hundred-foot swim. The trouble was that I had walked the few hundred yards down to Eddie's rig without gear, so when the blitz became visible from the campers I grabbed the nearest surf rod on his bumper spikes. I wasn't thinking about it, but he had just told me about his rod—it was brand new with a squidder right out of the box. Soon I was dog-paddling across the eight-foot depth behind the bar and getting tired, so I stopped, shoved his ten-foot custom rod straight to the bottom, and held it just below the tip for a rest. Moby stripers were playing in the shallows of the bar as I continued the remainder of the way. Once my feet picked up the slant of the bar edge, I walked up onto it in three feet of surf and began to cast. Hooking up right away,

I looked back at Eddie, who seemed both concerned and miffed about me using his new outfit. By the time I got the fish to me— maybe a twenty-five-pounder—the rest of the school had moved out. Eddie wasn't thrilled about me christening his new rod, especially when he realized that the reel was loaded with sand. But this had been, after all, an emergency.

That night I walked him through the routine of fishing plugs behind Long Bar, along with a subsequent drive to Chatham Inlet, but not because I loved him. If there was to be any hope of having Eddie drop my fish at the fish company on the way home, he'd bet-ter have some of his own.

Eddie left that Sunday with more fish than he had ever carried before, what with our take—Dickie's and mine—added to his. It was delicious not to have to drive off, risking flats, spending money on gas, and losing a day of sleep that was supposed to make up for the night before. Often, especially early nights in the trip, I used to hope that we wouldn't find the fish so that we could stay to swim in the day and sleep at night. I used to fantasize about lying in my bunk in genuine darkness. Sometimes my Joyce would move a certain way and I saw her as a woman and I thought about making love to her. Still, this was the life that we had chosen—without knowing that consequences lay in the trade-off between our old lives and what we had inexorably become destined to live.

A gaggle of buggies using tin boats hung out on the Pleasant Bay side of the Second Coast Guard—an abandoned building that had been used a century before as a lifesaving station for Nauset Beach. Rumor was that the guys regularly took their catch to a dock that was almost in sight across the bay. One morning, with a couple of hundred pounds in the back, I went looking for a fellow I knew who was part of that crowd. Walter was an inland mink trapper and a member of my fishing club. Anyway, Walter took me across, with my fish. There they lowered a bucket from a fancy hoist, which had to save a lot of people from hernias. This thing was so strong that they could hoist a good night's take in one pull. On the dock I casually asked the lumper what he figured they might be paying, and he said twelve cents. In shock and disgust I shouted, "Stop the hoist!" I wanted to cry. Here I was paying Walter to take my fish to town after being up all night to catch them and Walter's contact was going to screw me. Twelve cents per pound? Give me a break.

Inside, I asked the boss the same and he answered the same. And I, in no mood—no sleep and now the added expense in time and money of a failed mission—called to lower the hoist.

"That's what gets my ass about you people," the boss said. "You come out here to play, making good money on a job all week, and you want to be paid for everything."

As Walter started his outboard, the fish-guy townie and I glowered at one another while I handed Walter a five-dollar bill. It was money that we would miss.

A few weeks later, we hit them pretty well on consecutive nights. We filled the boxes the first night and put the fresh, second-night stuff in the aisles without ice. The catch came in looking nice—half of it really cold and fresh. Moreover, it seemed certain that we would take them in these numbers for more nights to come. All I could think of was how easy it was for Walter, with his boat, to take us across Pleasant Bay. With that gone, and I wanted no part of local low prices, we drove in to Chatham to Old Harbor Fish Company where I asked the guy taking our load if the boss was around. Pointing to an area with glass walls, he led me to a room with four telephones where the man in charge was working. He was a Greek or a Turk named Joe, with a cigar and a dark mustache, the boss.

I pointed out that our problem was that we couldn't handle the grueling trip the full length of the beach and that bringing fish in was both cutting into our fishing and compromising the quality of our catch. Joe listened with interest, with genuine concern.

"Joe," I asked, "what if you sent a boat every two days to pick up the fish? For you guys this is a short trip, and I could pay your man a few bucks for his trouble."

Word spread like fire over the beach that Frank Daignault was catching so many striped bass that the fish buyer was sending a boat every two days to pick up his catch. Naturally, good fishing was as much a curse for the others as it was for us because they, too, had all the same problems. A few people expressed some interest, but when they saw a boat come in and take our fish away, everybody wanted a piece of it. I was paying five dollars for this service, but I told them that while it was very convenient, it cost a ton of money. The gang had a meeting while I walked away pretending not to care, and they offered a five-cent-per-pound handling fee. I bumped it to a dime.

The next week, a Sunday afternoon, while I was fast asleep with the wind blowing through our quarters, the buggies started coming in. Jimmy dropped off a cow he had taken the previous sunset—no problem. Three truck campers had fallen into line behind him with fish, one with nearly two hundred pounds. I had to recruit Dickie to write down the names and amounts while I dragged the bass into the shade of my buggy and Joyce counted out the money to pay them for their catches. Cash lit the fishermen up. I don't know why that is, but they would rather have forty dollars now than sixty dollars next week. They seemed blown out at the thought of heading straight home with the money for the weekend in their pockets. Rusty pulled in with almost four hundred pounds. This thing was getting out of control.

"Frank," Joyce called, with urgency in her voice that I had long known was worthy of my attention, "we're out of money."

"No problem, Frank," Rusty confided, "pay me next time."

"Let me give you an IOU."

"We don't have paper," Joyce blurted.

Once the last buggy drifted out of sight in the haze to the north, the thought of what was under the truck started to sink in. The girls were too small to sense the potential of what was at hand, but Joyce and I looked at one another, fully aware of the situation. Dickie had a way of reading it when something got heavy with Mom and Dad. What if Joe forgot to send somebody? What if he couldn't find someone to make the trip? *What if we had more fish than the boat could carry?* Fighting a grin, Joyce tipped the cookie jar—a secret hiding place no outlaw would ever think of—and we all laughed at its emptiness.

The next morning the inlet was so shrouded in fog that you couldn't see a Rebel hit the water. We didn't think there was any way that someone would be able to motor across Pleasant Bay. At nine-thirty I began pacing, looking out over the gray, wondering how we would live on the Cape the next seven weeks without money. How would we live anywhere? Then, at the agreed-upon time, a sixteen-foot aluminum sounded a handheld air horn at Chatham Inlet. The six of us all ran to the boat to be sure it was from the Old Harbor Fish Company. Then we dragged, carried, pushed, and even threw more striped bass than we had ever seen at one time. With barely enough room for the kid to sit, the boat from Old Harbor was loaded to the gunwales. Moreover, the thing was so heavy we had to lift up on it to get it off the sand. The young man could tell that we were relieved to see him take the catch off. Just as he got clear, I asked him if he would come in two days.

"I don't know," he said, "give me a call."

Dickie and Carol both laughed, and Joyce put her hand lightly on Carol's shoulder to silence her. The young boatman, still not aware of what he had said, only that he had missed something, was unable to dope it out. I pointed out as patiently as I could the fact that buggies on the beach don't have telephones, and then we all shared equally in the joke. He had to think the trip to Chatham Inlet was fun, and the girls all liked him; he seemed to enjoy their grinning and staring. Everybody was waving as the little tin boat motored nor'west toward Chatham into the fog, its young skipper probably experiencing his first mission of importance. I wanted to hug Joe for buying the fish and sending his boat out to get them, for making good on a promise. Keep in mind that this was in the days before credit cards—at least for us—and we didn't even have enough money left to get home, let alone finish the summer.

The fish business was a great thing, but it brought a new set of logistical challenges. I knew enough to hustle drinking water from people leaving. Favors were easy now that I was buying fish. Still, we had never stayed on the beach this long. By the fourth day, there was no more fresh meat. One day I watched Joyce mixing powdered milk with what was almost the last of our water. What was left of that went into Kool-Aid. As meal planner she had a bunch of reliables tucked away—survival food such as fruit cocktail and canned peaches. Another was a huge, maybe two-quart can of "Chicken a La King" that had a scrumptious-looking picture of a chicken dinner on the label that bore no resemblance to what was really in the container.

One night, with a late high tide due around 2 A.M., we prepared dinner after sunset in candlelight and mixed powdered Kool-Aid with the last ice from the fish box. As I ignited the truck parking lights, I called the kids from a one-foot shallow where they often bathed during the week with a bar of soap. Starved, they came running.

Of course the first thing they asked was what was for supper. When Mom told them that it was Chicken a La King, they erupted into a feigned vomiting. Another time, when again without suitable protein for a growing family of six, we debated eating a striped bass. In the end, when we finished figuring what bass was going for, it would have been cheaper to take them all to one of those inns in Chatham where the ladies dress for dinner in gowns.

Long patrols were not necessarily starvation. Our camper was equipped with a small oven, and English muffin pizzas were a favorite. Spaghetti, which was dry in a box, could be boiled anytime there was water. Occasionally we ate bluefish, which went well with the pasta. Sand dabs were easy to catch and tasted just like flounder. Canned beans were good with just about anything. You don't know food until you've had beans and sand dab with Kool-Aid.

After a week on Nauset Beach, the stuff that needed filling was filled and the stuff that needed emptying was emptied. In other words, biological conversions were complete. While Mom foraged the aisles of the supermarket in Orleans, I dropped down to Chatham with my able-bodied field assistant, Dickie, to fetch a check and drop a few bass. Without credit cards, Mom took her time because she had no money. Joe was seated in his telephone-rich office, and when I came through the door, he greeted me by name and told the person on the line that he would call back. We shook hands when he stood.

"Frank, good to see you," Joe said.

Then he handed me a check for just under seven hundred dollars, which was a lot more than our summer grubstake, and I glanced at it trying not to let on that I was about to lose my bladder. We made small talk until I felt a little more relaxed, though I doubt I had this guy fooled.

"Joe," I asked, "why do some of these guys pay so bad?"

Rocking back in his chair to blow some cigar smoke, Joe explained: "Cape people don't want to pay for striped bass. They have too good a price on cod and haddock. Do you realize the money bass brings on the floor on Fulton Street? With New York Jews bidding up the price, nobody on the Cape can compete. I don't even carry it in my case unless I get a special request. Even then I get New York prices. The guys who offer low prices aren't screwing you. They're dealing in a local market."

North in Orleans, we found Carol in the supermarket parking lot watching for us. She told us that Mom was waiting on the other side of the cash register for us. Across the street at Cape Cod Bank and Trust, where we didn't have an account, they refused to cash my seven-hundred-dollar check—seven weeks' pay at the time—because nobody knew us at the bank. Our entire bankroll for the summer had been used to pay out to fishermen, so we were broke. I told the bank manager that we had no other money, and I asked her if she would call Old Harbor Fish Company to verify the check so that I could feed my family. She finally agreed, providing that I open an account to prevent this from happening again. Once Joe told her that we were okay and that he had just handed us the check, we left five hundred in the new account and had enough left to buy groceries for the rest of the summer.

MAY 1967, WOONSOCKET, RHODE ISLAND   Bob Bibeault's Flying A service station was one of those places where local stripermen hung out. More importantly, it was the place where the solutions to all mechanical problems could be found. It was home of the valve job, oil change, dirty joke, and, never to be overlooked, camaraderie that we surfcasters shared. One particular Saturday we planned to undertake a monumental engineering problem: A fifteen-foot Monitor trailer was going to be removed from its trailer chassis, then hoisted on the lift. After that a bridge was going to be welded to the chassis of a Jeep FC 170 pickup. After *that* the pickup was going to be backed under the lift, the trailer lowered, a few adjustments made to determine symmetry, and the two were to be married—truck and camper—what we used to call a chassis mount. Bibeault checked me out to be sure that I had worked the measurements and had brought the beer. He had looked at the elements of the assembly to be sure everything fit. Even the characters there who weren't in the play mulled their opinions. We had everything but a welder. Then Bibeault remembered Sammy, a hangaround who had just come out of a tour at the Adult Correctional Institute after doing two years for a B&E conviction. Sammy was good with a torch.

Sammy was at the Flying A within minutes of Bob's call, walking around looking at the tools he was going to use, the parts to be welded. Silence fell over the garage bay as Sammy walked toward the back, crouching, turning his head, looking where he was going to tack things down. The hiss of a beer bottle being pried open broke the silence, and Sammy threw his open hand behind him for it as he stretched the band of the goggles. Then he scraped the spark igniter, pulled down the glasses, and proceeded to tack home to vehicle, giving birth to a beach buggy.

A letter that my mentor, Frank Woolner, then editor of *Salt Water Sportsman* magazine, would later write, included a great chronicle of early beach-buggying that preceded the momentous occasion on this day:

> Beach buggies began to flourish in 1947, most of them jerry-rigged Model-A Fords. We cooked over open fires or on Coleman stoves stuck on tailgates. When midnight tides were poor and winds were cold, a lot of us slept in slit trenches dug in to the high dunes. This wasn't a reversion to wartime usage under fire but simply an effort to ward off cold and brisk winds. Even in sultry June and July, it can be damned cold under the stars. There weren't many women and kids on the beach then but there were some, and the big walk-in jobs came shortly after, likely the early 50s.

In the evolution of beach buggies, it was natural for them to later be larger and more ostentatious to accommodate the family. The names of those pioneers among the early practitioners of "family fishing" are a virtual Who's Who in the history of the striper surf. While it was a Massachusetts happening, many of them came from New Jersey, Long Island, and Connecticut. Thirty years later I got this nice letter:

Dear Mr. Daignault,

Oh, the memories your books bring back. We, too, had an old bread truck—it needed so much work and attention. I made pink and white checked curtains with matching print contact paper for the counters—an old rug covered the beat up floorboards. It was the most beautiful piece of junk you ever saw (at least we thought so). One time, coming home from the Cape, it wouldn't release gears from second to third, so we traveled all that way in second gear—very slowly. We came home on a wing and a prayer, so to speak.

My husband, Ray, was the fisherman in the family with our two sons following close behind. I always liked sitting on the sidelines, watching and getting just as excited as he did when it was a great catch. He's been gone almost twenty years now—but reading your books brings it all back so vividly—all those lovely memories when we were all so young and life was good and forever.

I have to enclose this poem, which we have all seen. It is just so appropriate. And once again, thanks for the memories.

Sincerely,
Evelyn Talvy

I pray that I may live to fish
Until my dying day.
And when it comes to my last cast,
I then most humbly pray
When in the Lord's great landing net,
And peacefully asleep,
That in his mercy,
I be judged
Big enough to keep.
—*Author unknown*

Woolner was primarily concerned with how men move around all night looking for linesides in what would come to be called a chase vehicle, while Mrs. Talvy's comments speak of families who enjoyed camping together in greater comfort along with the fishing. Today both still have a place.

JUNE 1967, NAUSET BEACH, CAPE COD   Reaching down to lock the hubs on our new-to-us Jeep was one of the most memorable experiences in my life as a beach fisherman. We were never to get stuck again. Even if the going got tough, we could let still more air out of the tires. Flats, which had been the curse of our life on the beach, were to become one-tenth the problem they had been because of tubeless tires. With a good-sized oven, English muffin pizzas would be a pushover. We had a gas refrigerator that made ice and had room for a pint of ice cream or a pound of meat—maybe delaying Chicken a La King for one day. We had twelve-volt lights without an electric bill and a gas lantern that provided light and heat, saving the truck battery for starting. We even had a heater.

There was something delicious, festive really, about starting a summer. The kids were fresh out of school and eager with a vitality that was less evident at other seasons. The only thing I disliked about June was the shortness of the nights. You could get into a decent night of fishing, carried away with time and tide, take a break, then be disappointed when the dull fire in the east lit off far sooner than you expected after 4 A.M.

During the first weekend, we had a lot of questions from the other regulars as to whether we were going to buy fish again that season. However, I feared the kind of risk we had taken a couple of times the previous year because of fog. Also, one of the gang had slipped me some really old and poorly kept bass that had left Joe bitching about quality, and it had embarrassed me. The new buggy was cooler, more reliable, and actually fun to drive by comparison, making it less of a chore to go off, and I didn't want to risk the summer money on operating a buying agency. If I engaged the boat for only my catch, it would be needed less. In addition, even here, amid the finest surf fishing on the planet, it was often possible to go many nights without stripers.

We also became conscious of a pattern in how the stripers ran the inlet. It seemed that when the tides were high at six, seven, or eight, the fish ran through like gangbusters at sunset. Sometimes they hung right in the rips in front of us. Other times they came through in pods. As with all inlets, there was a lag between when the tide out front was high and when it was high in the back. For instance, with a high at seven o'clock, the water slacked at nine-thirty. Rules were not hard and fast, but it seemed to us that the linesides often changed feeding positions at the turn in tide. Thus, slack water was no time to be scratching your butt. We often speculated as to why they did this six-to-eight evening routine so much. Maybe they wanted a low tide in the deep night in order to have the cover of darkness for feeding the shallows of Pleasant Bay.

There was a gang of weekenders with whom we fished two nights a week. They served as a welcome reminder of what night it was— otherwise I would never have cared about time until September. I knew that they disliked like me because of our freedom on the beach. In a way you couldn't blame them, but whenever a tone of polite resignation dripped, I reminded myself that we were all born with the same potential and the same choices as a result. Anyway, the children suffered less from these lifestyle influences and truly looked forward to seeing the others. Kids being what they are, it slipped out that Danny, one of the older boys, had broken off a monster in the inlet during the deep night. In itself this had no effect upon me, but that Sunday, when the others were all going home, Dick said that he had seen a couple of huge fish in one of the buggy fish boxes. Another of the boys lamented that he was exhausted from plugging all night. I knew that this crowd never knocked themselves out; they must have had something going that we had not learned about ourselves—low tide in the inlet.

That night, with the weekend crowd gone, after fishing high through slack, I napped for a couple of hours and went out into the inlet at low tide. The bay was running out, but the ocean in front was slack. There was only one person, a friend of the other crowd, and he, sure that the others were gone, was apparently uneasy being out there all alone. I didn't know him, but he had me figured and was what I call a midnight cuddler—a person who must have a buddy after dark. He told me that they had been taking a steady dole of big fish from the channel every other week since early season in May. I understood immediately that he told me all this to gain my favor, but if the others knew what he was telling me they would not have approved. With some people, what you catch is something that they cannot.

With ten-foot tides, the inlet was so different between low and high tides that it would have been impossible for a person who fished one to recognize the other. For instance, at high water the inlet had a sweeping surf and current left to right. At low tide, on the other hand, there were one or two hundred yards of wet flats ending in a deep right-to-left channel that dropped right down. You could hear the steady dull, distant roar of the surf to the east, but in the fore there was the quiet of an inland river dumping into the sea. No fish could feed the surface in this calm undetected. Apparently the big bass that had slipped into the bay to feed had found a haven in this deep channel. What monsters they were!

Using a three-ounce trolling swimmer—a ten-inch swimming plug with a mackerel paint job—I hadn't fished ten minutes before hooking up to a big striper. What with the channel current, I had to follow it downtide for some distance, stepping over a forty-pounder the other guy had lying on the wet sand, before trapping it in a shallow indent. It was about the same size as his. What you must appreciate is that during those years, we caught a lot of fish but few that made it to forty pounds—and I was out of my head because of it. Still, I never let it show. I wanted the cuddler to think (a) that I caught such fish all the time, and (b) that I did so at low tide in that very inlet. After all, I lived there and had an image to maintain. Also I didn't want it spread all over the beach that Daignault always had so many fish because he had an army of kids.

Two weeks later, the same tides having cycled back, the weekend warriors slipped out into the inlet during the late night and were horrified at finding Dick and me there ahead of them. They were fishing Rebels, the same hardware that we all used at high tide on the small fish, but Dickie and I hooked two to their one with the monster plugs—Gibbs Trolling Swimmers. On many beaches you'll often hear the old saw, "Big bait, big fish." I don't know if it's always true, but it was this time. That first night, I heard drags slipping the whole time we were out there. Yet out of six of them, I don't think they *landed* three. Danny, the young boy who had broken off a monster two weeks before and who had inadvertently alerted us to all this, was the first person downtide just below me. I heard him yell for his father, his drag zinging like crazy. His father, probably too far in one direction or the other, was not coming; the boy was in such panic that I felt sorry for him.

"Take it easy," I urged, "you have him. He doesn't have you. Slack off a little on that drag or the line will break."

It was a good bass, like the ones that had been there on the last set of late-night low tides—maybe forty pounds. Still, it wasn't that far away yet, as I could hear it thrashing in the channel. Naturally, once the boy cracked open the drag, it raced seaward, taking line, convincing the kid that he was doing the wrong thing. Then he reached for the top of the reel, and just as I started to warn him "Nnnn". . . *pow* the line parted. He mumbled something, and I went back upcurrent.

With fish this size, it isn't always hot and heavy. Dick and I had one apiece, and one of the other guys had a top fish in the low forties when Danny hooked up again. Same story: He was breathing heavily and yelling for his father. This time Dick heard him and passed the word up the line for Dad while giving freely of his advice on fighting a decent striped bass. "Too tight. Too loose. Easy. Be careful," Dick urged. Then Dick splashed out with a gaff in hand into the same shallow indent we had been using to corral tired stripers. When Danny saw that huge striper—over 40 pounds—flailing wildly with its back out of the water, he clamped his hand down on the spool and *pow*, broke the freaking thing off again. Guess something happens to some people when they see a great fish.

That Monday afternoon we took a small load—less than two boxes—to Chatham, leaving Joyce at the grocery store. Dick was now at the point that he filled the boxes at Old Harbor with ice without even being told. At ten, he was not yet strong enough to heft them up into the camper, but he would wait dutifully for me to come out of the office with the week's check, even gauging its value by the smile on my face. It was so near the evening meal that we decided to have dinner in town—twelve dogs with the works and four large Cokes. It was dark by the time we went back on the beach, the four kids asleep in varied patterns of arms and legs in the back. As we loafed south along the waterline trail of Nauset Beach, I couldn't help but notice that the east horizon was dotted with the lights of hundreds of trawlers, mostly Russian, looking like a distant city. It occurred to me that this fishing thing was a big business.

The tides had gotten too late for the evening highs that usually produced. I planned to sleep some and pick up the low water in the channel, but that was a good rest away. That night I sagged into my sleeping bag at the same time as Joyce and the kids. The inlet was silent except for a soft, sudsy sibilance that faded imperceptibly in the lowering tide. A gentle sou'west lifted the curtains of the buggy, and I could see Monomoy's low profile in the quarter moon on the same horizon—a lonely, foreboding finger of sand where no one ever went after dark and few ventured during the day. I felt a sense of serenity as I listened to the sleeping sounds of the children, the warmth of my sweetheart's rhythmic breathing upon my shoulder, and the notion that we perhaps had found something that would ease the burdens of life that we had known. Sure, there was the incessant concern that perhaps another baby might be on the way, there were two mortgages, the college thing all winter, and one side of the house to paint each spring. On the other hand, we had no truck payments, and we all had our health. With four beautiful children, we had never known the pain of having one of them handicapped or seriously ill, had never really wished for anything except the silly things that might have gotten us into trouble. Dickie and I had inexorably so bonded that he walked like me, talked like me, even cast like me. Anytime Joyce was more than ten feet away, Carol imitated her, even filling in for her with the twins, now seven. As I drifted off into a sleep that I had not known since a storm the season before, I could not help but think how lucky I was. Surrounded by the people in my world who mattered most to me, I was providing for them in a way that gave us more pleasure than we had ever known—the kind few people experience in a lifetime.

The first thing that I heard the next morning was the soft giggle of surprise the kids expressed at finding Dad *asleep.* The aisle of the buggy that led to the toilet bordered my bunk in that very small submarine, and I could feel the subtle motion of somebody getting up to head there. With one eye open, I spotted Sandra slipping out of her bunk as silently as a cat. Eyes closed, I rolled over and flopped my arm across the aisle, blocking her way, and a muffled giggle blurted from one of the others. Staring up at the ceiling and the arm of death that could crush her little form at any moment, she lowered herself to the floor and tried to wriggle through the space.

"Gotcha!"

That was the first season that I encountered the relationship between pleasure and accelerating time. One night—probably a Friday, because a lot of vehicles were coming on—the girls were playing with their sand pails near the buggy. Of course, it being the beginning of a trip, spirits were higher than at other times, and each buggy, it seemed, would stop and ask the girls if there were any fish on the beach. And they, apparently conditioned to what people seemed to want to hear, rebelled at the notion, so when each buggy stopped to greet the little darlings they would say before even being asked, "There are *nooooooo* fish here. *Nooo* fish."

That's another thing about the twins. Susan, born three minutes sooner, usually talked first, and Sandra had a strong tendency to repeat her. This had the reverse effect upon the fishermen coming on, advancing the notion that the girls had been rehearsed—especially with an echo in the background—to discourage fishing, to tell others there were no fish.

"What are they not hitting?" one surfman asked.

"Webels," said Susan.

"Webels," said Sandra.

One time, late season, nearly time to buy school shoes in Orleans, I mentioned that food was low and that maybe this would be a good night for Chicken a La King. Knowing that this would inspire an organizational meeting, I warned Joyce of the ploy, so she put a can of the stuff on the counter for them to see. I'll tell you, there were some long faces in the camp that afternoon. Around four, right after my pre-surfcasting-night preparation sleep, a din of chanting broke out. The four of them had little driftwood sticks over their shoulders, bandannas filled with sand attached to the ends like little bags packed forever.

"Unfair, unfair . . . Us kids need real food . . . We're gonna eat worms:

"First you bite the heads off.

"Then you cut the tails off.

"Then you suck the guts out.

"We're gonna eat worms."

The horsing around in camp was really a ritualistic recognition of the seasons: *Almost time to go back.* It was our way, it seemed, of coping with the real world. Joyce was the only one of us *not* going back to school. There was no justice in this, because when we had met more than ten years before, it was she—a letter of acceptance from Rhode Island College in hand—who had planned to be a teacher. When I went into education, she was amused at the notion that someone who could muster no greater justification for so noble a vocation than a summer to fish the beach would be there while she languished in an apron waiting for us to come home each day. Not that there was bitterness, but her gnawing sense of failing purpose never let up, never relaxed its hold upon us both. She had made out an application to work in the school cafeteria because she wanted the same hours as the kids, but word all over town was that these jobs went to friends of the politicians. She waited to be called.

Labor Day weekend, before the great exodus, without any goodbyes for anybody on Nauset Beach, we slipped the buggy north while the four kids slept and stopped at an opening on the back track for one last look. Joyce and I walked silently toward the front, our short boots left beside the cab of the pickup, the cool sand of Nauset massaging our toes. At the opening, someone had placed an old refrigerator and some battered pallets, both to keep buggies from going there and hopefully to trap some of the sand that moved at the whim of wind and an often desperately wild sea during winter. Thinking that its porcelain and galvanized finish would allow it to last forever, it began to sink in for both of us that summer was over.

3

COW COUNTRY

NAUSET BEACH, 1968 It's surprising how little time is needed to become an "old-timer." After only a few years, driving the beach no longer was a challenge. Predicting stripers was an uncomplicated ritual that related to the season, the tide, and the time of day. Even our methods had begun to formulate themselves: We now tied a Rebel directly to the mono and fished it moderately in moonlight while ever so slowly in the "fire" of phosphorescent plankton. This good life was comprised of two key elements over which we had no control: a continued stream of stripers from Virginia and the Chesapeake, as well as a beach from which to fish them. This latter component had begun to concern me.

I first heard about the budding problem from one of the guys who had moved from a place inland to Orleans. Apparently, a commentary had appeared in one of the Cape papers about how the interlopers from inland had gone onto *his* beloved Nauset Beach and ". . . fouled all that was beautiful in this garland of nature." Some had been saying that one of the greatest dangers we faced was that townies were not fishing the beach, which meant that the towns could close the beaches and run everybody off without danger of discriminating. If, on the other hand, there were local people surfcasting, few laws could be devised to control us without creating a storm within the community. One guy from Orleans fished the beach, a guy named Mac Reed, and though he was there a lot, he was rarely seen. A steady stream of letters was printed in the newspapers, but not a one represented over-sand vehicle use. With such an overwhelming force of public opinion against us, it's not hard to see why many, if not most, of the businesses in the sister towns of Orleans and Chatham—towns in common ownership of the beach—opposed the use of vehicles there. With that kind of consensus, people who for years had been ferried across Pleasant Bay to bathe and sun themselves had devised a tactic intended to put an end to the "transgressors" driving the beach—tank traps.

We first learned of them one weekend night at the inlet during a stage in the tide when things were slow. It came from Swede: "Aw, ya, Jeezus, the bastards dug 'um near the Second Coast Guard. Goddamn things was three feet deep, they was. They put poor Maggie damn near through the windshield. They was all lookin' when we jacked up. It was like hittin' a fooking stone wall, it was. Maggie, she got a bad gash on her forehead. Some was grinnin', others was ashamed, I think."

There was widespread belief among the buggy people that some of the business owners were behind it, although we could never prove it. The reason for this was that most of the tourists were from off Cape and less likely to be rabid about beach use. It just didn't fit that a vacationer would dig a hole in the beach trail, cover it with storm fence lattice—this stuff was all over the beach for erosion abatement—and newspapers, then sand. If you were looking too closely at the bathing suits, it was a thing you could miss. Even at six miles per hour, driving into a deep hole stopped you cold.

The striped bass appeared in a continuous stream with different year-classes coming along. The old sixteen-to-the-box gang had grown into ten-pounders and we still had a group of sixteen that usually made the "select" cull, paying top dollar. Often, when we had a fish slightly over that, Joe's lumper would raise one eyebrow, wink, and toss it into the big-money cull. Most of the gang was selling by then, with a majority making drops at Old Harbor, which continued to ship to New York. A few holdouts took less from local restaurants and dealers for cash money in the hand. There was a little talk about taxes, but it seemed to me that if the IRS ever opened that can of worms they might regret having to deal with all the "losses" the fishermen would have, what with boats, buggies, and tackle thrown into the equation.

The morality of clubbing stripers all night got some attention, but it was always from the handful who either couldn't catch any

number of fish or from those so ass-deep in money that they balked
at staying up all night after working all week. The argument that our
state had banned netting allayed the notion that anything wrong
might be going on. The rod-and-reel commercials had applied for
and received licenses from the Division of Marine Fisheries, which
kind of legitimized the activity. We commonly heard the saying, "If
you're a sportsman, you don't sell, and if you're a commercial, don't
call yourself a sportsman." Few of us gave it much thought. We also
had some conservationists going around to the striper clubs preach-
ing that linesides had lost their ability to reproduce, but there was no
evidence of that.

By this third season, all the girls had developed skills with surf
rods. Even Susan and Sandra were beyond laying into a cast with a
closed bail. Carol, because she talked incessantly, was kept "need-to-
know" on any fishing information. And Dick, now twelve, had landed a forty-plus-pound striper one night in the inlet.

It wasn't a blitz, but we had all been drawing from a steady flow
of bass when the boy came by tight with the thrashing of a good bass.
Dick happened to be using the light schoolie outfit with ten-pound
line—something I had repeatedly cautioned them all about using too
freely. The problem with this light tackle was that, while it was a joy
to use, if one of those rare good ones—say, more than twenty
pounds—latched on, it took too much time to bring in at best and
broke off quickly at worst. With water flying by the inlet at full rise,
Dick's fish slid into Pleasant Bay as if it wasn't even on a line. By the
time he was at the bottom of the spool, a gallery of us had gathered
to see what was going to happen. Once he was out of line, I told him
to grasp it with his hand and hold, hoping to avoid the spool bottom
where knots tend to be marginal. His line lifted from the dark and
placid sea, stretched but didn't break. Unaccountably, his fish pivot-
ed right, allowing the storage of some line. Close to an hour had
passed when the situation had begun to stalemate, with only small
amounts of line stored—though it was enough to take on a run
should this monster once again come alive. Gingerly, the boy began
to put on line, the drag slipping slightly with each pump. It was
another of those situations where time wore against the angler,
enhancing the possibility that something might go wrong, might fail,
with the gossamer thread that attached them to one another.

Moreover, with his spool filling somewhat, the drag slipped more easily; Dick tightened it a quarter turn, making it easier to gain on the moby fish. With the passage of time, the tide had slowed, giving it less help from a rising sea. Here on the end of the beach, the last finger of sand hooked north into a back pond that dead-watered when full. We could see the line leading into it, which relieved us all greatly. After a few minutes, I checked his spool. It looked good to me.

"You're going to see it soon, Dick," I urged, thinking all the time that if the tide started out, this moby lineside could again have the advantage in the other direction. "When you do see it, don't change anything. Don't pressure it when you see it. Don't panic."

All I could think of was the kid having an anxiety attack—the kind young Danny would get every time he saw a good fish in the surf. Only this time, we had what amounted to a light freshwater outfit, with half the strength of Danny's.

The other problem was that we had no moon, and no inkling where the monster fish was. We could only estimate that it was somewhere in our fore after extending an image of where the line led. I wanted to put on a light, but sometimes a striper will panic when a light bathes the seascape. Still, I knew that the back pond could be waded. And if we didn't do something soon, the tide would change and this fish—however the hell big it was—might go out with it if permitted sufficient rest in the interim.

Having decided to light up the pond and wade for it, I turned to the others and asked a few buggies to move up and face the back pond.

"Light them up!" I called.

The four-foot white belly of the cow lay motionless on the pond's surface twenty yards out. Wading to the top of my waders, I reached over it, its gill covers rising rhythmically in exhaustion, and pulled the gaff toward me. I could feel that the weight was more than anything any of us had taken that season and more than Dick had ever caught as I sloshed to shore—a forty-two-pounder.

One weekend that season, a fellow named Bobby came out on the beach in his mother's Wagoneer. Ours was one of those curious accidents of association through mutual acquaintance: We had grown up together, and his widowed mother had ended up marrying a widower and surfcasting mutual friend, Charley Murat. Before all that, Bobby and I used to bunk school and go to Horseshoe Falls every April for trout, finding the preponderance of our fish in the skunk cabbage of a swamp adjacent to the main flow. Then, in 1947, we fished with cane fly rods, mostly Montague, which were outfitted with level lines and permitted us to drift worms in the current. We liked the floating lines because you could see if something stopped the drift. Thus, solving fishing problems was something we had done a lot of together. By the time I was fishing Nauset, ten years out of high school, I wasn't seeing much of him anymore. In the meantime, he had lost his leg in the air force and, according to rumor, had done so falling down whorehouse stairs somewhere.

"How many ya got?" he asked.

I didn't answer.

"You fly fishing these things?"

"Been thinking about it."

"They're suckers for flies."

"I'll fix you up with something good, the whole rig, for a hundred."

"Bobby, I'm here for the money, not to spend it."

"Fifty bucks—rod, reel, and line and I'll throw in some flies."

Finishing his coffee, Bobby said that he would come back that night at low tide—which he did, around 1 A.M., after worming the front beach. Telling me that he wanted me to see a spot that the townie Mac Reed had shown him, we bounded over the clam holes of a low-tide Pleasant Bay to a spot called Scup Hole.

When we got there, we could see the rotations of Chatham Light straight west across the bay, the water millpond flat. Bobby shoved a fly rod into my hands, playing it down, as though it were something I had to do for him. Leaving the Jeep parked on the flats, we waded out onto a finger of sand in the bay shallows. Bobby hobbled on his wooden leg, chattering about having just heard one. Admittedly, I was a trifle uneasy in this new spot; I felt that if I took one bad step the currents would have me.

The fifty feet of ten-weight fly line slid through the guides, settled on the bay surface, then drifted left, followed by a swirl.

"See that?" Bobby exclaimed.

After it swung a few more feet, I lifted the line and dropped the fly to the upcurrent right—where it was then inhaled by a brute that made the placid waters of Pleasant Bay bulge before it ran off into the reel's backing.

Summers on the beach were great for the kids, who found both play and adventure.

Now with a four-wheel drive under our home, we would never get stuck again.

We found monsters like this fifty-two-pounder in Charlestown where, according to Beaumont, they had "stocked the pond."

"Jeezus!" Bobby yelled as he backed, dragging his gimp leg. Then I reached for the reel, the handle dusting my knuckles, causing the line to lift higher . . . before the leader broke.

"What happened?" Bobby asked.

"Shut up."

Trading use of the fly rod back and forth with me until dawn, Bobby rambled on about how Mac Reed had shown him a good spot. He said that I could have the use of it all week and that the fly rod—now down to a buck a week for a year—was the way to fish Scup Hole. Limping back to his mother's buggy in the gold glow of a new Cape Cod day, with my share of the night's bass, he called to me like a brother as I dragged my weary body into the camper, "Keep the freakin' fly rod, butt face."

SUMMER 1969   After a winter of selectmen meetings, the towns settled on requiring all self-contained vehicles to leave the beach daily in order to renew permits. This meant that whatever energy we had expended fishing the night before, we had to pack everything up, drive the length of the beach, renew, then drive back to the inlet—a total of twenty-two arduous, over-sand miles. Still, the guards who administered beach-use regulations, conscious that the selectmen had established these rules to harass us, were sympathetic. We learned this when one of the gang took two friends with him to renew his "daily." Once word got out about the loophole, almost everybody teamed up. This meant that only one in five had to make the drive, with four others riding in the back. By midseason, trading favors with fresh fish, one fisherman made a run on Saturday with a *stack* of permits to renew without even bringing the drivers. Of course, the hostility of the townspeople, upset with the increased level of beach traffic that the regulation had caused, seemed to grow. The tank traps continued but were far less effective because everyone was alerted to the possibility of encountering one while drivers looked for smooth, artificial-looking wheel grooves in the track.

In the newspapers, there was another round of editorials and commentaries by the same people. Outraged townies screamed to selectmen about the greater and greater numbers of off-Cape vehicles "camping" on the beach. Now, instead of fish, the all-abiding concern of every beach-buggy jockey on Nauset was how much time we had left before they made it illegal for us to be out there at all.

Joyce had been attending classes at Rhode Island College in the elementary education program as a nonmatriculating student for a couple of semesters now, and the costs of out-of-state tuition had taken all of our savings and much of the fish money from the summers. We had made arrangements for her to take her SATs at the high school in Orleans, a requirement for full-time acceptance at college. All we could think about, what with all four of the kids in grade school, was the potential of having *both* of us bringing home a salary. I had seen some positive effects of this among any number of faculty couples—such as two new cars in the parking lot to take them to a cottage in the country. In contrast, we were so poor that even the house we were paying on—some sheet metal diverting water from the attic leaks when it rained—had two mortgages. It may have been a great life, but we knew that if one element—our health, the stripers, our economics, our relationship, or beach access, for instance—fell out of the picture, everything could crumble. We had never liked Nauset in midsummer, because by late July a red weed or mung would come down from Provincetown to kill the fishing. With one cast, so much of the stuff could gather on your line that you could not retrieve and it could take quite a while cleaning it off. When the mung arrived, we went to Rhode Island, where the water was clean and we could almost always count on a big striper. Regulations at Nauset Beach had so constrained our lives that it felt good to leave the Cape.

EARLY AUGUST 1969, CHARLESTOWN, RHODE ISLAND
Squid Beaumont's aluminum Starcraft swung lazily at its mooring while he slept in his walk-in on the east bank of Charlestown Breachway. Squid lived in the next town over from us through the winters, belonged to our striper club, and had shared dinner with us a few times. Not that we were close, but a mutual respect had grown out of the realization that each of us had committed most of his life to the pursuit of linesides. Few knew how he had ever gotten the nickname "Squid." He had been baptized Emile in Woonsocket, Rhode Island, but Beaumont had never liked the name and had made no secret of it. When he was around fourteen, he often fished with an uncle whom he dutifully called "Mon Oncle" in French and who was to Squid really the father he had never known. One time at Point Judith Light, bait fishing with his mother's only brother, he

took a nice bass close enough to forty pounds for the old man to call it that. Emile, convinced that it was the squid that really caught the fish, would say whenever they went fishing, "Mon Oncle, can we find some squid?" In school he raved about the magical power of squid as bait. When trout fishing, he would lament the absence of squid in the sweet-water environment. He talked about them so much that the name took hold and, by the time he was eighteen, only his mother and his uncle still called him Emile.

As a striperman, by the time he was twenty-five years old, Squid was as good as they got. This was so because Beaumont had learned to enjoy an intimacy with the hostile sea that few fishermen ever master. He could smell the difference between upwind bunker and upwind bunker that had already been through the stripers. He never needed to look up the tides, yet he always knew what they were doing and when they would do it. One spring in Matunuck, where first schoolies had always shown mid-April, he pulled up along the west wall in a raging sou'west to talk to me while he kept one foot out against the stones to hold his little Starcraft in position. It made me nervous, but you could tell Squid was at home because he even killed his motor while doing it. When it came to stripers, Squid Beaumont was a very savvy person and good to have on your side when you were just coming in from a strange land like Cape Cod. Consequently, whenever we arrived in Rhode Island, seeing him was the first thing to be done once the buggy had been leveled.

Sure, six of us spent the best of the season on the Cape catching hundreds of bass. That was for the money. Eddy's fifty-five-pounder was the only true monster we had ever seen out there, and even he had ended up fishing in a boat by that season. Still, for the pure sport-fishing glory of catching a moby striper, Rhody had all the marbles. In a better world, you could fish for money and glory at the same time. But at that point, we fished for money on Cape Cod and for glory in Rhode Island.

Walking the quarter mile east to Charlestown Breachway, I had to suppress the excitement remembering what I had caught here in Charlestown. In 1966, a year when fewer than twenty "surf fifties" had been taken in the whole country, I had beached a fifty-two-pounder. A year later, a night when all my live eels had disappeared—let go or stolen by some other surfcaster—I had cast a Junior Atom and taken another bass over fifty.

Once at the breachway inlet, I called across to an angler who was working on his boat and asked him if he knew Squid. He disappeared among the gaggle of campers and returned with the man. After he motored both ways across the inlet, Squid sat with me in his camper and whispered confidently, "The pond has been stocked," which was his way of saying that fishing was good. All the local regulars who were out for blood like the rest of us had taken monsters. And while he admitted that most bass were small—in the lower thirty pounds—the number of monsters was extraordinary. After we finished a beer, Squid offered me a ride back west to my camper, and I, a surfcaster who hardly relished the brisk southwest sea running, was neither up for the embarrassment of refusing nor for walking back. As we bounded through the opening of the breachway that is flanked by jetties, a five-foot sea greeted us, fouling my Polaroids and wetting my cotton shirt. Once we were opposite the gaggle of beach vehicles in the dunes behind a gallery of surfcaster wives in lawn chairs, Captain Squid put the bow of his small boat into the running sea, allowing it to back us down close to the shore. Sliding my jeans off and rolling them into a ball, I waited at the gunwale for word to go ashore. This was foam-tipped Rhody surf, the kind of water that was an old acquaintance if not a friend. My plan—I had never executed it, but I'd thought about it many times—was to leap straight up with my pants held high for dryness. Squid watched the southwest seas. Frank watched the beach. The ladies on the shore watched a fool with no pants on. Captain Squid was in control as the small tin boat bobbed ever closer to the deadly surf. Riding up on the foam of breakers that took their turn assaulting the beach, Squid tooled his Starcraft so skillfully that it lost ground without turning its stern to the weather. Nobody, boat or shore, was saying anything. There was a sense that something interesting could happen as we approached the curling, crashing surf. Then Squid, the friend from my striper club whom I had learned to trust and admire, kicked me square in the butt over the side as I held my pants high over my head in twelve feet of water. It must have looked kind of funny as Squid gunned his boat to get out of there, because all the ladies on East Beach were laughing as I came ashore.

Rhode Island and Cape Cod were different in that the Cape had the charm and money fish in numbers while Rhody yielded monsters

that were almost too big to sell. Often you ended up taking a catch
to the taxidermist for two weeks' pay instead of to the market. It was,
in the words of Beaumont, the friend who had kicked me in the butt
and nearly drowned me, about glory. Rhode Island striper fishing
was a shot at catching something so big that they would put your picture in the paper. Most important, Rhody was good when all else
was bad, so it filled the niche of having what was important when it
was important. For a commercial, a person who sold his fish, there
could be problems.

Unlike the Cape, where trawlers were unloading in Chatham, P-
Town, and smaller ports, there were few places where you could sell
your catch in Rhode Island. The best one, over in Galilee, had some
lumpers who removed your ship-direct tags and put their names and
addresses on the boxes of fish so that the check went to their
homes—which robbed you of your load. You, the owner and shipper
of the fish, got a wordless look when you came asking about it. Sure,
you could deck the bastard, but first you had to know who he was.
Anyone who knew anything about how to sell fish in Rhode Island
treated the Harbor of Refuge as the Harbor of Getting Screwed. All
the regulars knew this; it was such old news that nobody even talked
about it anymore. Policy with rod-and-reel commercials had evolved
into taking the fish to Stonington, which was out of the way but safe,
fairly safe. The other problem was that often you would end up with
only one or two stripers, which, while decent in size, were not
enough in poundage to drive to Stonington. Beaumont had dealt
with this more than I and had approached me one winter to go partners with him on an ice cream cooler that was headed for the dump.
I paid the twenty-five bucks for the cooler, and Squid muscled the
thing to Charlestown where we kept it plugged in at a bait shop run
by Tom Sanders, who supplied us with live eels. Sanders was of that
lovable New England Yankee tradition with the jargon and inflection
that goes with it, saying "Ieeupp" between all sentences—whether
yours or his. He trusted everyone, handed out a farmer's dozen when
selling eels, and always covered himself when asked about the fishing by prefacing his remarks with, "Dunno how it is today." If we
were on a slow pick of stripers, the ice cream cooler enabled us to
freeze them until we had enough for a trip to Stonington. We pulled
the plug on it the night before so that they were nice for shipping. A
kosher market drove New York prices, and it was said that there were

a lot of Jewish people in New York. The result was that, unlike the
Cape where locals wanted to keep bass low in price on menus, even
with a middleman who handled your catch, shipping direct to New
York brought in the real money. Some days, if there was no blitz anywhere that loaded up huge numbers and lowered the price, your
catch was on the Fulton Street floor creating a bidding riot. In addition, the fish companies were so happy about receiving your shipment
that there would be a printed note with the check: "Thank you for
shipping to Ballantine Sea Food. Your product is always welcome and
we have enclosed some tags for your boxes so that you will be sure to
ship the next time where you will once again get the best prices."

To me, it had to be a weekend because there were a lot of buggies in the self-contained area. Kids were all over the place, and our
children were hard to find. Butch, a state trooper whom I had
befriended in some wild fit of self-abuse, was on the beach holding
up a beer so that I could see it as I came back from checking my eels
in the back pond. I had teased him about being a retread Quonnie
rat because he had been part of a bunch from Connecticut who had,
at one time, been driving nightly to that spot five miles to the west.
He had had some bad experiences over there in the rotation where
ten surfmen took turns if it was slow and twenty-five rotated when it
was good fishing. He liked the peace of eeling the beach, the open-
ness, the camaraderie that sprang from doing the same thing. Most
of all, he was enamored with the very big stripers that could be hoisted out of the surf in Charlestown, with far less risk of losing a dream
fish. You only had to play a drag way short of the line's breaking
point, and time was on the angler's side. The ritual of starting a night
of surfcasting was always the same: Suit up after dark, get the eels
from a personal wire basket in the back pond, place them in a wet
canvas bank bag, walk the beach, and cast and retrieve. With Butch
or my brother, Norman, you could spread in one direction where
each caster passed the other so that no one ever cast in the same
place twice or where another had fished. I used to needle them,
though I know now that they loved it, "This is the Russian Trawler
System. Keep casting, comrade." Man, could we cover some water.
One night, a slow one, when we had not made contact, we ran out
of sand on a four-mile beach. You can say whatever you want, we
were professionals.

Unlike the Cape, there was no structure—no bars or places for the water to slide through. It was straight, with no change that could be observed. The only distinct thing Charlestown had is what we called the "rut," which was a little step on the bottom, maybe eight inches deep, that you could feel if you were wading in a swimsuit. Often, but not always, the bass would swim that rut or take your eel just as you passed it. On calm nights you had to be careful not to spook the rut, because it was just outside your rod tip. When you lit a cigarette, which was something we all used to do at the time, it was mandatory that you flashed the flame of that Zippo with your back to the water. If you didn't, your reason for being there would scurry hell west and crooked, although you might never really know what you had done. When an eel died, we marked it with a piece of driftwood in case we ran out of good baits later so that it remained an alternative. In the bib of our waders, we also carried a plug in its box because, every once in a while, the bass would refuse the eels while splashing and thrashing in the surf close enough to hit with a stick. We were good, we cared, and we wanted the money.

That August, we had a steady enough pick to make a night of casting pay—say, one or two per caster, twenty pounds and up. The ice cream cooler was empty, because Beaumont had taken all the fish in. Norman had gone back home for work, and it was just Butch and me doing zero until midnight. There was no storm, but it was a big-water night with a sou'west humping in on our quarter left, foam sliding up the beach so that you ran down to cast then retreated. You didn't notice it at the time, but it was very tiring. I heard a motor coming down through Charlestown Breachway, walked a little higher and stretched. I could see Beaumont book seaward, smack a big wave, slide up, take air in his little Starcraft without losing a beat. The night began. Talking Butch into a change of pace, I suggested that we jig the breachway both to give eel fishing a break and to introduce a look at something other than a washboard horizon. We weren't there ten minutes when Butch was fast to a nice lineside on his fifty-pound-rated outfit. This cow was pulling line off his dry reel making a snapping sound while poor Butch tried to find a place with better footing. A monster wave broke over the end, sending a sheet of foam onto us and dumping green water in our fore. It was the elemental fury that my old editor, Frank Woolner, always used to talk about. Guess we should have thought of that before making a cast.

Getting nowhere with this fish, Butch was trying to keep line from leaving the spool because of a huge rock on our jetty side covered with barnacles. It was the first time I had ever seen him afraid.

He had a dream fish on and he was staring into the gray haze of night, not doing a thing to change the situation.

"Let's cut it and get the hell out of here."

"You stay right there," I admonished. "You have it, it doesn't have you."

"I can't bring it back against that tide," he yelled, against the sound of another breaking wave throwing water all over us.

"Butch, crissakes, relax. We're not going anywhere. You got a promise or something?"

"It stopped!"

"Good. Put some heat on the fish. Don't let the bugger rest."

"I'm gai . . . ," he began as another foamer cracked over the end of the jetty.

"Can we look?"

Putting my thumb and forefinger over his line, I got a feel of the angle, which told me that his fish was still seaward. Meanwhile, I tried to get a sense for the sea's timing, tried to get an idea of how she was breaking while Butch stored more line. At least he had stopped trying to abort the situation, and he truly had the look of dedication for which I had grown to admire him. I always called him John when things were serious.

"What's cookin', John?"

"Check the line again, Frankie."

When my fingers closed around the line, I could feel that it was straight down, roughly ten feet below in the current. Then I reached for the long gaff, looked south and seaward, and threw the switch on my light before climbing down.

"Did the light make it crazy?" I called as I lowered myself on the stones, waves breaking and buckets of green water lashing sideways.

"Okay so far," Butch answered. "Frank, don't go down there."

It was everything happening at once. I saw a flash of white belly, heard a wave burst over the end, knew that I was not low enough or close enough, then felt the weightlessness of bulge lift me before dropping and revealing exposed rocks in front of me and another view of the fish. Then, sensing a pause, one that surely would be followed by another foamer, I scurried a few steps down, reached past the fish with the gaff, and pulled toward me seconds before another wave broke shoving me and Butch's trophy against the rocks. I tasted salt and started climbing up the rocks and up the gaff handle that Butch was holding. He hugged me and we looked at a fish that was no big deal, low forties. The current and tough conditions had made it seem like a much bigger bass.

The best that we could figure, the ice cream cooler held more than a thousand pounds. The problem was that there were too many of us putting fish into it. I had consulted with "Captain" Beaumont—a title from a six-week course that he had neither sought nor aspired to acquire—and his feeling was that as long as the guys took their turn taking fish to Stonington when it was full, it was okay with him. Butch and I had a pick going and Norman's days off as a police officer had come back, so he was on the beach fired up like a Friday-night sailor. August was down the tubes and we had to get school clothes for the kids, shampoo with fresh water, and get haircuts—mine was down to my shoulders. It broke my heart to leave Charlestown: I had only fished for seventy-four consecutive nights and I felt in my gut that those buggers were going to do something memorable without me. Reluctantly, as we prepared to go, I instructed the troops.

"Listen, you must know exactly what fish are yours in that cooler. We cannot, I repeat, cannot, allow any simple mistakes to hurt Beaumont. If in doubt, we give him the benefit. Without him, there is no Charlestown. Now, when you get to Stonington, Dinkie, who is the guy who manages things, is going to try to hornswaggle you on the fish. He always comes up with something—fire, flood, earthquake, something. Just laugh and tell him you're shipping the fish, no matter what he says. Take these tickets and be sure they're tacked on the boxes. Now, repeat after me:

"'Wweeee aarree sshhiippiinngg tthhee ffiisshh.'

"No beer drinkin' before 2 A.M. No lighting up facing the water. Loving in the afternoon. When people ask about the fishing, you haven't tried it yet. *Staizitto.* Now what are you going to say if you make the run to Stonington?"

Norman pulled off a beer tab. "Huh? Oh, ah . . . We are shipping the fish."

I wanted to cry driving off the beach. God, I love to fish.

4

THEY DID IT WITHOUT ME

THE HOUSE WAS STALE and a hundred degrees, with rust in every faucet. Six of us took twelve showers and put on clean clothes, then Joyce took the children shopping while I slept because I had not yet broken the day-nap habit. When I awoke, I didn't know where I was. As I poured the coffee, all I could think about was my brother and Butch in Charlestown doing a job without me—a nightmare!

The two of them were alone on the beach on a weeknight. One buggy with an older couple was also there, but the guy cared more about digging clams and drinking beer than fishing for stripers. At full dark, the two forms of Butch and Norman were superimposed on the white sand so that anytime Beaumont looked at the shore he could make them out, even figure what they were doing. Butch hooked up first—midthirty pounds. Then Norman dropped a decent lineside but hooked up right away on the next cast. By 10 P.M. they had four bass, but they noticed that the farther east they went, the more hits they were getting, so they began to cover the beach more quickly. It was what I would have done. By 2 A.M. both of them were exhausted, but they had enough stripers to top off the cooler and still have more than they could store. Knowing that they had to drive to Stonington, they went to bed with stripers all around them—which is something that I would *not* have done.

The next day, stripers in Butch's front cooler and stacked in the aisle of the living space of his camper, they carted just under fifteen hundred pounds of jumbo striped bass—slightly more than half of which were Beaumont's—off the beach. Bound for the Fulton Fish

Market and timed perfectly for the Jewish holiday—Rosh Hashanah—they had the two desirable ingredients, price and pounds.

Dinkie's Stonington dock was quiet at midday, so unloading at the shipping platform was both easy and festive for a couple of off-duty cops. Dinkie stood over them shaking his head.

"Hope you don't think you're shipping those to New York," he said. "They'll be mush by the time the strike is settled."

"Strike? What strike?"

"Lumpers and fish handlers is on strike again. Ain't nothin' goin' into Fulton Street this week."

Norman looked at Butch, as both envisioned taking the fish back, refreezing them, maybe losing them, and trying to explain it to two others who might not believe what had happened and who might, just might, think they had sold the bass elsewhere and kept all the money for themselves.

Chewing the inside of his cheek, Dinkie appeared to be looking for a solution to help these guys out—poor buggers, stuck with all that fish.

"Listen," said the wharf manager. "I'm thinkin' of sendin' a shipment to Philly because we got a lot of people like yourself don't know what to do and it's our policy here to help out whenever we can. I'm not doing it for nothin', though. I get to pocket a dime a pound if you play it safe with me. At least you'll have it on the barrelhead today with me. Say thirty cents."

All they could think of was what they might do with close to a ton of fish, less than half of which belonged to them. The longer they stood there, the more appealing Dinkie's offer was getting.

"You going to help us weigh them and box them?" Norman asked, thinking that might sweeten the deal.

When they left Stonington, Norm was counting $430 in tens and twenties, and the farther they got from Dinkie, the nicer the money was starting to look. They even started joking about it, with Norm saying that he could picture all them New Yorkers chewing on striper fillets.

When we came back out on the beach, Norman called me over to his buggy for my cut and what they figured Squid had coming plus a little extra to play it safe. Squid's cut was for 765 pounds—$230. Butch and Norm split four hundred pounds, all jumbo, and my share, while it was accurate, reflected a horrible disappointment for me at a hundred bucks. They were excited, but they had never sold bass before and were simply thrilled to be paid to play. I was sick.

"Butch and me saved the load. Came close to not shipping because of the big strike in New York, the dockworkers or something. Guess it's bad. Anyway, we're off the hook and the freezer is ready for another blitz. You bet."

"Norm, did Dinkie tell you that? What did I tell ya about that skunk? Did I tell ya to ship the fish? Did I tell you to ship the freakin' fish?"

I could feel the veins popping out of my neck. Here we were, two brothers, and I wanted to choke him, the poor sap. What was I going to tell Beaumont? I started walking east to the breachway with Squid's share. He was doing chores around his boat—bailing, draining his splash, and rinsing his live well.

"Pilgrim," I called. He came across and we talked.

"Sorry, Squid, the two cops got screwed on another of those Dinkie deals, coming out with thirty cents. I don't know what to say. I tried to warn them, but the little bastard is so good at it that he could talk his way into a convent with no pants on." I couldn't hide the frustration.

"Frankie, c'mon, anybody can drop a fish." Squid began staring south. "The pond's been stocked again," he added, his voice lowered more out of habit because we were alone on the uninhabited side of the inlet. "A lot of fish. All my rock piles are loaded with them, all taking eels. Candy from a baby."

It was another big-water night. Suds were blowing over the end of Charlestown Breachway so badly that neither Norman, Butch, nor myself wanted any part of it. Even on the beach, the water slid high enough so that you had to time the cast by running down with a back slider, let fly, and back up in free spool while making sure that you had retreated far enough to be clear of the next breaker. Even so, stripers were in over by Split Rock pretty decently. Norman was first.

"You bet," Norman said, more to himself than us—he had a habit of announcing that a lineside had picked up his eel and was running. The way it always seemed to be, you would feel the line tighten, reach across the reel with your left hand to throw the antireverse open, and the bass would swim off carrying the eel while line tumbled from the spool. Our habit was to count to ten. Quite often, though, Norman was known to rush the last four numbers of the count so that it took six seconds to count to six and one second to recite seven through ten. Butch and I, much as we loved Norman, spent more time laughing about the things he did than anything else during a night of midwatch hunts. One night, when a sand shark was dropping down from an inlet on Jamestown, Norman turned, startled by the splashing, and ran, yelling all the way to dry land. Another time, while crawling around in the breachway in his waders and looking for crabs, he spotted a striper, which later weighed in at fourteen pounds, in the beam of his light. He trapped it up against the rocks with his body and managed somehow to grab it. Butch and I agreed that we didn't think a person could do that sort of thing, and Butch added, "Only Norman."

Back to the memorable night when Norman said, "You bet." With the two of us on either side of him, we both closed toward him with our eels in our hands to see what he was doing. The spool of his squidder was tumbling wildly, as line lifted under slight tension on a rising wave—"eightnineten." The line tightened, lifted, and Norm came back so hard that his fifty-pound braid parted, giving off a report like a rifle.

"Jeezus, Norm, what the hell are you doing?" Butch said, half laughing, as Norm fell back in the sand from the line's sudden parting. I wanted to scream from seeing him pull so hard on what could have been a decent striper. Trying to cover for him, I mumbled something to Butch about us all doing it. Butch said, "I know, but . . ."

Soon after my eel hit the water, I felt a take. I tried to deal with the cresting sea so as not to have too much slack and have a wave break and tip off the bass. Deciding to hit early, I hauled back and hooked it. Looking east at Butch, I could see that he was fighting a bass already, and poor Norman was nervously re-rigging. As I slid my bass up on a high wave, Butch was already bending over a fish and Norman was talking to the eels in his bag, a clear sign that he had finished attaching a hook and leader to the end of what line he had left. Making one empty cast, I was dying to know whose boat had just run out of the breach. I ran to the breachway and jumped rock to rock seaward until I saw a small craft rising and dipping out of sight off the end. Whoever was out there had me silhouetted against the light on the nor'east horizon. Once he saw me, he started yelling.

"Millions of 'um. Millions of 'um."

The hiss and boom of breaking sea drowned out all noise. Nevertheless, between those waves I could hear the slap and clap of breaking fish that sounded like slow-frying fat.

"Holy Christ!" came the call from the little boat, which you could sometimes make out and sometimes wonder if it would survive.

Hiss, boom. Clap, clap, slap, slap . . . "Jeezus! Millions of 'um."

It was Beaumont.

Although I couldn't see any fish, a kid from Ohio could have told you that we had a lot of striped bass in that Rhode Island surf. What was better was that there were two lights on the beach over near Split Rock—clear indication that my partners were doing a job while I was taking attendance on the jetty. I bounded back to the sand, and when I got there, Butch and Norman were standing over a major cow, a moby striper.

Butch's voice was cracking, and Norm was breathing heavily. No jokes were exchanged as they both stood there looking at the fish.

"I think you got it, Norm," Butch said, gazing longingly at the trophy.

Wouldn't that be nice, I thought. *Norman could have a fifty.*

When you see a fifty-pounder in the surf, it looks as big as a man. I've seen people cry when they were a pound short; they cry with happiness when they make it. No one can tell you why that mark is so important, why forty-five pounds wouldn't be good enough. After all, on average, a forty-five-pounder is only two inches shorter than a fifty. It's one of those things to which surfcasters always seem to aspire while seeming never to understand. This kind of striped bass, a fifty-pounder, is the only thing, short of impending childbirth, that could stop three commercial killers from staying in a blitz. Did Norman have it?

Taking turns dragging it back to my buggy where I kept the weighmaster's scale, we were all sweating when we got there. Butch opened a beer, drew long on it, and tapped Norman on the shoulder to hand it to him. Hoisting the bass, it pulled the needle down to 50.4. I bounced it and the scale dropped to 50.2, causing Butch to step back and shake his head, "No," for fear that one more bounce would take poor Norm's fish away.

Offering his hand, Butch told Norm that few surfcasters catch a striper like that in a lifetime. Norman was in shock. He kept looking at the fish and shaking his head. Cracking open a couple more, we just stood there looking at this sow. Then, after a long silence, Norman walked the couple of steps over to it and proclaimed proudly, "You bet."

Butch grimaced, as though he had no inkling whether he was on the edge of a good laugh or a good cry. Walking over to touch Butch was my way of saying that we were all brothers. Dawn came quickly after that.

Beaumont's little tin boat held in the current of Charlestown Breachway under a strong idle while he waited for me to walk the hundred or so yards from Split Rock where our bass were piled.

"How'd yuz do?" he asked, in characteristic Beaumont-speak, standing among a pile of the biggest stripers any of us had ever seen. At the numbers end, I suppose, *three* of us might amass a catch like that from the beach—but not from the size end. Two fish stood out as well over the magic mark—later weighing in at fifty-four and fifty-eight. The other dozen spread from thirty-five to the high forties.

"We got half a dozen decent ones, and Norman got a fifty-even. We kind of screwed up, I guess."

Squid was grinning, that look of a bad joke coming over him that I knew so well. "My boys are going back to school this week. Guess that means the teachers are going back, eh Frankie?"

Waving back to him, I said, "Nice fish," and tried not to think about summer's end.

Beaumont's early-October haul was taken to Stonington around midday. Dinkie was sitting at the desk reading the paper when Squid pulled up, bass tails in clear view on the tailgate of his station wagon.

"Squid, ma man, got a little load for the road?"

Beaumont went about boxing and shoveling ice onto the fish without even looking up. After placing them in roughly hundred-pound groups, he nailed the prefitted soft pine covers down over the mix and tacked on blue-and-white cardboard shipping labels—BALLANTINE. With a black marker, he scrolled SQUID BEAUMONT with a skull and crossed-bones icon on each box. In the office he dropped twenty dollars—which was the five-dollar-per-box price of the box and ice. Shipping costs would be deducted from his check at the other end on Fulton Street.

"Dinkie?" The little wharf rat looked up from his paper.

"You got your checkbook?" Squid asked.

"Ya, huh? Checkbook?"

"You open that checkbook and write one out for $560 to settle that bogus New York lumpers strike they had on Fulton Street last month. And if you ever screw one of my beach guys with your phony, two-bit disasters again, I'm gonna bait my eel pot with your balls."

"Beau, c'mon," Dinkie said, trying to smooth things. "You don't know. There could have been a problem."

"The problem was right here in Stonington. I had more than seven hundred pounds in that load!"

"Squid, buddy, nobody told me it was your fish." The little rodent opened the desk drawer; Beaumont moved closer on the outside chance there was a weapon in the drawer. Dinkie wrote the check for $560 that reflected the premium difference on the Rosh Hashanah price, the other forty cents per pound that Fulton Street had really paid.

AUTUMN 1969, CHARLESTOWN, RHODE ISLAND

Sometime in early October, the monarch butterflies showed all over the Charlestown, Rhode Island, dunes. In full orange-and-black regalia, they fluttered over the grass against the wind in what seemed like a futile effort to head down the beach toward Montauk. They labored in what appeared to be an unorganized way on a route programmed a million years ago, a route intended to take them to Central America. I often sat smoking on the dune edge and wondered how they all knew it was time. I would think, *How do they know which way to go? Why, like waterfowl, don't they travel together?* Instead, in full migration, they were spread by the hundreds, advancing ten feet west, then blown back by prevailing winds four feet east, always gaining. *Where they're going has to be a long way off.* So, too, does another clarion call echo, first from the Maritimes, then from the Maine rivers like the Kennebec, then Cape Cod, setting the entire Striper Coast into migration at once. As though at some divine signal, word is somehow passed that it's time for linesides to head south.

Having been back to work a month, I had no firsthand knowledge of Charlestown striper trends. With only two fish in the cooler, Butch and Norm had added a few and Beaumont had taken all of it into Stonington. Our Friday-afternoon arrival was punctuated by my jumping into the top bunk to store some sleep—an exercise of nebulous value. When I came down at sunset for coffee and dinner, Butch came over to tell me about his big night.

"Frankie, my only regret is that you weren't here. If I live to be a hundred, it was a night I'll never forget. Norm and I worked our way to Split Rock, and he beached one in the midthirties. Twenty minutes later I had a pickup on my eel just east of the rock, and I had a fish run me to the end of the breachway. I put the brakes on it, worked it partway in, had it run some line off, finally got it back. Norm went down for it, clamped his hands on its gills, only to get thrown on the beach when a wave broke. There, Frankie, and the Lord is my judge, Norm was rolling in the foam yelling his head off, wrestling with this monster. When I got to him he was choking and hollering. I lifted the biggest striper you've ever seen away from him before the two of them got washed back down the hill. What does Norman say once I got this fish high and safe?"

"You bet."

"IT WAS A 'YOU BET,' ALL RIGHT—FIFTY-FIVE POUNDS!" That night, with late-season vehicles now allowed on the front beach, we left Joyce and the kids in my buggy, and I rode with Butch in his. We drove west to the beach limit at Fresh Pond Rocks and began working our way back. An hour of casting eels had not drawn a solitary take. Then, around midnight, near the "mound"—a spot that was used as a landmark where a short sprawling juniper grew—I could see repeated dark stains appearing on a gray sea at the rut where the surf broke. It was clearly working fish, but they wouldn't touch the eels. Suffering the same frustration, Butch saw them also but he couldn't hook any either. Finally, cutting the eel hook off, I tied on a floater Rebel, cast down the beach, and hooked an eighteen-pounder. Once Butch changed over to a plug, he took a pair of around ten pounds each. Then the school moved out—or down or up—leaving us. After heading as far east as we could, we knocked down a pot of coffee that his wife, Sue, had put together for us with some sweet cakes, of which I woofed three. Then Sue crawled into bed, and I joined Butch in the cab to drive west again, stopping here and there to fish. Inasmuch as we found nothing with the plugs, we both went back to slinging eels. Butch knocked down a thirty-eight-pounder around 3 A.M. It kept happening to me in the striper surf; I had said over and over that I would never let myself get that weary again, but this time I was falling down exhausted. The way it had been, there had to be fresh migrants coming in from Cuttyhunk, the Vineyard, who knew? Butch put on another pot of coffee, and I sat on the back bumper of his truck sagging, drifting in and out. I got up after a while, looked in to see Butch with his head on his arm next to a boiling coffeepot, and walked down to the water.

The eel was dead and dry, so I bent it first this way then that, listening to the cracking of the vertebrae. I rubbed it with sand until it was blue and bent it some more. Then I cast it just west of Split Rock, pumped it wildly, allowed it to settle, then pumped it again. On the second cast, something took. I waited, allowing time for the eel to be swallowed. I let the count run to ten before setting the hook. To me it was a good fish—something better than forty, I hoped. I didn't want to rouse Butch for a smaller bass than the one he had because I knew he was dog-tired. In the light of the quarter moon I could see it lying there, finning, kind of shot. When the next wave broke, I pressured it and it slid up. I stood on it, hoping someone was around. It was awfully big. I carried it up to the canvas on which Butch had spread the other five bass, and mine dwarfed them all.

"Hey, Butch," I called, and he pulled his head up. "We going to have coffee?"

He poured for both of us, and we went outside so as not to disturb his family.

"What is that?" Butch asked in astonishment over the large white belly.

"Buddy"—I tried to seem as nonchalant as I could under the circumstances—"I think what we got there is a fifty-pounder."

"You sonovabitch."

Putting in a halfhearted effort, we didn't take any more bass. However, at dawn in a Rhode Island fall people are all driving the beach. A gallery gathered around my buggy, where the scale was drawn down to fifty-two pounds. Spotting the crowd from the water, Beaumont came ashore to admire the fish. One of the LaForest brothers remarked that my striper was so big, it looked like a cod. Then Squid reached down into the gullet, his sleeve as high on his arm as he could roll it, and buried his arm and hand to feel what he could about the stomach contents and proclaimed the moby striper clean. It had *not* been stuffed with additional weight. So much for anglers keeping their eye on one another.

The excitement with which we greeted the arrival of big bass in Charlestown had us flying. What we had was the best of both worlds—the chance to pack in some money fish *and*, with luck, grab a little glory in the form of moby stripers, maybe even winning a striper contest. Here's how it worked, and how it was shaping up.

Each season the nearby Connecticut clubs held an October holiday weekend striper tournament that paid prizes for the biggest three stripers in boat fishing and a lot of less important angling merchandise for the three best surf fish. Because the officials feared cheating in the form of boat fish being registered in the surf, they never offered anything that made cheating worthwhile. Still, the biggest bass, the contest winner, brought a reward of a five-hundred-dollar savings bond, which in those days was serious money. Of course there was no way to win by cheating because when you showed up at contest headquarters with *the* fish, that was it. Almost no way.

"Frank," Squid asked, "how we going to get that five hundred?"

"You have to be a bigger cheat than the tourney officials," I cautioned. "Look what they did to Gus Lawton. He comes in with the biggest cow in the state, so they stick some sinkers down its throat after he weighs in and announce the next day that Gus was beat by a few ounces—then display the same fish, Gus's fish, as the leader. After that the prize money goes to their boy, who doesn't take it, and the club keeps it all without a payoff."

"Gus wasn't ready for them," said Squid. "We can mark the fish and bring it in with witnesses. What can we do for an edge?"

Squid was grinning, but he was dead serious. "This isn't a fishing contest. It's about who can screw who with the best combination of lies for money and glory. This is *better* than a fishing contest."

"First," I urged, "the winning striper is going to be a boat fish. Second, the prize money is going to lure every glory glutton in the territory—the Snug Harbor bunch, our crowd, and even the Hartford bunch."

"Don't worry about Hartford," Squid reassured me. "Holiday weekend, they'll be cocked out of their minds by sunset on Friday. Our problem is the ones who can fish and want to win."

I looked at Squid, who was standing at the front end of his buggy staring out over the sea as if trying to unravel the future so that he could alter it. *This guy really thinks that he can win,* I thought.

"There are only a handful of people who can produce the kind of striper that will get the five hundred. Our edge is time."

"Time? Huh?"

"The derby starts at midnight," Squid mused. "The boats will be pouring out at sunset, three hours before the start, to get an edge. I know, I've been watching it for five years. They cheat by three hours."

"Squid, if they cheat by three minutes, they're cheating."

"That's what I say. If we start a week before the tournament, there's a good chance of overcoming any stray luck they might have from their cheating."

"Oh, I get it," I said with my most facetious parlance, "all we have to do is put a fifty-pounder in the back of our truck, then bring in this rotting striper, with maggots crawling out of its ass, for today's fish. Do I have that right?"

"Frank, don't be stupid, we'll hide it for as long as we have to."

"Where do you hide a fifty-pounder? How do you keep it alive without the enemy finding it first, and then seeing *them* end up winning with your fish?"

Prying the cap from another beer, he slid it across the table, eyes back out the window. "Jeeze, some freaking tourist from New Jersey will probably win it. Money and glory, gone. I got a better idea. I'll register, pay the ten bucks, you don't, and if you get a brute, you give it to me. I get the glory and you get the money."

The whole thing was stupid. Squid was muttering about tying a fish, which he didn't have yet, to an engine block on the bottom of Ninigret Pond.

"Forget it," I urged. "We're not talking five hundred here. It's a bond, which is worth only $375. It ain't five hundred until maturity. By the time it gets to five hundred, we'll all be dead."

"The bastards! Tournament ain't even started and they're cheatin' already."

FRIDAY NIGHT OF COLUMBUS DAY WEEKEND, CHARLESTOWN, RHODE ISLAND Once it was dark enough to offer the slightest cover, the boats came out of the breachway between the stone jetties in an almost solid line. It was three hours early, but it was still tournament time. By full dark you could see the running lights, green pointing this way, red that way, sprinkled on the horizon. About 2 A.M. strays started returning for a short sleep. Each striperman did what he could to win the tourney. Some drifted dead mackerel. Others motored west in search of live menhaden. A few drifted live eels. Stripers were hauled over gunwales—many in the thirties, a few in the forty-pound class, which everyone pretty much knew would take a miracle to win.

Late Saturday word spread about a fifty-one-pounder that had been taken somewhere east, maybe around Matunuck, no one knew for sure. As had been the situation for so many tournaments, the benchmark was in place: a fifty-plus. It was not Squid's. It surer than hell wasn't mine. The fish was brought in by George Cosgrove, who, along with his wife, Connie, was one of Charlestown's top rods. Everyone knew their capabilities, and we'll never know how many regulars secretly prayed for them both to come down with the flu at tournament time.

The second day Connie Cosgrove was live-lining a hickory shad with fifty-pound line along with George, the one leading the tourney with the fifty-one-pounder. It was one of those feel-good early-fall mornings where you get to take off your sweater around 8 A.M. and go swimming by noon. She felt good. George had the lead and she had George so it kind of made her, through some perverse transfer of power by association, a highliner. All they had to do was accept the unlikely possibility of getting another fifty-pound-plus and look down from their lofty position upon all those others quite likely not getting another. It was a picture-perfect morning on Rhode Island's picture-perfect coast. Fifty-one pounds of striped bass was—given past tournament results—none too shabby.

Connie's shad had begun to falter after swimming in circles for twenty minutes with an 8/0 Siwash hook in its mouth. The bait was alive, but bleeding had drained it of all energy. Still, the scent transmission continued as the east-moving tide carried it toward the dusky form of a great striper. The fish pumped west in a slow search pattern, looking for the shad that by now had lain on its side drifting toward the bottom. Connie was working on her acceptance speech when the cow bass picked up the shad and continued west. The mono lifted and the ratchet announced the take. *CLICK* . . . *click, click, click.*

"Connie, grab that!" George urged.

The thirty-five-year-old housewife, who had probably taken a dozen decent stripers in her life, muscled the boat rod and set on the cow striper as the line tightened precipitously.

"Back off, Connie," George warned, "your drag is too tight!"

Confidently, Connie opened the star drag control on the crank side of the reel, but she opened it too much, and the monster, pumping and pulling in a wild, desperate effort to escape, caused the reel to backlash for lack of suitable tension. As the line lifted on the spool, crossing and gnarling and knotting upon itself, tension did rise, but not enough to break fifty-pound mono. It rose enough and gnarled enough to *cut* the mono right at the spool of the Penn reel. Connie's dream striper was free, towing a good two hundred feet of monofilament line in the morning sun of Green Hill, Rhode Island. There was a long silence as the poor woman contemplated the notion that a husband and wife might, just might, have won the tournament—one and two, husband and wife. Her lip curled. George muttered, "Jeezus Christ, Connie." And she began to cry.

They were barely in sight when Squid came bounding west toward the breachway in his Starcraft, two fish in the midthirties up front for ballast, money, and a saving of face for half a night's effort. Looking toward the shore, he noticed a splashing in the waves on the beach and cut the throttle. Wearing Polaroids, he looked down into the green depths and could make out a strand of mono leading from the beach. He snagged it with his boat hook, pulling some of it in— enough to connect this line with the splashing in the surf. Hand over hand, Squid eased the moby lineside toward his boat and then gasped at the sight of as big a bass as he had seen in quite a few months. It was no world record, but it was a good bit over fifty-one pounds, for sure. When he got it to the gunwale, he could see that the cow had been choking on a shad. Unhooking the shad, he removed the hook, then stuffed the three-pound bait back down the striper's throat.

Meanwhile, Connie and George had seen Squid stop and go through the whole procedure, and they knew that this had to be *her* fish, the new tournament leader. They beelined it over there to confront Squid.

"Beaumont!" Connie yelled. "That's my fish!"

"Your fish? I don't see a collar on this fish that has a name on it. This fish is mine," Squid said, trying to seem casual.

"I am going to scratch your @#$%& eyes out, you @#%$# skunk, you freakin' cheater!"

Of course she had had time both to digest and to contemplate as a result the fact that her loss was dethroning her husband's tournament-winning striper. All she could think of was Squid, whom all three knew did not—repeat, *did not*—catch this monster. And Squid, hoping to bring it in for the $500, or was it $375, and the joy of winning, the glory, could see that his prize was going up in smoke. Connie was about to have a stroke. George could imagine his fifty-one-pounder sliding into second, or maybe even third, place the way things were going. George could see that Connie was trying to figure a way to get at Squid and make good her promise to scratch his freaking eyes out. Whatever was going to happen, Squid felt that while it was really neither his fish nor hers, it was, after all, in his boat. George flat-out told Squid that if he tried to register the fish—whose ever it was—he would inform officials that it was a found fish, and therefore not a caught fish. It was a standoff. Here was the kind of striper that few of us ever catch in a lifetime. Here was the kind of striper that some years might yield ten from Virginia to Maine. For one of them it was a chance to be remembered, pictured in the *Hartford Courant*, the *Providence Journal*, the *Boston Globe*, that fleeting fifteen minutes of fame.

"Connie, shut the f— up!"

"I'll kill that guy!"

George shouted angrily at Squid, "You did *not* catch that fish."

"Neither did you, neither did she."

Connie yelled, "I'll kill the bastard!"

"You can't bring it in."

"Neither can you."

"I'll kill him!"

Squid pulled on the starter cord and motored back with the lineside tucked into his Starcraft. He shaved, put on a clean shirt, because you never knew if the press might be at tournament headquarters, and took the fish in. Seeing George and Connie when he got there, Squid sensed they had already told officials what had happened.

"This isn't mine," Squid admitted. "I found it and didn't want it in the wrong hands."

Puzzled, the officials didn't know what to make of it all—and I doubt, to this day, if anybody really knows or even cares. That Monday, with the tourney ending at noon, word was sent for Squid that he was wanted at the awards ceremony. Squid stood shyly in the crowd, knowing that George's fifty-one-pounder had done the job and had garnered the five big ones. Beaumont saved face with a forty-eight-pounder that hadn't won anything. Just before they called George up for the winner's trophy, Squid was asked to come forward for a special prize—"Sportsman of the Year." The master of ceremonies from Connecticut told the story of how Squid had found a fifty-four-pound bass, but—because he hadn't really caught it—had turned it in fair and square. Everyone clapped for Squid, and Connie, smiling broadly, planted the nicest kiss on Squid's cheek while he blushed with delight and was presented a trophy. The next day every paper on the Striper Coast ran a picture of Connie's warm congratulatory smooch. It gets no better. Beaumont later told me that Cosgrove would probably be dead by the time the bond was worth a full five hundred dollars. He was, after all, over forty.

Late in the fall, I got a personal letter in the mail:

Hi Frank,

It's me, Squid. It's too bad that yuz had to go hunting in November but I suppose that it's only fair that a person could like to do other things besides fish. We had a nice stocking of the pond early November, but the price was not good because the Long Island haul seiners really mowed them down when the fish went by them and the floor on Fulton Street must have been ass deep with not enough buyers. Still, it was good to put my Starcraft up for winter. The rivets are all loose anyways.

October I made a social call to Stonington to discuss the dock and lumpers strike with Dinkie. He was very sympathetic to the idea that having his nuts cut off before I killed him stood a chance of being the low point of his season. With that in mind, Dinkie wrote a check for you, Norman, and Butch, along with my share, saying that he had misread the situation, and I'm just getting around to catchin' up with business.

You take care of them guys—their share with this money I'm sendin yuz. I look forward to another season next spring when we can again knock down a couple and talk about the bass and how they move.

Your friend and partner,
"Squid" Beaumont

5

P-TOWN: CLOUD LAND
OF THE CUCKOOS

DURING THE WINTER of 1970, the managers of Nauset Beach, comprised jointly of selectmen from Orleans and Chatham, put an end to the summerlong "squatters." Updated regulations required that anyone using the beach in a self-contained camper had to stay off for three days when leaving the beach. Fishing all summer, as was familiar, was over.

PROVINCETOWN, TIP OF CAPE COD, JUNE 19, 1970
This place is unique for a number of reasons. It's a fishing village that has been home to rogues since colonists extracted the first salt from its waters more than three hundred years ago. Even now you can stop by any smoke-filled bar and see the fishermen brawling with leather-sheathed knives on their hips, yet it remains unthinkable to use one in a bar fight. Boys hold hands with boys and girls hold hands with girls. Summers on Commercial Street, a "Disco Cop" falls to his knees and begs people to move across traffic while he belts out "Jingle Bells" with a police whistle. He bows from the hip for some and snaps to attention with a full-starch military salute for others. Some folks talk to themselves on the street, or they sell religion or preach against war; others are in rags with a 50K-limit VISA in their pocket. When your mother told you that it takes all kinds, she must have just gotten back from P-Town.

Beach sand is coarse and gravelly, not soft, which is an inaccurate expression used to describe a level of driving difficulty. The term *surf fishers* has a slightly different meaning here because, along with surfcasters who actually cast from shore, there are surf fishers who launch boats right into the open Atlantic, pushing off with one foot as though the tin boat were a scooter. In P-Town many families populate the beach using two vehicles and a boat from which to fish. The larger "buggy" is home, with all the creature comforts needed to keep the gang fed, healthy, and protected. The "chase vehicle" is utilized to run the sand trails into town for supplies and to take sellable catches to the dock, but its most important use is to push the boat bow-first for a launch and pull it high onto dry sand when it returns. Not that there are rules, but generally speaking, we can also say that those fishing in boats fish primarily in the daytime and those who cast from the beach fish mostly at night. In the final analysis, the area is not famous for its surfcasting; it is better known for its good boat fishing. In the 1950s Captain Ralph Gray boated one of the biggest linesides in forty years—in the high 60s—and Kay Townsend, then a short while later Rosa Webb, caught the IGFA Ladies All-Tackle World Records at 63½ pounds and 64½ pounds, respectively. Regardless of your choice of angling technique, you have to say that the place is steeped in striped bass traditions. A displaced Nauset Beach family, out after stripers, could do worse.

Beach distances in Provincetown were rarely more than two miles and usually only one, whereas Nauset was over ten miles. A popular Provincetown spot was half a mile west of the Coast Guard Station called the "Second Rip." The boatmen parked at the high end; at the low, surfcasters would form up at high tide to catch the rips, which formed from the falling of Cape Cod Bay. With prevailing winds southwesterly, it was possible to cast a large swimmer straight out, throw the clutch lever of your reel, allow the line to tighten, and feel your plug drum in the current until a moby striper ate it. The best tides started with a midnight high; but a few nights later, still influenced by either a new or full moon, the water would still be falling with the first light. On those "morning tides," a fire lighting off in the east with a strong current—the big stripers, often more than forty pounds, but only rarely over fifty—would drop down from Race Point toward the Back Beach, which was a stretch of wild sand dunes that were less inhabited. Sometimes—and you could always tell by the bent rods they left in their wake—the stripers came from the Back moving against the current. Ah, but the realities of surfcasting, which somehow seem always to be forgotten, were that most nights there was nothing.

For that reason, you could help pass a long uneventful night by standing beside someone who was talkative and pleasant. However, because you were swinging ten feet of rod blank with almost that amount of line, you never wanted to stand too close. Thus, casters threw their lures, then sidestepped toward each other to chat. One person there stood out favorably: George Carlezon was a left-handed caster. This enabled us both to cast all night shoulder to shoulder without even moving our feet. George was pleasant enough, but it was his left-handedness that made him popular. He was also old guard, which meant that he had gotten to P-Town after the war twenty-five years before, had fished with Frank Woolner, among others, and knew how to fish from the beach.

I recall one night on the drop when all the gang was setting like mad on "ghost hits." It was happening to me, too. Your plug would be moseying along or swinging and *bang*, you'd get a hard hit, but there was nothing there when you set. Fine if it happened once. But after a while, you'd start to notice that it was happening to the others also, which kind of blew your mind. Anyway—and I hope I'm not taking too long with this—George banged one, and he was the only guy out of about twenty of us to hook up. It was maybe a thirty-five-pounder.

Coming back down to my left shoulder, he whispered, "Frankie, when you feel 'um hit it, don't do nuthin'. Just wait. He'll come back."

For a meat fisherman wanting that fish, not setting on a hit is like holding your hand on a hot stove. I got a bang, and my arms—functioning independently—hauled back, and all I could think of was kicking myself in the butt. When I checked to see if Carlezon had been looking, he was laughing at me—which made it even worse. I rushed the retrieve because the notion that they were passing way on the outside was in my head. A guy downtide fanned soon after his plug hit the water. After my cast, there was a bang, a hit just like the others, and I did nothing but picture my Atom plug lolling in the current. Then I felt a solid take and I was on to a screaming, drag-taking striper. *Oh God, how I love to fish!*

Later, while standing around, we worked out the theory that the stripers were batting or killing or spearing with their dorsals, then returning to pick up their kills. When surfmen were automatically setting, they were taking the plug or prey away from the bass, so it moved on looking for another. If you left the plug there, it was where it was supposed to be and they came back to pick it up. George and I were the only ones with bass.

The Second Rip, or "Telephone Poles"—as it was named right after World War II—was a starting point for newcomers like us who had been displaced from another beach by regulation. However, it lacked the kind of numbers needed to keep commercial fishers out of the poorhouse. With six years of full-time summer surfcasting, we had all grown used to more action, which often happened somewhere on the clock other than from 1 A.M. to dawn. The girls didn't even try to deal with those hours, and Dick was sagging pretty heavily by the third night. Even that activity took place only four nights out of each set of tides—eight nights per month. What was needed was a filler trip. Because we were still allowed three nights on Nauset, we could time a weekday run that minimized exposure to others fishing there, allayed any concerns of being turned away because of beach maximums and raised the possibility of getting some money fish on the dock. I think the slow beach fishing in P-Town bothered me most when I thought about what the boatmen could do trolling wire line jigs and bunker spoons. Their Jeeps would pass with bass tails hanging off the tailgates, making me thirst all the more for some of the high drama to which we had grown accustomed. We needed a Nauset trip.

Making my case with Mom, I had us figured for Tuesday afternoon. That timetable would allow us to dodge those who stretched the weekend, and also have us coming off Nauset on Friday when people would be arriving. Except for a stray vacationer, whom we could cold-shoulder away from, we would be fishing largely alone. The tides there would be in the evenings at seven, eight, and nine o'clock, which we had learned were the best when water was rising into Pleasant Bay under a lowering sun—a twice-per-month situation that we knew to be the most productive. Low tide out in the channel was in the middle of the night, so we could fish almost around the clock. It fit nicely outside the Second Rip's place in the tide chart. The high command, Mom, was game for some commercial fishing.

Late Tuesday morning we left the Cape Cod National Seashore and bought provisions on the way to Nauset Beach. The septic tank had to be emptied at the town dump. At Warren Roderick's Tydol

Station we gassed up, pressurized the tires, and filled the water tank. With Mom still buying groceries at the A&P with her helper, Carol, the rest of us went to the dock and shoveled all the ice we could carry into the permanent cooler on the front bumper, which held three hundred pounds of bass. Portable coolers were also filled and slid down the aisle of the living quarters. By 1300 hours we were driving south on the mid-Cape highway, the kids singing "We All Live in a Yellow Submarine" from the living space. At a place in Wellfleet that is known for great foot-long dogs, we pulled up and asked for twelve with the works and four large Cokes. The girl who came to the cab and took our order, knowing that no two people could eat twelve dogs, looked perplexed: "Twelve?"

"Twelve," Joyce responded. "Four Cokes, large."

Later, when she brought them out, I was reaching for the change from three dollars and bumped her hands as she set up the tray. One of the dogs fell to the ground.

The clerk, sensing a minor disaster that was certain to beckon a need for defense, said, "They were all right when I brought them."

The kids fell silent in the living space, because they knew somebody was going to have to make do with *one* dog, and pressed their noses against the glass. Joyce excused herself, opened the door, and picked up the dog, which had fallen to the gravel, carried it over to the barrel, and disposed of it. I lifted the change from the tray—all of it. None of us wanted to stay there, so we drove a short way to a rest area, where all the kids complained weakly that they couldn't finish theirs. Four half dogs slid across the beach blanket on the side of Route 6 to Mom, who had taken one—the contributions were way more than she could possibly eat. It was one of those times when, while I cursed being poor, always reminded by our number, I wondered if being rich might have been a greater nuisance. Most of all, it was the way we all looked at each other.

Checking in at Nauset, the guard wrote down our permit number and collected the small fee, while—without being told—Dick rummaged through beach trash Dumpster for sea worms left by other surfmen. By the time all four tires were aired down, the thirteen-year-old had consolidated the living remains of several tomato cartons of very expensive striper baits and placed them in the forward cooler on the outside chance we would need live bait. Ice had settled enough to allow room for the carton in these eighty-five-

degree temperatures as it always had. An hour later we leveled the
buggy with the radiator into the sou'west, and the camper door,
where light could filter onto the surf, faced away from the water. We
all slept until after 1900, the sun lowering south of Morris Island, a
cod boat heading home after a day at sea, gulls trailing and diving for
the evening gurry. It was kind of Patti Page, kind of Olde Cape Cod.

When we finished dinner, Mom, with Carol's help, picked up
and I took the others outside to get the fishing gear ready. Water hurried into the bay now, swinging left to right on a rise, mare's tails
blowing off the bars as waves broke, their rainbows fading on a low
sun.

"Dick, I want you at the high point plugging that corner where
they sometimes stop. I'll send a runner from time to time to check
on your action. Take your kit. I'll tie on Rebels for Carol and Mom.
You girls stay near them in case one of you needs help with a good
one. Sandra"—our youngest by three minutes, and nine, turned
around at the sound of her name—"have Mom set up at the eddy to
the right of the main rip, and I want you both to go wherever you see
fish being taken. Stay with the action and don't touch the fish.
Change rods when you have landings and leave them."

When Carol, age ten, came out, she was wearing Mom's hippers,
and Mom had waders with a surf belt. The purpose of the belt was to
keep her from taking on water in a trip or a bad step and getting too
heavy. The twins were barefoot, because there was nothing made that
fit them; this was only their third season surfcasting and two of those
years would not have counted had God been looking. Don't worry
about Dick. Only a fool would have failed to have given him the best
of everything; he could outcatch any man, so the return on invest-
ment was a no-brainer. All professionals, they had their stations and
their orders. "Carol, be sure to open the bail *before* you cast."

Dick's uptide whistle was first. I turned in time to see him backing with a bend in his stick. Carol set and dropped hers, and I was
on in a sequential set of hits that was clearly an arriving school coming from the outside toward Pleasant Bay. Susan was on, as was
Carol, and I moved my bouncing six-pounder up to the truck. Joyce
slid out of the eddy over to the main current to join Susan and
Sandra, and she was on immediately.

Patow! A rifle shot from parting monofilament line was heard
from Carol's stick.

"Just take another rod," I told her. Carol's lip curled as if she was about to sniffle.

They all needed a ghillie. Our policy was that no one, other than Dick or myself, was to touch the fish because of the inherent danger of someone getting an errant hook to the hand or foot. It was both for their protection and for the continuation of the blitz. Walking about them I passed out new surf rods, which, by design, were identical so that no familiarization was needed when tackle changed. Dragging two bouncing fish back to bumper spikes, I stood the rods in them, clubbed the bass, removed plugs, and turned in time to exchange gear. I never made another cast, and it seemed like forever before the tide slacked enough to offer us a break. Carol counted forty-seven schoolies, including the ones Dick had strewn all over the high point. Knowing that these ran sixteen fish to the box, we had to have more than three hundred pounds. Rinsing them all free of sand, we packed them head to tail in the front box after we topped off the other boxes with ice from the front.

It was a system that we had come to know. The ice melted quickly in the wind of driving and the heat of the day. With our combination of coolers, I could keep close to five hundred pounds of bass iced. Still, by the end of the second day, there was barely enough ice to keep the catch. If the mix of fish and ice was right, there was no room in the coolers for the third night's catch. However, if we left the beach first thing in the morning, the third night's catch didn't have to be iced. It could be stowed in plastic trash bags—a recent invention in those days. In a less perfect world, you could come off the beach with most of your ice gone and no fish to put on that ice. On the other hand, you could also catch more stripers than you could stow, which would necessitate an early run off the beach. With the new three-days-off regulation, it was never advisable to take fish off from a good night, because you couldn't come back for three days and the bass would probably have been gone by then. The beach rules of Orleans and Chatham were killing us.

Late afternoon of the second day, I could hear the girls talking outside the buggy.

"Maybe we won't have to stay the whole three days," Carol seemed to wonder.

"Well, if you didn't break so many off, Carol, we could fill the boxes and go back to P-Town," admonished Sandra.

"Does Mom have enough food?" Sue asked.

Dick, who had been sharpening the knife in his kit, heard them talking and chimed in. As the oldest, Dick was the big brother who could always explain; he always had the advantage in age that gave him a grasp, a clear comprehension of our delicate balance of food, water, gasoline, ice, and even money.

"Girls"—he spoke in his most authoritative voice—"if we fill those boxes, Dad *has* to go off to sell the fish."

Mulling the whole thing, Susan said, "Fill the boxes."

Sandra-Pete-Repeat echoed, "Fill the boxes."

I climbed down from the bunk, nodding at Joyce—who was reading a paperback in her bunk—and asked, "Got any Chicken a La King?"

"Frank," she said, "we have enough food, we don't need that."

"Just go along with this."

That night at dinner, when the kids came in, they kept looking at each other and at the ominous can—a clear sign that food was in short supply and that dinner was not likely to be exciting. Mom served hamburg patties and spaghetti, which seemed to surprise them, but the message was clear that the quality of life for the next few days hinged on taking a whole lot of striped bass. When we finished dinner, Carol helped Mom clean up while the other three draped plugs over the windshield wiper for quick change. Dickie was teaching the twins how to clinch-knot a plug to a mono line. All the rods were retied and lined up for the evening rise.

With the sun low and a little less water, the stripers came through the inlet again that night like they had done the previous one. Again, all of us hooked up at once and all of us had fresh rods in less than two minutes. I dropped out of casting to ghillie for the fifteen or so smaller bass, with another around eighteen pounds that Mom beached before it was even dark. Disappointingly, on this night the entire catch came in that one flurry; none of us had so much as a sniff after that. At 2200 I whistled them in, and judging from how quickly they responded, it was no sooner than they wanted. In ten minutes all three girls were in bed, and in three minutes more I could hear the slow deep breathing of sleep. A partial moon hung over Morris Island as Joyce and I walked barefoot in the powder of Chatham Inlet. Dick, who was standing on the best stretch of the rip that formed as water turned to flow into Pleasant Bay, cast a swimming plug. He seemed to be enjoying the quiet, almost pleased to have the place to himself without fish. It was, though at his age I doubt that he consciously knew it, the contemplative way that surf-casting is supposed to be.

NAUSET BEACH PATROL, DAY THREE   At noon during lunch I laid out the situation for the family.

"We're going off tomorrow because of the new regs. Whatever we get tonight goes into the aisles. If it's dead, I'll whistle you in before midnight. Everybody is on bonus, which means that if the four of you beach a hundred pounds and they pay fifty cents per pound, you get to split twenty-five dollars four ways, which is six and a quarter each."

Dick was the first to pick up on the numbers. "Isn't a hudnred pounds, at that price, fifty dollars?"

"The first half of the catch goes to the 'boat' for expenses—gas, food, line, plugs." They all looked at Carol. "It's the way all commercial fishing operations do it. Half for the boat," I instructed.

"But, Da-aad, this isn't a boat, we're not a boat," Carol complained.

"Six dollars?" asked Susan. "We never had that much money."

"Six dollars?" chimed Sandra.

Now my clutch of commercials was out for blood. The twins would surely be planning a major attack on Provincetown's penny candy shop. You could go hog wild with six bucks. Too bad nobody told the stripers. That night we all stood on the rip that hurried to Pleasant Bay, where it would shimmer in front of the Christopher Ryder House to impress couples in dress clothes having dinner. We caught nothing. We were in bed by midnight; tomorrow would be a long day unloading fish and replenishing everything else.

Late that morning, near an abandoned building that had once housed first a beach patrol and later a Coast Guard Station, an eighteen-year-old boy from New Jersey was shoveling in the sand. He had crossed Pleasant Bay with his mother in a boat used by a Chatham motel to ferry guests to the outer beach. For him the freedom to be able to dig a hole in the beach of any size, feel the shovel penetrate, and move so much sand with abandon was a new experience. They say he dug down eight feet; you could have put a Volkswagen in it. He called to his mother to come take a look, and when she arrived at the edge of the hole it caved in on him. The frantic middle-aged woman sought help but, by the time she got some others to come, she could no longer remember—as everything looked the same—where it had all happened. He was dead and was not found for many hours.

We were passing the place on our way off and saw the police beach patrol there. The kids all listened as the police officer told us about it, and I could see their noses pressed against the glass; I could tell they had heard the story; I could see the terror in their faces; I could only imagine how the mother must have felt.

The drop at Old Harbor Fish in Chatham was uneventful, and I was flattered that the floor help remembered me. Our drop was 396 pounds of select and 18 jumbo. The price could vary anywhere from twenty-five cents to sixty. At the high end of that range, our load would fetch more than a week's salary inland, which, whenever I weighed the value of our efforts, always brought me comfort. Most of all, fishing was what we liked to do and it was something that we could all do together.

A fast run of the beach before the noon heat was a favorite way of ours to deal with the change-of-beach and reprovisioning drill. With the fresh food gone, the Nauset patrol was usually topped off with a load of supermarket-cooked rotisserie chickens and Arturo's Portuguese bread, which we ate in the camper parked in the large A&P lot in P-Town. With no breakfast and noon bearing down, any of us could have fought a full-grown gorilla for something to eat. You should have seen those girls run across the parking lot to greet Mom and push her shopping cart back to the buggy. Even if they had no memory of the chicken, you could smell it. We pulled chicken off the bones with our hands and ripped fresh bread into chunks. Mom pulled the tabs off pop cans for them, and there was not a single word, as all eyes smiled.

While the new Nauset regulations had forced us to P-Town, we had all begun to like it there. For one thing, the short beach run was welcome after eleven miles of sand and thirty of highway. With a 10 P.M. high tide, the Second Rip had doubtful potential for at least two more nights—which was all right with me after a tiring run to Nauset.

July 1970 was the date of release for my first writing effort and subsequent sale—an article about surfcasting for stripers that appeared in *Salt Water Sportsman* magazine titled "Montauk on My Right." The next month another article of mine was published there called "Block Island Safari"; it was about "monster" bluefish up to ten pounds. Still, bluefish were an exotic species then, and few of us had ever seen one over that size from shore.

The set of morning tides on the Second Rip had not been this dead all season. Carlezon landed a bass in the twenty-pound class, and Dick beached two one night when twenty other anglers couldn't catch any. Several times the boy was seen removing conchs from the treble hooks of his plug, and one of the New York crowd asked Dick if he would swim or float his swimming plug for him so as to see its action in the hope of imitating the lure. When Dickie swung the artificial softly into the water's edge to demonstrate, the Atom plug sank like a stone. What the boy had been inadvertently using was a leaker. It was fairly common at the time, because the tools or molds that Atom was using then were turning out products that took on water, causing the lures to cast well but sink. Apparently, the few fish that came through were deep, and the boy's offer was the only one seen. Despite this small revelation—which raised a slight buzz with surfmen—fishing was just awful, and few regulars were showing up mornings.

In early August, on a midnight tide, the first good one as dictated by the P-Town traditions, there were perhaps four of us fishing and six more watching, smoking, and drinking coffee beside their buggies when fish came in. All four hooked up in sequential order, west to east, while the others ran to cast and a sixth wader-clad man ran down the line of campers pounding on the doors, shouting, "The fish are in, the fish are in!"

I was on to something that felt good and was taking line from the reel when I looked at Dickie. I could see him hunched over his reel picking at a backlash when his line went tight from a hit. It pulled so hard that it ripped line out of his tangle. Luckily he mended in time to throw the clutch and recover. One of the early surfcasters to hook up shouted "bluefish" and, as each landed his, he would confirm that indeed we did have a run of blues. When I shouldered over to Carlezon, he told me that the previous year they had taken many of better than fifteen pounds, some up to nineteen. He suspected that the same fish were back. *Nineteen pounds?* I thought. *Do blues get that big in this part of the world?* The all-tackle world record was twenty-four pounds, but it had been taken off the coast of Africa some-where—the Azores. What was worse was that my article on bluefish, "Block Island Safari," which had just come out, spoke of monster blues weighing ten pounds. When I saw a person beach a piddling twelve-pounder, it hit me how much of a fool the article stood to make me appear. If these surf fishers could routinely land fish near-ly twice that size and, when looking down at a twelve, say, "I never saw one that small"—I was none too happy to have written it.

Dick carried a small billy club or "priest" in his kit, and before whacking a bluefish, he put the wooden club into the fish's maw, then heard the wood splinter as it closed its jaws on the club. "Whoa," the boy exclaimed, "what teeth!" Action held up until the first light at about the time when the tide slacked. Bluefish were strewn all along the beach, some in neat piles beside tailgates. Needless to say, not one of the blues was released. This crowd, which had always utilized money from the sale of their catch to offset the costs related to going there, wouldn't dream of releasing a fish, even if it fetched only twelve cents per pound. These were commercial fish that were being landed by sport fishermen.

We had one person fishing in the crowd who hadn't gotten it yet. It doesn't take long for the gang to put a label on somebody, espe-cially if he's new and lacks an appropriate title. Allan had pulled up on the beach with a Pennsylvania license plate and had asked ques-tions about the fishing—a battery of questions: "What do they catch here? Have any been caught lately? Do they pull hard?" Holding up a lure, he inquired, "Is it okay to use one of these? Do you think they will come tonight? How do the fish see in the dark? Do they always bite at night?" Kind of makes you wonder, doesn't it? Allan's failure to wait for an answer to each question immediately placed him under suspicion, which more than likely contributed to his being assigned a name. What was worse was that, being from Pennsylvania, he was a foreigner. Thus poor Allan, because of his propensity for questions, was dubbed "the Pennsylvania Wonder Boy" and it stuck. Later, he became known as "PWB."

The second night, now with fifty surfcasters on the rip because word had spread of the bluefish blitz the night before, blues came through right on cue at the top of the tide. The gang was all guffaw-ing and pulling and yelling, "Fish on," and passing one another excitedly and yelling, "Coming down, fish on." Then, at the height of all the excitement, we heard a voice in the darkness: "It's okay, fella." Then again: "It's okay, boy."

Womp! A small baseball bat came down on a bluefish head not far from him downtide.

Thump. Another bluefish met its maker.

Still, a friendly voice of hope came out of the darkness. "Hold still, fella, I'll have ya back in the water in a jiffy."

Sidestepping to one another, the guys started quizzing each other about what they were seeing but not believing. "Is somebody talking to the fish?" asked one surfcaster.

"Easy, fella."

"I wouldn't a believed it if I didn't see it with me own eyes."

"There's a guy over there talkin' to a bluefish."

Then one of the clowns muttered, "Ya have to talk French to 'um."

"It's the Pennsylvania Wonder Boy," somebody shouted in a kind of stage whisper, "he's talking to the fish!"

"Talking to the fooking bluefish?" said Swede. "I can half understand talking to striped bass because them is kind of special wid all of us, but a bluefish?"

Allan paid no attention and probably didn't hear what was being said about him. Maybe he didn't care. With so much standing around and so many casters tied up with removing blues, it was easy to walk back down into open water. My plug had been cast and was drifting and swinging off my rod tip into the current while I daydreamed about Allan. Here in the striper surf, all these people were sport fishers. And Allan, who was certain to be a Catskills trout fisher—probably a branch of the Delaware River—was bringing the angling ethic that he knew from his inland sport where people rarely killed a fish, especially a trout. In a way it was he who was doing things the way they should have been done, but here, where hauling protein from the Atlantic was an established tradition, sport and commercial fishing ethics, if not in conflict, were certainly jumbled. As for talking to fish, I doubt that works anywhere except to impress upon those around you that you have no hostile intentions.

The bluefish blitz was really getting to me. Many of the blues, though none of ours, were dangerously close to twenty pounds. One night that week I beached a twelve-pounder, and a surfcaster passing by me with a fish by the tail so as to avoid its teeth said, "I'm not trying to hurt your feelings, but it's been a while since I've seen one that small."

There was strong rumor circulating about a woman in a boat from one of the buggies on the Back Beach having taken one weighing twenty-three pounds. Keep in mind that we had all caught hundreds if not thousands of linesides. Still, these blues—which admittedly brought a low price in the market if you were thinking commercially—were so new, so rare in our experience at that time, that they were thought of as an exotic species. The last time "exotics" had visited Provincetown I had been in grade school.

Back then, during the early 1950s, thousands of bluefin tuna had stormed the area between Wood End and Highland Light for the entire summer. In boats, these tuna—often approaching two hundred pounds but more likely "school tuna" that were less than a hundred pounds—would tow the fisher around on a Nantucket Sleighride kind of pull. At least in boats it was possible to catch up with the fish and win. On those rare occasions when a surfcaster hooked a tuna, however, no one ever caught the fish. Usually the angler was spooled; and always that person had a story of high drama that caused him to lament the last encounter while looking forward to the next.

Back to our own exotics—the bluefish. With few exceptions, during each night of a dropping tide on the Second Rip there would be no blues and then—as if by divine signal—a gangbusters run of jumbo blues would pass, inhaling plugs. Our son, Dick, was one of the lucky ones. Many fishers think that they can tell the size of a fish by the spirit of its battle. This is true to an extent, in that you will usually be correct in any appraisal of size when judging a medium fish and a large one or a small and a medium. The boy figured his fish was at the high end but, once he slid it onto the wet sand, he could see a greater thickness and a full girth, and viewing it left him flush with excitement. He slammed a dent into its skull and was certain that the thing could not bite him so he bent over it to remove the hooks with the pliers from his kit. When he did, it flopped hard, head then tail, driving one of the previously sharpened treble hooks into Dick's forefinger to the bone.

"Oh brother," he whispered to himself, distracted now from what he hoped to tell his dad about this monster. Then he felt the deep penetration of the hook and how it made him sick to his stomach on even the slightest move. Dropping one wader-clad leg onto the blue-fish's body to hold it down, he tried to make out the severity of the injury, but his hand was all blood. Reaching for the small knife in his kit, he tried to sever some of the skin in the hope that it would relieve the hook's grip, but the barb was buried deep. Nothing he tried suc-ceeded—it instead imposed even more pain. This was rugged stuff for a thirteen-year-old alone on a dark beach with his father some-where downtide. His final effort, based upon his bloody view of the injury, was that little flesh was preventing the hook's removal. He just bit his knife case and pulled hard—really hard. "Oh brother!" he tried to say through the leather, and the hook was free. He washed his hand in the surf again and again until the blood stopped, wrapped it with tape, and went back into the action. After daybreak, with a pile of bluefish all over the beach, Dick disappeared to find his hidden trophy buried in the sand. Casters, mostly from New York looking for affidavits for their clubs, were lined up at the scale as I filled in numbers and signed slips. Every one of the boys gasped at the sight of the kid's bluefish. When we weighed it, it pulled the scale down to twenty pounds and a shade. It is easy now to think of the world record as thirty-one pounds, but that happened many years later. The morning we weighed this trophy bluefish, the record was a mere four pounds away.

The bluefish were okay, and for us they saved the season on Cape Cod, but my heart was on East Beach, Charlestown, with Butch and Norman, and having a beer potlatch with Squid Beaumont. Cow country. That day, I put my proposal to Joyce that we head there for some money fish while there were still a few weeks of summer left. Anybody who knows her appreciates that just about anything is fine with her, so we left.

CHARLESTOWN, RHODE ISLAND, AUGUST 1970   Waving my arm at a boatman who was making a wide sweep in the Charlestown Breachway current, I called, "Buddy, you know Beaumont?"

"Everybody knows Beaumont."

"Tell him his striper-fishing instructor is here."

"I can see him," the fisherman answered. "Come with me."

It was still the wry Beaumont that I knew, and I could see that he was being careful not to mix the idea that he was glad to see me with the idea that it would have been better if I had stayed wherever I had been fishing.

"Frankie, the pond is awful, ma man. Nobody even fishes here anymore. All the action is in the harbors along the Connecticut shore. We're all trailering our boats to Stonington to the pogies."

"Pogies? What the hell is a pogy?" I asked.

"I'm not sure," Squid answered, "but when the bastards show up somewhere they sure don't come alone."

Irritated, because he still was not telling me what they were, I pulled on the warmish beer to give him time.

"It's awful. All you have to do is find the schools of pogies and drag a weighted treble through them to foul-hook one, then let the bugger down and a cow eats it. People who don't know how to fish are down there doing it."

"Right in town?" I asked.

"The theory is that the pogies have caused the big bass to concentrate with the schools of baitfish; that everything is with the pogies. That's why there's nothin' here. Frankie, you know I love you like a brother, but I wish you'd stayed on the Cape. At least there you had half a chance at some action."

Walking the half mile west to our buggy, I tried to imagine a Charlestown without huge stripers, but I couldn't.

6

THE MOBY COD MYSTERY

THE RHODE ISLAND SURF, MARCH 1971   Have you ever wondered what's around during those harsh winter months when no one would even think of surfcasting?

Back when cod were a viable species, most people thought that they could only be caught in boats, miles at sea. Little was known about seasonal saltwater fishing, and even less was known about what happened along our beaches in the off season. There were suspicions about what could be accomplished angling but, for the most part, what happened in our ocean was a big mystery. Much of what was believed at the time was based upon a mix of hope, experimentation, and conjecture. For instance, it was presumed that a surfcaster could fish bait on the bottom all winter and catch cod; yet few knew anyone who did it. What was happening in our surf was largely a mix of accidents.

There were, however, a few things that were commonly known about fishing the beach for cod. Plum Island surf fishers used to fish the warmer winter nights—that they could stand—usually for small fish, table stuff. In late October on Nauset Beach, when striper anglers found it too cold to plug, they would often fish bottom with sea worms and occasionally take small cod.

One June morning on Nauset Beach, while driving off in the family buggy, I saw a cod of about twelve pounds struggling in the low-tide surf. I ran down and grabbed it for the table.

At Matunuck, Rhode Island, in 1964, April school striper fishing was an entrenched activity that had always received more than its fair share of attention. A few constants at the time were that at dawn and at sunset you could cast a small bucktail jig attached to a chunk of broom handle and catch schoolies from fourteen to twenty inches on practically every cast. After dark a sea worm could be anchored to the bottom, and you could catch the same small stripers. As is still the custom, many of us fished both methods early in the season, often before the first fish arrived. One night while bottom fishing, I had a take that pulled the rod down so hard, the sand spike leaned toward the water and I came close to losing the whole rig. When I got the fish in, it turned out to be a cod of about twelve pounds that dwarfed any linesides we sought that early. Unusual occurrences will often happen when fishing in salt water; I simply blew off the experience as just that.

A few years later, still in the 1960s, we had a blitz on the beach in Charlestown. It was one of those November events when the first wave was strewn with bait and birds were whacking the water while gamefish swam through it all. I say *gamefish* because the foam was laced with bass, bluefish, weakfish, hickory shad—you name it. My brother, Norman, had our biggest fish that time—a cod over twenty-five pounds that had taken a bucktail jig. You bet. For most of us, this month represented the last of the fishing and served as a signal that winter was trying to approach. There was nobody at home in my cod-fishing mind. I still didn't get it.

On East Beach, Charlestown, Rhode Island, the LaForest brothers—all hard-fishing Frenchmen who used to cling to the beach season by fishing all winter—had previously dropped hints of their winter fishing. I mention ethnicity because as a Frenchman myself—one who stayed in the first grade two years because I couldn't speak English—I know full well where these guys were coming from. They hammered up their French Canadian background in many ways. For instance, they installed a full-sized flagpole on the beach and raised the Canadian jack every Friday afternoon when they arrived for the weekend. Naturally, their pidgin English was laced with just enough French words and adjectives *after* the noun to make listening to them comical and fascinating at the same time—especially when they talked about the fishing, and enthusiastically when they talked about the cod.

"Awe, ya. Crissakes, the cod, them. Pull like a bastard. Big as ya leg, ey? All winter, nobody. *Pas un chat à toute la mer.*" In winter there isn't a soul on the whole ocean.

Again, because it was not the first time I had heard them, I dismissed their excited stories of monster cod as just more of what you're often apt to hear fishing. Then came validation.

At one of the local all-night diners, a Crisco joint that served a pound of homefries with every breakfast, where late-night drunks and early-morning commuters jostled for counter space, there was a chef who often talked about cod the size of outstretched arms. The talk would have gone right by me but, one February morning when I was sitting at the counter, I overheard the name *LaForest*, the apparent source of fresh cod fillets. What was it with these guys?

That past season on the striper beach, in August, I had met one of the brothers and he had told me that much of the previous winter they had taken cod up to forty-five pounds using bait on the bottom. What stuck to me the most was how he talked about the conditions—the cold, the ice in the guides, the failure to watch offshore weather that frequently resulted in ruining their hundred-mile round trips. He talked about drying gloves on the manifold and lamented big fish they had lost or had broken off. Bob, who had been working in a junkyard where they piled flattened auto bodies onto trucks for shipping, had a load drop on him that messed up his legs. Despite numerous surgeries and many months of rehab, he could walk forward all right but couldn't back up—which is tough when you're a surfcaster. Because of his condition, Bob blamed the tragic loss of what should have been his biggest cod on his accident. He said that after the take, as he shoved the surf rod to his left and started walking frontward toward the dunes, the fish spun him around, spooled him, then broke his forty-pound line. What kind of fish does that to anglers who are in the habit of landing cod over forty pounds? Remember that this was winter.

Among the difficulties the LaForest boys had experienced was acquiring bait during the winter months. Most bait shops were closed for the season, and even those infrequent ones that stayed open would not have evening hours when surfcasters would be driving to the shore. Consequently, the brothers had stocked their freezers with all sorts of bait: shad, pogies, or skimmer clams that they chunked on the bottom. In a pinch, they told me, squid could be bought as seafood. Keep in mind that in those days few people, and certainly not many Frenchmen, ate calamari. Many of us didn't even know what the delicacy was and if we had recognized it as squid, we were unlikely to have considered it appetizing. We later learned that there is a big difference between squid intended for bait and that which is marketed as table fare. Squid was expected to smell; however, if it does smell, it isn't good to eat and also makes poor bait. The stuff from the market was great, but it wasn't as good as skimmer clam meat that could be packed in kosher salt, then frozen. The salting process toughens the baits this side of soft leather, and the effect was that the skimmers stayed on the hook much better.

The pieces were falling together. I had on occasion caught cod in early spring when it was still too cold for stripers; we had seen cod arrivals just when the last stripers were migrating in late autumn; and four brothers whom I trusted raved about fishing for them in between. With evidence of cod being around during all the colder months, the situation screamed for examination. What more information did I need in order to investigate a fishery no one—save the LaForest boys—knew anything about? Then came inspiration.

Herr Daignault,

In your articles you have made occasional mention of outsize cod from your Rhody beaches. Is there a viable fishery there? If so, what are the details of this activity, the nuances of surfcasting for cod? Do you have enough information and suitable exposed film to work up a piece for SWS? *Remember that when I give you the go-ahead, it is money in the bank.*

Best regards,
Frank Woolner, Editor
Salt Water Sportsman

I have always loved to fish because of its primal nature as well as some agrarian need to harvest protein from the environment. My first fishing safaris occurred when I was seven years old: They involved angling with devil spoons for pickerel and also with earthworms for autumn-yellow perch spawning in gravel along the shores of lakes. As a writer, I thirsted even more to learn things that few others knew, because such information would form the basis for a story. Obviously, you have to know language and how to string the words together, but your greatest asset when outdoor writing is the teaching of something about which little is known and which raises interest. In addition, you have to validate what is being presented with a strong case that you can defend. Every story has to withstand the test of truth. For instance, I might say that striper fishing is good—and that would be easy to say in the year 2002, because such information is common knowledge. Yet what would an editor have thought thirty years ago if I had told him that a fisher could go down and catch the cod of his dreams from a beach in February? It might have been a good story idea but, without pictures, it was only a claim. That was what my editor, Frank Woolner, was talking about when he mentioned "exposed film." Without pictures, little could be said that would pique reader interest. I had to catch cod from the beach in winter and then record it graphically. If I could do that, I would be the first to document it in print. It's hard to believe that at the time, most folks assumed that everything related to fishing had already been discovered.

Winter fishing was not then feasible with my family, because the kids had other interests and the winter beach was and is a hostile place. The cold and winter storms made even well-thought-out trips frequent disasters. Nel, a fishing buddy with whom I had done a lot over the years, was given the lowdown and—having always been delighted with any and all adventures—was ready for weekend bait dunking for cod. Moreover, he understood that we were not just fishing but also looking for suitable photos of cod. Sad to admit, but most of our early efforts were a disaster.

If you think about it, all fishing can be slow or disappointing. You can lay bait on a striper beach in July, wait all night, and still not catch a thing. Any season you can drive down to the shore and find the surf replete with weed or the water so big that you can't hold bottom with half a pound of lead. Some winter nights the skates abound, or there can be a million little bait-stealing critters that polish a hook faster than you're able to rebait. The worst of winter fishing, however, was the cold. We had to learn the nuances of keeping from freezing our butts off.

We had a buggy with all the heat and comforts to take on the frigid temperatures; still, the vehicle was slow and expensive for a night of fishing. With a small four-wheeler, today called an SUV, we could run out to make a cast and duck back into the cab to watch the rod tip against a light on the horizon. Most of the time, each of us fished a pair of rods with little fear of having two hits at the same time. We would cast gloveless with conventional gear so that the thumb could control the spool; as a result, our hands ached before we could find the inside of the cab. Retrieves were always done with gloves on, though because of this, the gloves got wet and often needed to be replaced. Cooking gloves on the truck's manifold was quick drying but it was also a fine art that was accomplished within a span of seconds. If you could smell the gloves, you were too late. It was slow and it was cold and it was dark, unpleasant, and frequently without promise.

Could they really be in our New England surf all winter? Was there a viable fishery for surfcasters? Beach fishing in the off season for suitable table fare was virgin territory for an aspiring writer. I just had to know.

One night in March, at a place where the LaForest boys had always done a job, one of our sticks went down flat from a good take. I ran to it and, as I did so, I felt as if I was in one of those dreams where you are pumping away and not getting anywhere. My buddy, Nel, got there just as I did. The rod was under so much tension that it was difficult to get the butt out of the sand spike. The fish didn't take all that much line against the drag, but it felt decent. It wasn't like what folks often said about cod fighting like an old boot. That assumption may have come from boats hoisting such fish from the depths fast enough to defeat the swim bladder. Here in the shallow surf, no such thing is likely to happen. Admittedly, a bluefish could tow a cod, pound for pound. Still, given the time of year, this cod had a lot of life. Regardless, I rushed it in so that we could photograph it. All I could think of was seeing this monster in the wash— only to drop it. Once beached, it weighed thirty-two pounds. Nel was as happy as I was over the event, to say nothing of getting his share of steaked fillets after the pictures were taken.

There is something that needs to be said about this first cod. Early evidence is always an accident. This marked the first time that we had ever taken a cod while actually trying to get one. Still, it was affirmation for all our suspicions about there being such a fishery, one viable enough to work from the beach.

A year later Nel and I went to Matunuck, Rhode Island, with his family station wagon and walked over the dunes to fish bottom. Around 10 P.M. our action began. I had previously noticed that cod never hit us soon after dark. It was as though they needed time to move into the shallows from deep water. At any rate, we beached a pair of so-so cod—about ten or twelve pounds—along with getting a lot of promising jiggles. Because of the way the lights at the Harbor of Refuge glowed, we faced the east so that we could outline the rod tips with the light on the horizon. After a while we noticed that there was a Coleman lantern glowing near Carpenter's Bar on the beach, less than a mile east. What really grabbed us was that the lantern seemed to be flashing, as though people were passing between the lantern and us. Now, why would people be passing the lantern so often?

Taking in all our gear and whipping Nel's station wagon down the East Matunuck Road, we arrived in time to find cod up to approximately twenty-five pounds strewn over the beach. One guy was passed out on the sand from drinking ginger brandy. The tide was coming up on him while his buddy was fighting another fish in the sliding foam. Nel and I set up just west of their better spot; we had no desire to be confronted for crowding them. We landed decent cod until high water, which helped to make up for all the nights that had been so slow. Even if I had been able to kick myself in the butt for not trying it sooner, I was so numb that I would have never felt it anyway.

All in all, I had finally accumulated sufficient know-how to write a story for *Salt Water Sportsman*, and I could back my assertions with suitable photographs. I had, to use the jargon of real writers, the whole package.

Once my article appeared in such an influential market, I began getting requests for more stories on fishing the beach for cod; the thing had taken on a life of its own. As the A-number-one cod authority, of course I had to have more fresh pictures. Nel complained bitterly, saying—smiling all the while to show me he didn't mean it—that he would need more gloves. It was an awful environment in which to try to have fun. Worse, we had a series of terrible trips during the few warm nights we could match with a weekend in January and in February. One of the nights that Nel couldn't come, I caught a cusk that weighed between ten and fifteen pounds. It had teeth like my neighbor's dog, but it was good eating. (I mean the cusk.) However, the experience that brought about my return to Christianity was the night I decided to try an old striper favorite of mine on the outside chance that cod were influenced in the same way.

By this third season, all the girls had developed skills with surf rods.

My brother, Norm, with his fifty-pounder. Three of us took four fifties that season.

Father and son growing up together on the Striper Coast. Dick and I saw the bluefish as an exotic species.

We found monster bluefish in P-Town, which the kids, Dick and Sandra, caught with little effort.

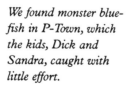

Just west of Rhody's Quonochontaug Breachway, when the rising tide gathers for the run through the flanking jetties, there's a good rip in which it can be a little hard to hold bottom. The extra lead needed is worth it, because stripers have been known to face the current there. My thinking was that cod might behave like their striped cousins. It would be easy to park there and fish bottom during the late night while Joyce and the kids slept. It was a school vacation week in late February. Bottom fishing the rise didn't produce—just as a lot of things we try don't work—so I turned in.

A short time later I heard a small buggy on the back trail, which at this time of year is unusual. I thought to myself, *A February weeknight, late?* Just as I was about to go back to sleep, I heard another rig. Ten minutes went by, and still another vehicle passed. It had me reminiscing about how "Quonnie" gets in the summer when there's little room to park and even less space in the rotation of anglers. Of course that's striper fishing, and my therapist says I'm not supposed to think about stripers in February. Peeking through the curtains of our camper, it became clear to me that much of the world had gone mad: There were several buggies shutting down behind the big dune. I found myself stealing through the dune grass at 2 A.M. to find out what was going on. I no longer knew who was doing this, the Frank who fished for cod or the new interloper burglaring through the dunes in my boots. After crawling like a marine in the stiff dune grass, I gasped at the sight of a *rotation* of surfcasters moving through the jetty stones like soldiers . . . organized, disciplined, serious. They were doing the summer thing and, because I was groggy from the hour, I truly believed they were striper fishing. Suddenly, one of them near the end stepped smartly toward shore then ran down the beach with his rod tight. It was just like it is in the summer. *It's a free country*, I thought, *ask*.

When I stepped upon the first Quonnie stone, a regular whom I recognized from many summers was obviously startled to see me. Rolling his eyes like a mother superior watching merchant seamen scaling the walls of a convent, he emphasized that there were no stripers around in February to take the Atoms, Dannys, and Gibbs Swimmers. Still, there was a thirty-five-pound cod at his feet, and it wasn't the only one that had been caught. I could see that it sickened him to imagine their secret plug fishing in some magazine or fishing book. Not only had they caught cod; I had caught *them* catching the cod. My concerns that he might have killed me for writing about it made it one of the best-kept secrets of the time. Plug fishing for cod in winter from shore. Hard to believe, isn't it?

SCHOOL'S OUT, JUNE 1971, PROVINCETOWN, CAPE COD One of the beach fishermen knocked on the door of our buggy while we were settling in on our first day of the summer beach. He was polite, but a burning question that he sought to have answered raised the hair on the back of my neck.

"I want to become a teacher and spend the summer on the beach like you. Who do you have to ask, who do you have to know?"

Trying to be patient and trying to sound patient, I explained, feigning sincerity, "Well, you have to know the state certification officer who is going to fix it for you with the registrar at the teacher's college." Joyce, who was making coffee for him, kept her back to us until we talked about the striper fishing. After he left, Joyce refused to let me open up even in the privacy of our buggy.

"Can you believe that guy?"

"Frank, he didn't mean anything. He admires what you're able to do."

"Everybody wants to be a teacher in June. Let's see if he comes back for more advice, more information in September. I have seven years of college nights in with two years to go. Joyce, should we wait to tell him that in September? Or might he not want to be a teacher in September?"

"Frannnk."

"Joyyyyce."

On the fourth day in P-Town, I was beginning to itch for some action. We needed groceries but I would have preferred to double the trip up with a drop of fish at the dock. Still, even without a load, I could get some ice. While there I could read the slips on the desk and see who was doing what. The dock was covered with pine boxes that held roughly a hundred pounds of fish each, with ice. The boxes were stacked four high and ten boxes wide for a hundred feet. All were jumbos from Billingsgate Shoals. No wonder we were dying on the beach. They can't be everywhere. The Second Rip was nearly a week away from productive tides. Boats from the beach had a steady pick going, so there were stripers around if a surfcaster could hit water that was twenty-one feet deep—which he could not. On the way back from town, we took the left fork in the back trail and continued on to Race Light.

There was a brisk sou'west and the lighthouse keeper, a Coast Guardsman named Charley, was swinging from the hips with wire line in a vicious chop. Every few minutes he would nudge the boat's motor into neutral and proceed to pump and reel a striper, gaff it, goose the engine into gear to spool some line out, and begin pivoting at the hips again, only to repeat the process; the bugger was tonging money fish. Dickie and I sat in the cab out of the wind watching Charley.

"He's got another one!" Dick said excitedly.

This went on until the tide slacked, then Charley went to his mooring, hooked the big boat to it, loaded the bass into the small boat and rowed ashore, got his Jeep and pulled everything up. *Great duty*, I couldn't help but think. That night around midnight, I came out after a short sleep and walked around. I heard a *pop*—the sound of a breaking fish that had to be a striper. Then I heard another. I roused Dick, who did not have to be told twice. With floater Rebels tied directly to heavy mono leaders, we walked the shores of Race Point Light together, casting into rips that formed from the water leaving Cape Cod Bay. Directly west, we could see the light, the rhythmic flash of a navigation beacon that had to be, but we didn't really know, in Plymouth. We didn't catch anything really big, but the two hundred pounds had us working on a check, and for me the excitement was in what we had learned. We could take fish at Race Light when everyone had been telling us it was a boat-fishing spot. This is a notion that must be emphasized: It's not only what you catch, but what you learn. The catch is gone in hours and the money not long after, but what you learn about where and when, dear and patient reader, will comfort your habit for the rest of your life. We were getting that.

The Daignault family went on red alert after the relatively small kill Dick and I had. The girls were in bed early the following night, because I had told them that we had a place with promise, all by ourselves. At midnight I kissed Sandra because she was nearest to the aisle in the camper and whispered, "Come on, honey, we're going fishing."

Susan stirred a little, but she responded to the urgency of knowing that Sandy had awakened. Dick and Carol climbed down, and

Joyce rose from her corner of our bunk to close the window and shut out the gale that was blowing through the buggy. Mom poured them juice, and I reached for a fresh pot of coffee. There wasn't much conversation, but there was an element of purpose among the six of us. We were commercials out to catch a lot of fish if we could. Somehow the kids had a way of knowing when it was time. Within a few minutes we were all outside, and we began the routine of cast and walk in a southerly direction toward Hatches Harbor.

"I'm on!" called Carol.

"Dad, Carol's got one," Sandra reported.

"No lights, hold your speed," I cautioned, "there should be more."

"Mom's on," someone shouted just as I hooked up.

I heard Dick's club, and so it went, as a mix of school stripers passed in the rip. Behind my right shoulder, I could see the rhythmic flash of each revolution of Race Light and, as I fought my fish, I counted thirteen seconds per each full 360-degree turn. I slugged my bass, and two of the girls were waiting for Dick to help them with theirs. We were really loading up. Then I saw something in front of Hatches that was the most startling sight I have ever seen in a lifetime in the striper surf. The sea for about an acre was shimmering and sparkling, glowing like a massive amount of phosphorescent plankton, causing the kids to back away from the water's edge. No one made a cast, and we all looked at it. It was a mix of sizzling and fat frying and marine sparks. It was really scary then but—as fast as it had appeared—it was gone. Then the kids resumed casting and began to hook up again while I tried to put it out of my mind. Clouds were scudding over town, and there was lightning on the horizon. It began to rain and the wind stopped. Meanwhile the bass kept hitting. The rain began to bounce off the sand, and the sea got very still. We were all still catching stripers, but we didn't know what to make of it. The kids were talking to each other in short sentences, which gave me the impression that they were as spooked as they were wet. The twins, shoulder to shoulder and fighting fish, seemed to be taking their time as though they knew that if they hurried they would only have to fight another.

"Mom," I called, "want me to whistle them in?"

Joyce responded by saying, "Yes, please. They are really wet. They'll be cold next."

The shrill whistle brought a response that told me it was what they were waiting to hear. Carol was still fighting one, but the twins came in right away and Dick began stringing bass onto his rope for dragging. It was pouring, so Joyce started toward the camper, taking the three girls to warmth and cover. We barely made it back to the buggy when the front hit, sending lightning across the beach with a loud immediate crack. The wind heightened so that the rain lashed sideways. All warm and dry in their sleeping bags, the girls pressed their faces against the glass to watch the lightning. It flashed so close to us that there was no time between what we saw and the booming. We have all looked up against a scudding, cloud-laced sky to see lightning. But this lightning was down on the beach, dancing off the sand. Every time it happened, someone would say, "Wow," and for the close ones Dick would say, "Oh, brother." Once, on a particularly close one, one of the girls asked if the lightning could hit the buggy.

"I don't know, dear, but the tires should keep the lightning from having a place to go. If it has no place to go, it can't hit us." (I don't really know if that's true, but it comforted her.)

Sandra began to whimper in a way that told me that she was frightened, so I crawled into her bunk and cradled her in my arms. Some of her hair found its way into my mouth, and before long I could tell from her breathing that she was falling asleep. Thunder rumbled harmlessly to the east, a clear sign that the front had passed. Our crew was finally in la-la land. An hour later, however, I almost said a Hail Mary.

Now that the storm had passed and everything was dripping, I went outside and could hear a buzzing sound from the front of the buggy. The air was very still and dank, with a scent of ozone like the eye of a hurricane. It was humid and quite warm. *Buzzzzz, buzzzzz.* The surf rods, all standing in the bumper spikes on the front of the truck, were glowing at their carboloy guides. At the glow, there seemed to be a flow of electric sparks lighting off, giving me the impression that if I touched any of that stuff I might get a shock. *Buzzzzz, buzzzz.* I thought, *How can I go fishing if I'm afraid of my rods?* Dick's kit lay on the ground, so I took the gaff from it and touched one of the rods, the wooden handle in my hand, but I was still afraid of getting charged or whacked. I'm not a spooky guy, but I have to tell you that I was spooked that night. Anyway, after touching the first stick, the sparking stopped on it; I touched another, and it stopped also. Then I realized that what we had was St. Elmo's fire.

St. Elmo's fire is static electricity that develops when two objects or environments have different charges or when these highly charged atmospheres pass each other. Tribes of early humans were frightened by this phenomenon, and some modern developments have generated it and have also left us spooked by it. In aviation, before much was known about it, many early pilots watched patterns of electric current formed by charges flowing on props or wing surfaces. Few surfcasters have ever seen St. Elmo's fire, and I'm just as glad that the kids missed it that night. Let's go fishing.

Traditions of the time dictated that there was little or no surfcasting at the actual Race, in front of the lighthouse. It therefore occurred to me that we might benefit from getting out of there when we were through fishing so as not to bring attention to ourselves. Rather than drive straight down the front beach to the Second Rip, we used the back trail so that it simply looked like we were coming from either the east or from town. The next morning, a lot of the people who were staying on the beach were outside their rigs examining the washed-up remains of either a small whale or a porpoise. Even if you cared, you really could live on Cape Cod for many years and never learn the difference. Along came a four-wheeler, and Allan, the Pennsylvania Wonder Boy, stopped and limped over to examine the carcass, which really hadn't been dead that long. Allan kept looking at it as though his mind were working a mile a minute. You may remember that he first came to our area from a sweet-water ethic and had never sold fish. After having towed this thing a little higher, he began digging into the sand, trying to make a loading platform. Then he jockeyed his buggy into position beneath it so as to roll this walrus or small whale, or fat fish, onto his tailgate. It was easily hundreds of pounds. With so many of the men standing around watching poor Allan, he seemed a little lost struggling with it. After a while it must have occurred to the guys that if they didn't help Allan it might just lie there and stink and ruin living there, so they helped him get it on the back of his buggy. A good third of the thing hung off the tailgate.

Swede asked, "Vot use going to do wit dis ting, Allan?"

"It is my claim under maritime law, Swede. I'm going to take it to the dock and sell it. They make perfume with these things."

Limping up the stairs in his waders at the dock at Seafood Packers, Allan told the head man there that he needed a hand to unload it and wanted to know how much they were going to pay. The boss shook his head to the negative, thinking PWB nuts, I'm sure. Allan then went over to the co-op, still wearing his waders in the heat of the day, where—from what he had already learned selling fish— they might not pay quite as much but at least they would take it. He was wrong. The co-op boss said they had no market for whales or washed-up stuff that nobody could even identify. Once he realized there would be no compensation, Allan drove down to the end of the dock and put his tailgate right over the water, hoping to dump the thing just to get rid of it. This move got the attention of the dockmaster, aka the "wharfinger" in Provincetown, who started yelling. "Hey, what the f— do you think you're doing?"

I know you might believe that this was a long time ago and environmentally anything went in those days, but the officials did not want a smelly navigation hazard in their harbor. In his defense Allan pointed out that it had come from the sea, and that's where it belonged. The dockmaster, who wore a tan uniform and a badge, and who by now, no doubt, was checking his hip to be sure that he was wearing his gun, spotted the Pennsylvania license plate. "Take it to Philadelphia," he told Allan. "They got an ocean there."

Here was a guy who last season talked to the fish and was now selling fish by the many hundreds of pounds with no buyer. He knew one thing, as the dockmaster jerked his thumb toward the beach— he had to get out of there. So what does one do with something that nobody wants? Take it to the dump.

Allan drove into the landfill, flushing a couple of hundred seagulls, and the dumpmaster spotted him right away. I guess these guys are trained to watch for certain things like fridges with the doors still on them and whales that are dead.

"Hey," the dumpmaster yelled, "where you goin' with that?"

Allan explained as politely as he could, standing there sweating in his waders, because he now was beginning to see his options shrinking, that this fish washed up on the beach at the Seashore Park and he picked it up to keep the beach clean and help his country. If you think the wharfinger was crude, you should have heard this dump manager; a Harvard man I am certain he was not.

"F— the country. F— the Seashore Park. Get that f—— thing the f— out of here before I call the f—— cops."

What do you do with an eight-hundred-pound fish in the ninety-degree heat of July? You take it back to where you got it. You don't say anything and you just drop if off where it was and nobody is the wiser. It is not your problem. Allan was thinking, *Hey, I didn't kill it.*

Then, as he was driving down the beach trail, a park ranger going off the beach pulled out of the way to let him pass. Allan waved and thanked him for yielding as he passed. When the official spotted the monster, he jacked up and turned on his siren to stop Allan. Now the sweat was beginning to run off his face, drops meeting from each side at the low point of his chin and falling into his waders.

"What . . . is . . . that?" asked the ranger.

"Well—" Allan paused, desperately trying to think of a convincing way of making the park ranger understand that if the death of this little thing was a natural event, it perhaps should be disposed of in a natural way. All the time Allan was formulating his explanation, the ranger was shaking his head no.

I know that when a story is told, the teller is supposed to bring it to an end. No one, however, was ever able to find out what Allan did with the whale. Months later, one of the gang asked about it. Allan just mumbled something, and nobody dared to seek elaboration.

7

MORE CAPE COD ADVENTURES

EVERYTHING HAPPENS ON CAPE COD. Whales were sometimes near enough to the beach that you could hear their deep baleful moans, followed by the sudden whoosh of air blasting out the blowhole. During the day, or if there was moonlight after dark, you would actually see the white spout; it looked like wind-bent steam. Occasionally, from the beach, with the a hundred-foot drop of the true race so close, you could actually see the whales. At times, many of the boat fishermen found themselves in surprisingly close proximity to these leviathans when they came to the surface—thankfully never under their boats. It made you wonder if the whales wanted no issue with the fishermen.

One morning the kids found squid washed up on the beach, and we drove for ten miles east, then southeast on the curvature of the Cape, looking at them. With some still alive, the children sought to rescue them by putting them into the gentle, waveless surf, but the poor creatures just turned around and beached themselves again. We thought, hoped really, that the squid were afraid to go back out into the water because perhaps some predator was out there, perhaps a bass. Disappointingly, after a lot of casting we made no contacts. You sure have to wonder.

At that time, in the early 1970s, the area was inundated with dogfish—sand sharks ranging in size from approximately four to seven pounds. There had apparently been some interest in imitating the British because of the popularity of their fish-and-chips market, which had been built largely around dogfish. Consequently, one of the local trawler skippers had received a grant to determine if this was a viable fishery, and he had leveled his boat with them in less than a day. However, before long, because the dogfish have such tough and abrasive skins, the automatic skinning machines broke down.

On one of the nights that we were heading to the back beach, we met one of the gang leaving. He stopped and told us not to bother because some strange occurrence was impeding the fishing. It didn't make a lot of sense to us; I even thought it could be a prank designed to prevent us from going there. We soon stopped at a pet spot to cast. When my plug hit the water, my line went limp, the plug gone. Going to the buggy for another rod, I met Joyce, who had a limp line.

"What happened?" I asked.

"I don't know," she answered. "Everything was just gone."

With two of us clean, I wasn't about to lose another two-dollar plug. For that reason, I moved the truck facing the water and turned on the headlights—never a good choice in surf where you hoped to catch stripers. When I did, I could see that the ocean was filled with thousands of glowing diamonds. The longer we sat there with the lights on them, the more sparkling eyes became visible. Spooked by all of the gleam and glitter, we left and went east a couple of miles, hoping to find better opportunity. Only this time, before casting, I put the headlights on the water. Here, there were even more of the same—so many that we could now tell they were dogfish, eyes glowing in our direction. Driving a mile, I turned the vehicle wide to shine lights on the water, saw the diamonds, then drove on. We met another surfcaster down near Head of the Meadow who warned us not to bother with south of Highland Light; it was all dogfish.

Considering the hour, I suggested to Joyce that we head the thirty miles south to Nauset Beach. After we had gone about five miles, in North Truro, we met Joe Crow facing us driving northbound and made a U-turn to catch up to him. When he pulled over, he cautioned, "Don't go to Nauset. There are dogfish, full length of the beach. You can even see their eyes."

The "Cape Shark," known as the spiny dogfish in the rest of the Northwest Atlantic, would in the next five years become a twenty-million-pound-per-year fishery. These little sharks, which do not reach sexual maturity until they are eighteen years old, typically bear litters of only two to sixteen "pups." Used as an ingredient in everything from beef jerky to soup, exports go largely to European markets where many of the mammals' parts are utilized in specialized products. For example, Germans regard the smoked bellies as a delicacy; "beef jerky" and soup rely upon the dogs as a main ingredient; and, of course, they are greatly enjoyed fried for fish-and-chips. I don't know how far seaward they were, but we had them for forty miles. Who could have ever anticipated that twenty years in the future, dogfish would have their conservation and future debated by the National Marine Fisheries Service, and fishermen would be seeking to keep them a viable resource for the six hundred boats from North Carolina to Maine that hunt them?

Few of the places I've fished were as dependent on conditions as Race Point. The tide had to be on the drop after dark for bass to show there, and the nearer it got to low tide, the better the fishing would get. When nature combined all this with a powerful southwest wind at night, it all got better. True, we had seen Charley clean up trolling in his small boat in the daytime, which to him must have seemed like he was a stone's throw from the light, but he was a long way out there. For us there was just no reaching those fish—or else our methods from shore could not match up with what was needed to make them hit. Like everywhere else we fished, you had to do whatever you did at night.

One afternoon, with a sou'west gale blowing whitecaps and a windswept sea of six-footers, it was way too rough for Coast Guard Charley to launch. Birds began collecting within casting range, and you could clearly see that something was brewing. All of a sudden, a burst of white appeared that seemed much larger than a fish breaking; it was more like a hand grenade going off. Soon after, there was another explosion, and the birds were rushing over to it. Within minutes it was like a berserk minefield. I had seen bass, bluefish, bluefin tuna, and albacore all do this, but never with such violence. Dick and I suited up with parkas and belts to protect us from the heavy sea. Waves were so big that when we stood in two feet of water, we were lifted off the bottom every time one broke. Once we got out in the surf, in the thick of the action, I could make out light-colored bodies scooting through the waves, the apparent targets of the predators that were blowing up the water—squid. What was different about them was that they were huge—the length of half a baseball bat and possibly two pounds. Books say that they have been found more than ninety feet long in the Pacific, so, on a worldwide basis, two pounds isn't *that* big. Unfortunately, we had no poppers that imitated these critters. It was a very busy ocean with all those waves tumbling, jetting water, squid scooting with cow stripers chasing them and catching them, often, but not always, in a burst of white when huge dark ink stains became visible, then dissipated quickly in the wave action. Dick and I were both on within three cranks of the reel.

We had previously caught stripers during the day, but it was never a happening upon which you could rely. Big stripers during the day, forget it—except for that day. Dick's bass was in the mid-thirty-pound class, and mine was in the high twenties. We dragged them high, went back in, and both hooked up right away. The laugh of it was, even with very castable poppers, we could barely manage a hundred feet in this gale. If you wanted to fish the plug the full distance, you snubbed down on the spool before the plug hit the water in order to tighten the line. Admittedly, your cast might be shortened five feet, but the plug—moving right away to allay any sinking—fished for ninety-five feet instead of sixty. Because he was smaller, Dick had to stand in shallower water and even at that he was bobbing like a cork. I choked with laughter as a wave broke in my face when I noticed that while he stood on the bottom he would make headway with one of these moby stripers. When a wave lifted him, however, the resistant bass towed him seaward a few feet so that by the time he had it in control again, he was in deeper water than he wanted under him. After a time, we each made a dry cast, which almost felt good, each looking at the other for reaction, and it was soon clear that the bass were gone. Between us we had close to two hundred pounds, which was a bonus because we always relied upon night fishing to pay the bills. Realizing that the upcoming tides stood a good chance of being productive, with a 2 A.M. low early the following morning, we decided to pass on our planned Nauset Beach trip for a much less demanding Provincetown situation already yielding. Most amusing was that Provincetown anglers, with all their dyed-in-the-wool knowledge of the striper surf, had no regard for Race Point because it was considered to be a boat-fishing spot.

That night we came down the back trail from the Second Rip, turned a sharp left after the lighthouse, and parked partway toward Hatches Harbor. When Dick and I got out of the truck, we could hear fish breaking, so we roused the girls, who came out running.

These were not the monsters of the previous day, but we stood a good chance of tonging as we moved north to the shadow of the lighthouse and a line of beach buggies with their tin boats pulled high.

Roughly twelve walk-in vans were parked on the arcing curve of the beach with all the inhabitants asleep. Silently, six of us spread between the trucks wherever we could find space to stand, the tide still too high for us to cast on Race Bar. Susan hooked up first, then Sandra, the twins shoulder to shoulder fighting fish. Still, the rest of us couldn't connect—which in itself was not that unusual, but what really got my attention was that the girls were arguing quietly as though there were some sort of territorial dispute.

"Susan has my spot," Sandra complained.

Whispering so as not to be heard by people in the vans (my concern not over disturbing them, but over adding company to our fishing), I cautioned them to keep it down and share the available space. Then I realized how their "system" worked. Each would cast straight out, permitting the plug to swing in the current from left to right. Moreover, every thirteen seconds, when the Race Light made its revolution, the seascape was bathed in light, creating a momentary shadow cast by the buggies lined up on the beach. The times when the little plugs passed into the shadow line just as the light was moving past, a lineside would hammer the plug. It was a timing situation: They had to drop the plug about half a revolution—six seconds— upstream of the shadow line and pretty much expect a hit six seconds later when the light passed. It didn't work all the time, because the situation depended heavily on counting to six and having your plug hit the water six seconds above the shadow line. Once I realized this, I set Dickie and Carol together taking turns, and Mom and I found a nice, fat beach buggy that was casting a huge shadow on Cape Cod Bay. We cleaned up. When the tide dropped, we moved out onto Race Bar; as we did so, the shadow weakened and its influence became less pronounced. Still, the more the tide fell, the better the fishing got—or perhaps the falling tide was allowing us to stand closer to the Race. These striper encounters always made me wonder what was in people's heads in these parts. Here we were in some of the best striper waters in the world, hundreds of hungries vacationing for that very purpose, hundreds more who had been born on these very beaches, and no one was fishing. I have yet to understand it.

One of the girls with this strange fish, dead of natural causes, which soon became the talk of the beach.

A fishery about which little was known, we found monster cod winters in our striper surf.

"Comin' down, Mister Buck." A little girl with a "spinner," in the milieu of old-guard surfcasting, is looked upon with more than casual disdain. With a nontraditional plug this is not only degrading, it is not even supposed to be possible!

Keep in mind that, while we knew few people in P-Town because of our Nauset Beach orientation, there was a lot of watching going on. Striped bass could be sold in a lot of places, but most of the fish were taken to Seafood Packers, which offered the highest money because they in turn shipped to Philadelphia and New York. The way it worked was that you weighed your fish and made out a slip, which was left on the desk. The accountant, Kenny, came down from the upstairs office every few days to round up the slips. If you saw a lot of bass on the dock floor, you could peruse the slips and determine at a glance who was catching what. It was the most accurate fishing report in the world—unlike the stuff you read in the newspapers when a tackle shop wants to sell gear and bait and drums up fake blitzes that are no better than the ski reports of "packed powder" when it's really ice. You could believe what you were looking at in fish and at what the slips were saying about where the fish had been caught. Even if you didn't know the person whose name was on the slip, it didn't take a Sam Spade to find out who he was. In beach fishing you are either at one end of a beach or another, or someplace in between, so if someone's looking for you, you're going to have company. Of course you can always drop your fish somewhere else.

Alternative buyers nearly always offered "cash on the barrelhead" for your fish, with no waiting and no tax concerns. Some fishermen liked this because they could go home, in some cases hundreds of miles, with the money in hand for fish taken the same trip. However, when Seafood Packers paid a dollar per pound, the cash-paying wholesalers offered sixty cents. Boat fishermen, who were often nearly impossible to find and whose methods could be a mystery to anyone not fishing in that very boat, were safe. On the other hand, surfcasters could easily be located, followed, and often imitated. It didn't take long for the Provincetown hungries to locate the "guy with all the kids."

A few weeks later, when the same tides came around again, two buggies we had never seen before pulled up at Race Bar while we were fishing. The tide was in full drop with a nice current left to right from Cape Cod Bay when Buck Henderson, a retread Long Islander who had moved to town ten years before, came down and got right in between us, not thirty feet from Sandra. Henderson was throwing one of those traditional blue Atom plugs, popular in the Second Rip and Back Beach, when Sandy hooked a lineside in the high twenties.

She excused herself as she passed him, and he was just as glad to have her below him so that he could continue fishing. What you have to understand is that this guy was wearing a hundred dollars worth of surf garb, including waders, and casting a conventional reel. He was a pro who'd been fishing fifteen years before this barefoot, short-pants little girl—with a spinning reel and a "Webel"—was even born. Going downtide to help her, I passed Buck who was casting and retrieving feverishly—which seldom contributes to angling success. Dick and Mom hadn't been around, raising the suspicion that they were doing something probably to the south, toward Hatches out-flow. Henderson watched carefully when we went by him, carrying Sandy's fish. Leaving it high, I slopped out into the surf to make a cast, Sandy delaying for some reason. Getting right below me, she lobbed a short cast very softly. I heard the slurp of a feeding lineside right away and Sandy's drag groaned as she hauled back. This time Buck, who had learned his ropes at Montauk, stepped out of the water as though he were being inconvenienced to watch "Short Pants" passing and calling, "Fish on."

I know the psyche of these guys, and it is not acceptable for a lit-tle girl to make them look bad. It's one thing to be lucky—they've all seen that and can accept it. It's another to be a kid, because that can happen also. But a little girl with a "spinner," which in the milieu of old-guard surfcasting is looked upon with a more than casual dis-dain—and even worse with a nontraditional plug—is not only degrading, it's not even supposed to be possible! This time I was delayed getting to her by a short hit and Henderson stood beside Sandra, following her downtide to—ahem—help out. I would have been too late anyway, and he had made up his mind that he was not going to get back into the action without first determining what she was using. As the decent lineside was slid onto the wet sand, Buck hovered over it both to remove the plug and to see what it was. Then he turned and walked casually toward his buggy, running between revolutions of the revolving light so as not to be seen, for some tack-le adjustments. In the time he was gone, our youngest daughter hooked and beached another fish. While I was taking it off her plug, I could hear her groveling in the wet sand, digging for bait. Pretending not to notice, I walked back to the water but turned in time to see her draping sand eels onto the hooks of her plug. This explained her short, softly swung lobs when casting; she didn't want to snap the sand eels off on the swing. When Buck returned he had a spinning outfit with a Rebel like the one Sandra had, but it didn't do him any more good than it had for me. The difference was that now I knew her edge—live bait. In apparent frustration over her inability to clear the waves with her little plug, when she felt the wiggle of sand eels under her bare feet, it occurred to her to dig a few and put them on.

"Comin' down, Mister Buck," she called again.

As I passed him, he whispered to me in frustration, "What the hell is she doing?"

I tell these stories because they provide some examples of how easy it is to remember only the good nights. Somehow the high adventure of us all being there together plays down the realities of the ever-increasing number of slow nights. As we caught fewer stripers, we began to look forward to the early-August bluefish blitz. In the back of my mind the notion that last year's bad fishing in Charlestown was some sort of anomaly and that those monsters would be back haunted me. I wondered if Beaumont would write a letter if the fish came back. Was he loyal enough? Did he care enough? The thought that I was playing with twelve-cent bluefish on the Cape with those Rhode Island guys cleaning up without me often had me glowering out the window of my bunk on afternoons when I was supposed to be sleeping. I have enough bad dreams without suffering new ones.

We had reduced our interest in Nauset Beach to nights during the week that had the more reliable evening high tides. The perpetual balancing act of resource management of water, compressed air, sewerage, truck battery capacity, propane, gasoline, and ice needed more attention on Nauset than anywhere else. For instance, if you filled the forty-gallon water tank without allowing the air to vent, you were not *full*. If you didn't leave some air in the tank to compress, there was no pressure in the system, and you had to pump water. Pumping was okay, but a pressurized system was more like home. We often resorted to a spark plug compressor to restore pressure to the limited water tank. We had twelve-volt lighting in the living quarters but if you ran the battery down, the truck wouldn't start when it was time to move or leave the beach. The propane lantern utilized the same gas that was used for cooking and also threw heat. We had a second bottle of twenty-five pounds of propane, but we always had to remember when one bottle was empty and get it filled before any major patrol. Then came the most profound addition to the comforts of a highly isolated fishing family—television.

Our little black-and-white TV was purchased used for less than fifty bucks. Equipped with a small switch that converted AC power to DC, we could plug it in for three channels of snow. It was not until one of the beach scientists told us we needed an antenna that we could muster enough reception—providing the antenna faced the right way—to make out the gray forms of people, which seemed to match up with the voices. Sometimes we had a picture with no sound, or sound with snow. We soon learned that the direction the buggy faced had a strong bearing on reception—and that this was not always the direction I wanted to face when parking the truck. We needed antenna rotation, for which I improvised by screwing a sand spike to the side of the truck so that the shaft of the antenna could turn. We got pretty good at refining our reception—so good, in fact, that many nights our surfcasting crew was curled up under sleeping bags with the wind blowing against the buggy, mesmerized by Jackie Gleason threatening Alice with his fist and asking, "Alice! How would you like to be the world's first woman astronaut?"

To us television had come to mean an inland, home pleasure and we had never equated its use with our lives at the beach. Still, the beach had its own problems for a family—which television could help to solve as well on the beach as it did at home. Along with bad fishing, there were storms or the need to relax and find diversion from the continuous pressures of fishing. Weather reports, for which we had relied upon our vehicle's radio, were in greater detail, which is always better for fishermen.

The other change in our situation was that stripers found their way less and less into the mix of our action. Conservationists had begun to warn of striper droughts. Long Island haul-seiners encircled schools of bass so heavy in the nets that vehicles had to be used to pull the gear and fish ashore. Gill-netting went on in one state, and in other places where it was not allowed fishermen gill-netted for bluefish and marketed "incidental" stripers. Commercial fishermen blamed sport fishermen. Rod-and-reel commercials blamed the netters. Each side pleaded a good case but never with any true agreement about what could be done to save the fish. The only thing everyone was sure about was that there were fewer bass and more bluefish, the numbers for the latter vastly different.

When we sold a striper, it was in the round, whole, for roughly sixty cents at the time. If too many bass were "landed"—a commercial term for bringing them to market—the price could end up at thirty cents. Bluefish had to be gutted, so 20 percent of their body weight was reduced to gurry. A good price for blues was twenty cents and a bad one was six. The problem was that the boatmen enjoyed a much greater catch advantage over surfcasters—they could bring in five hundred pounds when a beach fisher might have fifty. On a great night, we could beach a hundred pounds of blues, gut them down to eighty, be paid ten cents per pound, and net all of eight dollars. Worse, while you were doing this, the whole time thinking you were fishing commercially, a sharpie somewhere was catching *one* striper and getting paid twice that—with clean hands. Still, the exotic nature of fishing for something different was a constant distraction. Despite our penchant for running into town with a load of marketable fish, we loved the feel of live thrashing fish pulling line against the drag. There was some inscrutable drama in it, some cult sense of belonging when you were part of a gang of surfcasters all leaning into a bent rod.

A school of bluefish is not a large number of fish; rather, it is a system of predation comprised of a horde varying in size from a rough circle as small as fifty feet in diameter to as large as five miles long and one mile wide. The system is a cutting machine that functions through nature's most primitive design—teeth. When a fisher throws something into this mélange, he does not know the size of the system, the number of individuals of which it is comprised, or often whether anything is even there. Passing bluefish are not like passing stripers, which swim apart from one another at different levels of the water column. Passing "choppers," as they are so often called, are touching each other and competing.

Analysts see blues as angry, but they have no emotions; they just do what bluefish do—eat. Consequently, a cast into water where there are bluefish permits a fishing line to be exposed to teeth that just naturally cut or, worse, damage the line so that you have no knowledge that what was once fifty-pound line is now twelve or even less. A weed gets on the line before the line moves. Then when the line moves from the fight of another fish, the dancing weed is viewed as potentially edible, and any predator that takes too long in making that identification loses out, so the weed—and the line, as a natural consequence—is cut or damaged. If the line is cut, a fishing lure that can cost the worth of fifty pounds of gutted bluefish is lost and must be replaced. The last complication in dealing with choppers is that they are very strong and are capable of pulling great quantities of line off the reel, which forces the surfcaster to great exertion in subduing the quarry. We seek a profit for a low-priced fish that is reduced in size, that decays rapidly once killed, and that does its very best to destroy as much line and as many lures as it can, adding to the expense of seeking it commercially. No matter how new your equipment is, no matter how sturdy your hooks and lures might be, nothing can withstand the Atlantic's predatory system of cutting machines once it has had its way with your stuff. Take it from a professional, a rod-and-reel commercial, a person who sold fish for the money and still enjoys catching them for the fun.

One morning, dawn's dull eastern fire lighting off, I pulled up on Race Bar to a gaggle of chase buggies in which everyone was soundly asleep. Rods with bottom baits stood willy-nilly in a mix of distances from the water, which was clear evidence that most had arrived at different times. Walking quietly past the sagging, nodding anglers, I hooked up on the first cast and proceeded to knock off roughly a hundred-pound box of bluefish. It was no surprise that I lost a plug to a cutoff; there were any number of blues out there. My new Cortland braided line, known as white gold by the regulars who all used it, had numerous nicks and cuts in it. Driving east away from the snoozing casters, I pulled down by the water, dumped the box on the wet sand, lifted a well-honed gutting knife from my kit, and began to slit each one from vent to gill, which was a simple exercise. Then I went back and pulled the entrails from each one, cutting them wherever they were connected. Putting the knife down, I rinsed each bluefish in the surf and threw each one into a box on the tailgate of my chase, blood running down off my vehicle, blood running down off me. I rinsed my dirty arms in the sea—forgetting my fifteen-dollar, water-resistant Timex watch, which would stop running two days later. As I proudly drove east toward our big camper, it never occurred to me that a useful and efficient knife that I had used for years had been forgotten and would drift aimlessly with the tide in less than an hour. In the loss of a plug, a line, and a knife, I had accumulated more than fifteen dollars in expenses for eight dollars worth of bluefish. Fishingwise, I had not done very well.

The trick in making bluefish pay is to have them when no one else has them. The market situation for blues is very much like that of stripers, only it's a greater exercise in extremes. For instance, in July the blues dribble into the big-city markets at a level that falls slightly short of demand, driving the price up. Come August, the big centers where many blues are shipped will have a run, begin shipping, and knock down the price. There is a period, however, when all of us expect the blues when we're standing around on the beach on the best night tides, wondering if the explosion is going to take place that night, the next night, or the night after that. Each season, when the price is the subject of conversation on every midwatch hunt from Boston to Edgartown, the often repeated analysis of fishermen is uttered, most frequently with no small amount of contempt: "They could be payin' ten dollars a pound. If you ain't got none, what good is it?" The big money is for the *first* ones.

AUGUST 3, 1972, SECOND RIP, PROVINCETOWN, CAPE COD   With the water topped off at 1 A.M., the rip was pulling hard. Everybody was there. The New York bunch, mostly Long Island fishermen who alternately worked Montauk, showed up. Almost half of the Thundermist Striper Club from Woonsocket, Rhode Island, and some Connecticut fellows from the Hartford Surf Club arrived. Among the group was one woman, Kay Townsend, who had held the Ladies All-Tackle World Record with a sixty-three-pound striper for an hour; she had been splashed with enough perfume by her husband to signal that a lady was present. We had Allan, the Pennsylvania Wonder Boy, who had surprisingly become quite adept at all the buzz- and cusswords in dialectic Cape Cod surfcaster jargon to fit in as though he had never been an effete Catskills trout angler, along with Swede from Nauset and the ever-present Carlezon. Name someone who had ever fished the rip, and he was there that night—so it had to be a Friday. The thing is that for all the surfcasters standing around smoking, not one in five was fishing. Then all hell broke loose.

Every bit what it had ever been, the rods arced and bent in sequence left to right coming down from the Race with each of the casters in the water hooking up and the others running desperately to get in.

"I'm on!" one shouted amid the slamming of beach vehicle doors, dousing cigarettes, and thumping wader feet. Then there was the snapping sound of mono leaving against the drag of one reel and the distinctly different sound, determined by reel model, of a rapidly clicking pawl against a running fish. It was pandemonium; the only ones not fighting fish had a plug in the air. Soon what had been a crowd really too large for the amount of usable, castable sand was reduced by half as some fought to remove hooks, stow fish, or reattach lures. This guy backed with one and that guy was coming down to cast. It was what surfcasting was supposed to be—a lot of people with a lot of fish—what my old friend Frank Woolner had come to call twenty years before a "blitz."

Nobody missed out. Yes, there were catch differences where Swede had eight and Carlezon fifteen, but all had some fish to take to the dock. By the time it was light, many of the casters were exhausted. By then the boatmen knew that the bluefish had come in, and they were pushing their boats off right and left. They needed only to get clear of casting distance to start their popping plugs and we could see the bursts of white of their hits. It was old-home week, big time. To the east a couple of buggies that had been going off stopped just short of Coast Guard Beach and began tonging all over again. I could see them backing and clubbing in my field glasses. With that in mind, I propped the coffeepot in the sink, started the buggy, and headed toward the action. As I passed an angler casting, I heard the unmistakable whistle of his plug while his two buddies backed under the strain of moby bluefish. One, who was removing a plug, displayed the amber coloration of a Reverse Atom, which was a wacky development of the time in which a swimming plug was attached backward. The whistle was the distinctive sound the plug made when it traveled at casting speeds. I knew what they were using, but we all assumed that bluefish were dumb animals and any popper would do. My big popper was tooling along in the groundswell sweeps for which the Cape tip is famous—nothing. The three guys with Reverses were all on again. I changed to a Reverse—still nothing. Then Al, a regular from Long Island, called to me, "You got a bucktail on that Reverse?"

"Bucktail?" I asked.

"You have to have a bucktail or they won't take it."

Cutting the hook, I bent a new hook on in no more than a minute. I cast, threw the clutch, wound some slack in, popped it once, and an explosion on my plug saved me from ever having to say that I had been somewhere else that morning.

It was a summer Saturday at sunrise and the bluefish had raided Provincetown like a band of marauders. By noontime, I knew, tons of bluefish would be begging for a buyer. At the moment I could see people all around me on the beach in the sibilance of a tide dropping at sea and everyone, it seemed, was fighting fish. All of a sudden I had a thought that I had never had before and certainly had never acted upon as a result: *Leave these fish. Be the first one to market with less.*

Matt Costa's fish market on Shankpainter Road was one of the nicest, cleanest fish markets you could ever find. He had everything in fish except the smell. I had never sold stripers to him because he always paid local prices, but for bluefish it was the other way around. If you caught him in need, and he didn't have another source, you had what was known in commercial fishing parlance as a "seller's market." There might be blues piled in Stonington, but they would go west to Fulton Street. If they weren't in P-Town, they were in demand. I pulled in at the back of the store, then walked around to the case with all the crushed ice and looked at haddock and cod fillets, ocean perch, mussels, and oysters. *Hey,* I thought, *no bluefish.*

Costa greeted me and smiled beneath his black eye patch.

"Hi, Matt, want some bluefish?" I asked.

I knew he was interested because whenever he wasn't, and that was often, he would be shaking his head no before you finished the sentence.

"When did you get them?" he wanted to know.

"I just came off the beach. They've all been caught this morning."

"How many you got?"

"Box and a half."

"Thirty cents."

"Matt, c'mon, you don't have any and you'll have them sold before noon."

Costa pursed his lips, as if he were imagining a deal gone sour so early in the morning. "Okay," he said, "forty cents, but don't come back looking for that the next time."

We weighed the 154 pounds of whole, round bluefish and he peeled the sixty-two bucks in cash off a wad of green in his front pocket. As I pulled out of his parking lot, others began to arrive. Five buggies with bluefish tails hanging off their tailgates entered the lot. As they pulled around to the back of the store, I could see Matt shaking his head no. I drove away. At the traffic light that controls Race Road, other buggies—all carrying bluefish—were headed to town. They would find markets that would buy their catches, but they were unlikely to get the price I had. Mine had been first.

8

I BELIEVE IN HEROES

THE TYPICAL STRIPERMAN is a fearless, innovative, committed, patriotic, dedicated, hardworking, and totally lying sonovabitch. We are so bad that if we catch too many bluefish, we fantasize that we are fighting stripers. If we can't catch anything, we then deny that we had the experience. If we fish a hundred nights and catch linesides for five, we will talk about those five nights for the rest of our lives until our grandchildren recite each adventure—rolling their eyes for emphasis—in the back room of Grandpa's wake. It is also the nature of striper fishing to have a certain incidental contact with bluefish. At a limited level, a bluefish is a nice break from what is expected, and often a bluefish can save both face and a night of fishing. However, what we had in P-Town back then were bluefish in our cornflakes, bluefish dancing in our beer glasses, and bluefish on our plates. We could never start a night of fishing without stretching out the line of a cast and inspecting it for damage; we could not go anywhere without a fistful of wire leaders to protect our lures from being cut off. We never wanted to fish with any lure that was any good for fear that it would end up all teeth marks. Moreover, the worst side of this situation was that we were all striper fishers at heart and we weren't catching any—just bluefish.

The perennial Billingsgate slaughter had put a lot of stripers on the dock for all who brought their bluefish in to see. This can be a real grind when you think of yourself as a striper fisherman but you can't catch any, and someone comes along and proves that they aren't really extinct. Somehow the rumor got started that a "slug" of stripers had moved into the area and would probably show up in the Second Rip soon, which touched off a mild charge of angling enthusiasm; an example of a common spurt of optimism that never needed much encouragement.

Every surfcaster from Montauk to Muncton was standing on the beach in waders smoking a cigarette, waiting for someone else to make a cast so as not to be the turkey whom everybody watches. On cue, the bluefish came past taking everything in the water. Only this time, after everyone having been engaged in conversation about the inevitability of stripers in our surf because of what was seen at the dock, when each hooked up, each was dead certain that he had a striper. They said they could tell it was a striper by the way it fought. Bluefish are strong, but they have a tendency to shake the line. They don't drill off through the water like a small locomotive the way a bass does. Everybody knows that. This particular season, the way behavior had evolved, few cared about creating suitable fighting space by yelling "Fish on" when they hooked up because, with so many blues, there would have been no fishing if others stopped every time a fish was fought. Only now, minds all primed for striped bass, the first guy who hooked up shouted, begged really, "Fish on! Comin' down. This is a bass!"

Standing there with my plug hanging off my tip—I couldn't cast, because it wouldn't have been courteous to get in the way of a person who was saying, "This is a bass"—I stood watching the whole thing in kind of an embarrassed resignation. The next thing you know another guy came downtide shouting, "This is a bass." So many of the people above me passed tight with a thrashing gamefish that I was now the most uptide person, which gave me a chance to cast. Hooking up right away, darned if I didn't have a big striped bass on, of which I was certain. After a few minutes two guys walked past me returning from down below with huge bluefish. I was sure they were blues because almost everyone carries bass by the gills and blues by the tails, and these guys were carrying their fish by the tails. As I followed mine downtide, I called out, "This is a bass," but the next guy just cast anyway. Even Swede, who *always* yields to anyone needing it, let his plug fly. Now the guys who went past yelling, "This is a bass" were again coming down begging, "This is a bass." Still onto my "bass," I couldn't yield, so I apologetically said to them, "I have one too."

"Ya, sure," said Swede and he hooked up.

Later that morning, an orange sun shining on our beach among the dead bluefish, blood, billy clubs, and coffee cups, there was not one solitary striper. Of course for Dick it was his kind of action. He used to marvel at the power of a bluefish, and fighting them every cast was something that he could never have too much of. But at eighteen he seemed to be losing interest in the beach; he used to watch the Coast Guard forty-footers bounding through the white foam with a more than casual interest. It would end up being his last summer with us.

AUGUST 8, 1975, RACE CITY SELF-CONTAINED AREA, PROVINCETOWN Storms shut the fishing down for a much greater time than the length of the storm itself. In our part of the world, there was no such thing as a short, or one-day, storm. Once the weather turned east, we had to figure on no less than three bad days and nights. Said differently, that could be a week of storm duration. Then, depending upon intensity, the surf could stay big and mean, or there could be weed in the surf to the extent that it was impossible to fish until clean water had swept the material away. We had such a storm, and frankly I was kind of glad because I just wanted to lie back and sleep in darkness, wash and shave, and play catch-up without surfcasting. One night, rain lashing sideways, we even took a ride into town to walk the streets.

Then on a Friday night, amid scudding clouds, damp air, and an east drift with fog and haze, the storm ended, and we noticed the usual weekend bunch coming onto the beach. At the Coast Guard Station a petty officer monitored the radio. Off-watch seamen clustered in front of a television. Except for the storm, it was a quiet night. The blue strobe lights of Provincetown Airport only a quarter mile away over dunes flashed eerily through the mist, marking a blue flash. Out over Cape Cod Bay to the west, a light plane struggled against headwinds. Seeing the airfield, the pilot radioed for routine clearance and asked that the strobes be turned off. Familiar with the field, he preferred to use the white lights that lined the runway. The switch was thrown at airport control, and the radioman watched for the beacon of the approaching aircraft. Near sunset we heard the roar of something pass very near to the buggy. At first we thought it was a vehicle going by way too fast and too close to a small village filled with children. I looked outside but didn't see anything other than people hanging their heads out their camper doors for the same reason. Two minutes later the roar was upon us again—only this time we saw a light aircraft leaving to the west very low over the dunes. Those distances always seem greater, but it appeared that the plane had buzzed us very close, very low. The little plane banked for a turn and continued east. Then, as it swung around for another pass, it fell suddenly, as though it had slipped out of its lift, landing pancake flat in the water with a dull thud like the sound of a tin boat coming off a wave top. There was the ominous hiss of an extinguished engine before everything grew very still. The plane seemed to be floating, but the light was failing and we could hardly see. We would not have believed what we were seeing, but everybody who was outside saw the plane hit the water and was yelling to get help at the Coast Guard Station, only half a mile to the east.

About a quarter mile out, the plane's beacon heaved, first high in easy view, then hidden behind the towering seas. As a surf fisherman raced to his jeep to report the mishap to the Coast Guard at Race Point Station, the plane's beacon either failed or slipped beneath the sea. With Race Station in sight, five minutes had passed since the crash. Time: 8:55 P.M. and very dark. That night's new moon was generating major spring tides when there was more water than usual—when all the North Atlantic, it seemed, was trying to move around Cape Cod. A sandbar lay fifteen feet below the surface, causing the vicious nor'east sea to bulge right where the plane had hit.

9:00 P.M. Duty Officer William Chambers was startled from his radio room desk as men burst into the station to report the crash. At the duty officer's shout, seamen bounded down stairways. Boat crews were dispatched to the pair of forty-foot station boats moored in town. Informing Provincetown Rescue, Chambers desperately sought to think of all the options at their disposal. Race Station's newest piece of equipment came to mind—a thirteen-foot outboard-equipped rubber boat—an Avon sea rider.

"How large was the plane?" Chambers asked. "Where did it hit? Is it close to the beach?"

It was crossing his mind that they might give the new boat a go, given delays in getting the men to the forty-footers in town—not to mention the summer tourist traffic choking the streets. Worse, in these heavy seas it could be many miles of hard going. One of the reporting beach fishermen had a trailer hitch on his buggy that could tow the rubber craft on its trailer out onto the beach. With no real time to think, Chambers sent his three remaining men, who happened to be the lowest ranking, to the beach: David Kelley and "Ned" Rogean, both seamen, along with Apprentice Seamen William Beard. They were young men whose rank and age seemed inappropriate for what had to be done.

9:15 The rubber boat arrived at the encampment. A few hundred people were standing on the wet sand, some holding their hands over their mouths as they listened in horror to a baleful moaning from the gray, storm-tossed sea. They heard a cry for help, a cry from a man who was dying. In town rescue boat crews strained against the traffic.

9:30 Total confusion reigned on the beach. Representatives from every possible authority piled in, among them state police, park rangers, volunteer firemen, and local civilian rescue. The small rubber boat slid down the banking as Seaman Apprentice Beard argued to get aboard, but Kelley and Rogean pointed out that there was only limited room in the boat. Two sailors climbed on in the darkness; the sea bulged and turned white, leaving both of them flat in the surf. The little boat capsized, filled with water, and slid harmlessly in the shallow foam.

Too heavy to move for the tangle of beach fishermen who watched, they grunted and heaved to force the water over the gunwales of the craft. As an occasional wave slid it higher, the men succeeded in turning it over. Life jackets, paddles, and what was beginning to look like a gaggle of junk was thrown into the boat, as everyone hustled it down for another try. Both young seamen, Kelley and Rogean, had lost their vitality for the mission, and one of them was heard to say, *"I don't want to go."* One of them admitted under his breath, *"I can't do this."* These men—mere boys, really—were manning a lifeboat station, and this little rubber craft was a lifeboat that carried the full promise, the tradition of the sea. They were the lifesavers, the Coast Guard, and there was a man out there dying. Despite their overwhelming fear, they knew they had to go.

Between the two seamen, eight-foot combers broke steadily amid five-foot seas while a circle of beach fishermen held the Avon steady as it rose and fell with the water. Sliding chest-first, the two seamen piled in, while those on the beach walked through the suds as far as they dared, pushing it off as they ran for higher ground. Scoring two hits on the starter button, Rogean, his back to the huge swell breaking upon them, hit the water first, Kelley riding right over him, while the boat tobogganed crazily into the surf.

9:35 Preoccupation with putting the little boat in the water had become so desperate that men forgot and tried to match the sea with brute force. There wasn't room for another pair of shoulders. Finally, someone bellowed: "Wait for the sea. Wait, wait for the water!"

"Now," someone called as they shoved and ran and pushed until those up forward lost their footing in the buoyancy of neck-deep water. Rogean hit the starter and the motor took hold, driving the boat seaward just before climbing a ridge and slipping out of sight in a gray and dismal North Atlantic.

Kelley had a two-cell flashlight, if it wasn't wet. Rogean had a painful backache from their first effort at launching. They bobbed about aimlessly, idling down the motor in the hope that they might hear a voice from the blackness. None came. Rogean kept the headlights of the beach to his starboard so that he would not lose his orientation. What if the tail section was filled with air? Could they collide with it in the dark? Where were they going? What if there were more passengers than could be carried? If fear danced at the threshold of their minds, it had all but overcome a survivor who clung desperately to a part of the floating landing gear of the aircraft only yards away. How could he be there? How, after all that had happened, could this be so easy? Kelley would later testify that the person was suddenly just there.

Maybe the survivor, Arno, heard the sound of the outboard or felt its vibration; perhaps he was able to exert an audible moan that caught their attention. Rogean said later that he was just suddenly within reach. The odds were staggering that they had somehow been able to find themselves alongside each other in that black-and-white Atlantic maelstrom. Perhaps desperate men are capable of desperate things. Prying Arno's arms from the landing gear, the Coast Guardsmen hauled him over the side.

Turning the craft toward the lights, Rogean rode the breaking seas toward the beach, trying to gain a feel for how the waves broke for his final mission—to get them back. Meanwhile, Kelley urgently asked, "How many others are there?" There was no answer.

"In the name of God, how many?"

The survivor, one eye gone, a leg broken, nearly incoherent from shock, whispered, "One, one other."

An hour had passed since the plane had crashed. The rubber boat, sitting on the outside on the edge of the surf line, seemed almost stately in its smallness. Lights reflected out of the fog, breakers casting shadows upon the troughs. Fearing another launching effort, Kelley called for a line, hoping to send the survivor in on the beach so that they could turn and seek out the other man. However, they ventured in too close and a comber settled the issue, capsizing the boat and dumping the three men—Seaman Kelley cradling the survivor—nearly into the arms of the people who waited on the sand. The fishermen hauled them ashore quickly, but it was no dry landing.

After a brief application of first aid, Arno was hustled onto a four-wheel-drive pickup and driven to Provincetown Airport less than a mile away, where he was flown to a Boston hospital.

Spitting sand and aching from their ordeal, the two seamen knew their job was not finished. This time, storm seas having subsided and with more experience, the boat cleared the surf on the first effort. Hauling manually on the starter cord, Rogean felt the gravel in the outboard with every pull. With steering also inoperable, Kelley paddled frantically to keep her head into the sea.

AN HOUR LATER The searching wore on. An H-3 helicopter scanned the area with powerful lights, national seashore park rangers probed the waterline trails, and civilians walked the beach. Except for the rubber boat washed up, partially deflated, there was nothing.

Late the next day, a body was recovered by divers from inside the small, single-engine aircraft in forty feet of water. Station boats and the helicopter that had been dispatched from Otis Coast Guard Airfield had worked around the clock to locate it.

A DAY LATER Sun breaking through what few remaining clouds we might have had, I heard the beach fishermen talking about what they had seen.

"Ya, if you had not seen it," said Swede, "you would never 'ave believed those sailors."

"They was heroes all right," George uttered, almost reverently.

"The airplane fella, he's the lucky one."

From the moment the plane hit the water, I had been involved in some way. I had driven directly to the Coast Guard Station immediately after the crash, but another fisherman had gotten to them first.

I had seen the rubber boat towed out, had seen it launched, and had seen it return with a completed rescue. No aspect of the situation had gone on without my knowledge and view. Most importantly, I had photographed it in the kind of setting with which I had become familiar—the night surf. If the film was good—if it was crisp, properly exposed, and had captured the essence of what had been done—in the reporting vernacular, I had it all.

A MONTH LATER Having returned to work and having seen the developed film, I sent off a short letter along with prints of the rescue to Chief Petty Officer L. E. Houde, commanding officer of Race Point Station. The day after the tragedy, each of us had discussed what we had seen the previous night, so he and I had some knowledge of each other. He knew that I wanted the men of the Race Station to get a medal, but he was politician enough not to let on what the Guard was thinking. In my letter I had said that the pictures of what these young seamen had done spoke for themselves. Two months passed without any word from the Coast Guard about the disposition of the awards decision, so I sent a letter off to Captain R. J. Hanson, the group commander of Woods Hole, which oversees Race Point. His response follows:

DEPARTMENT OF TRANSPORTATION

UNITED STATES COAST GUARD

Dear Mr. Daignault:
This is in response to your letter of 27 December 1975 concerning the rescue case at Race Point Station on 8 August 1975.

On 19 October 1975 I submitted recommendations for personal awards for SN Kelley, SN Rogean, and SA Beard to the Commander First Coast Guard District in Boston. The recommendations for Kelley and Rogean may necessitate approval from the Commandant of the Coast Guard in Washington D.C.

I am aware of your interest in this rescue and assure you that I will contact you at such time as a decision is rendered concerning my recommendation for awards. If awards are to be given, I extend to you my invitation to the ceremonies and will advise you as to the time and place.

Sincerely,

R. J. HANSON, Captain, U.S. Coast Guard
Commander, USCG Group
Woods Hole, Massachusetts

With a bigger story and better pictures than anything I had ever done freelancing on fishing, I sent inquiries to just about every major magazine from *True* to *Yankee*. Eventually the sale was made to *The American Legion Magazine;* for the piece, I received two hundred dollars, which at that time was just short of a week's salary. The editor's acceptance letter was dated April 15, 1976.

Recall that regulations at Nauset Beach had forced many of us to utilize an alternate beach, which for us was the Cape Cod National Seashore in Provincetown. However, many other families were confronted with these same issues, which brought about similar choices. Whenever authorities who are seeking solutions come up with a remedy, they give rise to a set of consequences that generate more change—change begets change. In this case, an influx of surf fishermen from Nauset inspired a set of regulations that made it less attractive for them to choose P-Town as their alternate beach. Limited to three days, and required to absent themselves for three, Nauset fishers so inundated the seashore park that park officials limited the number of days on the beach to twenty-one. Thus, a routine emerged where vacationing surfcasters started with three days at Nauset, went to Provincetown for three, and returned to Nauset. For many people the cycle exhausted the twenty-one park days in six weeks, leaving them with no options in early August—a disaster for anyone hoping to spend the summer fishing. This was a minority group—made up of retirees, teachers, commercials, individuals with other winter employment, and the like—that carried no weight with the agencies charged with administration of beach use. A further consequence that sprang from all this was it became incumbent upon those involved to devise ways to "stretch" the situation. Many New England towns guard two things with guns: their landfills and their beaches.

Surfmen of the Provincetown beach push off a Coast Guard thirteen-foot rubber boat for a downed pilot.

Coast Guard seamen David Kelley and Ned Rogean motor out in a stormy sea . . .

Only to be pushed back by a vicious North Atlantic.

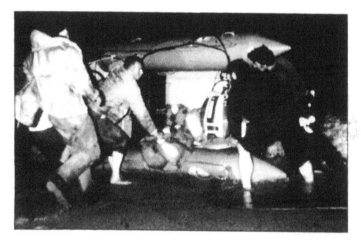

The surfmen of the beach dump the water and ready the little boat for another try.

After a miraculous find of the pilot with a two-cell handheld flashlight, the sailors bring in the pilot, Arno Groot, cradling him in their arms in the surf.

Whatever enforcement weaknesses manifested themselves, word spread quickly among the esoteric hard-cores of the rod-and-reel commercial world. For instance, the Nauset seventy-two-hour rule was as flexible as they get for those of us who knew how. You went on late at night so that your day of arrival didn't count. Three days later you could not be expected to leave late at night with a family. Further, the fourth morning, after sleeping short or fishing all night, a dawn departure, only seventy-eight or seventy-nine hours on the beach was no big deal to the old man snoozing or reading a paperback at the guard shack. The first rule in this abuse was to be as friendly as you could be with the guard—a kind of necessary symbiosis similar to that which often occurs between prisoners and their keepers. The obvious bonding choice was fresh fish, but in some cases just a bathing-suit-clad woman handling the details of checking off the beach was enough to garner immunity. There was one old-timer who so diligently fed a family of foxes that hung around for handouts all night that he could be bought with cat food for his foxes. The main thing here is that by making your stay at Nauset a four-day, the twenty-one-day Provincetown grant took care of business for seven weeks. Often a week could be spent at home during a spell of bad weather that served as a welcome break for surfcasting families not out for blood.

This may all sound good on paper, but the issue of dealing with regulatory days had no allowances for the fishing. Striped bass do not decide to spend three days here, then three there, to accommodate their antagonists. There was no way that you could get through a summer without having fish move into one spot or another for more than three days. Invariably, you ended up wanting to be at one beach for the fishing while regulations sent you to another. What was needed was a foolproof set of cheats for both systems. We did everything.

For instance, when going on to Nauset, we had to read our beach number to the guard. One of the girls would dutifully read a number from the previous year—a simple mistake for a ten-year-old. We could have had Dick make the mistake, but little girls were often given more slack with old men than little boys. Three days later we could go off, drop fish and provision up, and return with the right beach number as long as the guard shift had changed. Carol knew a favorite guard whom she called "Captain Klinger" from *Hogan's Heroes* who seemed always to melt over her because she reminded him of his granddaughter and was much more interested in her than beach days and beach buggies. Anything for striped bass.

The higher the government agency, the more arrogant and stupid it is, which is why I was partial to screwing the Provincetown Gestapo. On the day shift, there was a fat guy who was a retired navy boatswain mate chief with thirty years of service. He was working for the seashore so that he could have two full pensions, comfortable in the knowledge that he had hornswoggled the U.S. government for his entire life. The old fool loved being revered as a navy man. Although I had been a yeoman—which is, in my opinion, a profession requiring considerably more intellect—I never let on and just said I had been deck force, a group that generally lived in admiration of boatswain mates who "really ran the navy." The truth is that I felt then, just as I do now, that when the navy is assigning professions to wet-behind-the-ears youngies, they make the ones who cannot read boatswain mates; if they never learn, they make them *chief* boatswain mates. I lived to screw that guy and used to fantasize about it as a result.

When we were checking onto the beach, the pompous bastard all but wanted everybody at attention while we waited for a permit to be filled out. Had he had his way, it would have been in triplicate. Still, I always called him "Chief" with a false respect while eyeballing those blank beach passes and thinking of how I might grab a fistful for a lifetime of surfcasting. I later learned that it would hardly have been necessary—with the most rudimentary fourth-grade stationery, I could print my own beach passes, and did. So went the regulatory aspects of commercial fishing.

While salivating over the best surfcasting ever experienced by any family anywhere since the time of Peter, it was easy to forget the pressing needs of a family trying to support their Cape Cod habit. It was fine coming off Nauset at dawn on a summer weekday, but when you shared the mid-Cape highway with deer and rabbits there were no Dairy Whizzes or the like to keep the kids happy. Admittedly, most mornings they were so tired that they woke up in P-Town, and we relied upon what we called "Fidel Castro" jobs for breakfast. Here's how it worked.

Because we had left Nauset in the early morning, we were in P-Town, thirty miles north, too early to drop fish at the dock. Moreover, we were all famished from having been up half the night and traveling without sustenance. With everything else closed, the best way to wait for the dock to open was to have something to eat in the supermarket parking lot. There, at the A&P, the only market in town open all night during the summer, they had rotisserie chickens, cooked and ready to go, spinning around in those little lighted glass towers. When combined with Arturo's Portuguese bread, it was more elegant than a French restaurant. We dubbed it "Fidel Castro" because, only a few years earlier, when Cuba's Castro had been under fire at the New York United Nations, he and his entourage had subsisted on chicken in a cheap hotel. The market parking lot was not quite a cheap hotel, but then Castro was never a surfcaster either. There weren't many things we have ever fed those kids that inspired more pleasure than parking lot "Fidel Castro jobs." When you've spent your life listening to children talk at dinner, and suddenly all you hear is bones clanging in an empty dish, they have either been fed right, fed slowly, or both.

During those halcyon years, new challenges presented themselves almost more quickly than we could learn to deal with them. Our drop one morning was about two hundred pounds, which, considering there had been six of us casting for three days, represented dismal fishing. Nevertheless, when someone was coming in from the city and saw a slip on the desk at the dock for that amount, he didn't realize this; he thought that Daignault had caught all those fish alone. The mission became to find Daignault. After a particularly tough patrol at Nauset where everyone had pulled his or her weight, I decided to take the gang out for ice cream in town. You can't fish all the time. Passing the Provincetown Airport near sunset, I noticed a group of beach buggies parked there. As we rode the Race Road toward town, I saw that they were all in my rearview mirror. I thought it was kind of strange, but when you fish the beach you can get paranoid, so I kind of blew it off. We took a right onto Route 6, and they were still there behind us. It seemed odd to me. We continued left onto Shankpainter Road. They went left onto Shankpainter Road also. It was becoming increasingly suspicious. We pulled into the Dairy Mart for ice cream—one strawberry, two pistachios, a vanilla crunch, and two chocolates, all with colored jimmies. Nobody came by. I began thinking, *Where did they go?* Then, just as I started passing out the ice cream, four buggies passed the Dairy Mart and one of them said, so clearly that I heard, "The sonovabitch is eating ice cream!"

Another complexity of life was the balancing act over where to fish. The idea was to find out what everybody else was doing without ever allowing it to be known what *you* were doing—a reversal of friendly behavior that called for at least five years of diligent practice before you rid yourself of the guilt. Three places dominated my concerns for where they might be doing it without me: I could never forget Charlestown, because I just knew that dream fish would someday come back there and everything would again be the same. Some mornings, the dawn sun filtering into the buggy as I tried to think of fish until I slept, I would envision Beaumont riding on the waves in his Starcraft, standing in it as though it were a chariot. I would think of Norman and "You bet"—his line lifting and tumbling off the reel; Butch trying to tell me a story and laughing so hard he couldn't finish. Short letters from Squid came each summer to our General Delivery address, but they were always the same. "I love you like a brother, Frankie, but don't come." Nauset Beach was lean, giving up a small catch during only the best, neap-tide weeks. All Provincetown had was bluefish, and the New York bunch came on every full moon, going through the motions in some anachronistic tradition that imitated their fathers and uncles. The thing that was getting me down was that we had begun to lose our small stripers. Catching less and less, when you did get one it was pretty decent, always over twenty-five pounds. Because it was a lifestyle as well as an occupation, there seemed to be no change in the numbers of us living there. What changed was that people had stopped going out. You could drive the beach on a late evening and pass one darkened camper after another. Many mornings the fishermen slept in without launching their boats.

In September of that year, the article on the rescue came out in *Legion* and I called Race Station to see if anybody there had seen it. Rogean, promoted to third class petty officer, had mustered himself out of the Coast Guard on the expiration of his enlistment, but Kelley was still there. The chief running the place told me that something had happened to drastically alter the scheduled awards ceremony, which quite suddenly had been sent on to a higher authority. The whole thing puzzled me, and the CPO there sensed it. "Sir, each command, depending upon level, is authorized to go only so high with awards. Sir, if you promise not to quote me, that you did not hear it from here, I think this thing is being upgraded. Sir, maybe Washington read your article."

After we hung up I tried to put it together. Over a year had passed since the rescue and nine months since Captain Hanson had assured me that there were going to be awards. An upgrade was the only possible delay. Then word came.

DEPARTMENT OF TRANSPORTATION

UNITED STATES COAST GUARD

2 December, 1976

Dear Mr. Daignault:

Concerning the development of awards for SN Kelley and SN Rogean, The Commandant U.S. Coast Guard has informed us that they will receive the Coast Guard Medal which is awarded only to an individual who has performed an act of heroism in the face of great danger to himself. The presentation of these awards will take place in the very near future and you will be informed of the time and date of the ceremonies.

Thank you for your concern in this matter.

R. J. HANSON, Captain, U.S. Coast Guard
Commander, USCG Group
Woods Hole, Massachusetts

The Coast Guard awards two levels of medals: Silver Life Saving and Gold Life Saving. I had looked these up in my own copy of *The Bluejacket's Manual* while perusing the notion that the one the Coast Guard had chosen ought to be on the higher end. But my old copy made no mention of the "Coast Guard Medal," and word was indeed that it was new. A March 1975 copy of the manual said that the medal was new, had not yet been designed, and had not been authorized for issue; as the highest decoration bestowed exclusively for noncombat performance, the Coast Guard Medal is placed after the Distinguished Flying Cross but before the Bronze Star. It is comparable, an equivalent, to the Navy or Marine Corps Medal. It is awarded ". . . while serving in any capacity with the Coast Guard and distinguishing one's self by heroism not involving actual conflict with an enemy." It was possible that Kelley and Rogean could be the first recipients of the Coast Guard Medal.

Invitation

Commander, United States Coast Guard Group, Woods Hole, Massachusetts, requests the honor of your presence at an award ceremony, to be held at 11:00 A.M., 11 January 1977, at United States Coast Guard Station Race Point, Provincetown, Massachusetts, whereat,

Boatswain's Mate Third Class Edward Jackson Rogean
And
Seaman David William Kelley

Will be presented, for their acts of heroism on the night of 8 August 1975:

THE COAST GUARD MEDAL

A buffet reception follows. RSVP

4937

9

OUR BEST STRIPER SEASON

JANUARY 11, 1977 RACE POINT COAST GUARD
STATION (AKA ICE STATION ZEBRA), PROVINCE-
TOWN, MASSACHUSETTS When you have only known
Cape Cod summers, seeing the place in the stark dismal cover of
winter is an overwhelming disappointment. Only the frost-edged
Atlantic appeared the same. It was for Joyce and me a shock to experience the Outer Cape this way. Still, Race Point Station was decked
out in all its finery because this was a special day: No one could
remember award ceremonies ever having been held there.

There were lots of bluejackets and many civilians. Among the
civilians were parents of the sailors who were being honored. Two
sets of moms and dads were teary and nervous because it was not
something anyone had ever expected would happen. Heroes are in
books and movies and sort of abstract, faraway, even occasionally
suspect. That day, however, whatever anybody thought, whatever
suspicion might come to mind, for me, was a day that had been a
long time coming. I'd never really believed that heroes existed, but
Kelley and Rogean had turned me around. I had not heard that they
were heroes. I had seen it. Most importantly, I had made certain that
nobody had forgotten it. It was the first time, in my young career as
a writer, that I had had a chance to make a difference and my pen
had worked. As a result, I was as emotional as their parents were.

After a lot of unorganized standing around, we were all sum-
moned to the boat hangar, which was the only facility large enough
for us all to be assembled out of the wind. Seaman David Kelley was

in dress blue uniform. "Ned" Rogean, who, in the interim, had been promoted to petty officer third class, had returned to civilian life. The group commander, Captain Hanson, introduced Rear Admiral James P. Stewart, commander of the First Coast Guard District, who was to make the awards on behalf of the president. People were beginning to blink and gulp.

Admiral Stewart addressed all twenty-five of the station personnel, officials from the unit and district, local civilian dignitaries, and families. He pointed out that, "Preparation was useless without the courage and selflessness demonstrated by the two men who went beyond their training in the finest tradition of the Coast Guard, demonstrating the highest degree of professional seamanship, devotion to duty, and concern for the plight of their fellow man."

Certificates that accompanied the medals read in part, ". . . cited for heroism on the night of 8 August, 1975, serving as crewman (coxswain) of a 13-foot Zodiac test boat during the rescue of a downed aircraft in heavy seas off Race Point Light. Without navigational equipment he (they) maneuvered toward cries for help in turbulent seas that severely hampered his (their) efforts to rescue a downed pilot."

Seaman David Kelley of Plymouth, Massachusetts, was singled out for demonstrating remarkable initiative, exceptional fortitude, as well as daring, despite imminent personal danger in this rescue and for launching again while wounded. He showed unselfish courage and unwavering devotion to duty, reflecting the highest credit upon himself and the U.S. Coast Guard.

Edward Rogean, of Hyannis, Massachusetts, was cited for heroism as coxswain of the boat, showing complete disregard for his own safety, locating the survivor with his skill, and protecting the survivor with his body when the boat capsized.

As each young man stepped forward for pinning by Admiral Stewart, a mix of applause and verbal approval rose from the gallery. One look at those in attendance and you could tell who the parents were—as well as the author of the report that had led to the upgrading of their medals. A chill came over me thinking about how young these men were and how proud we were to have known them and to have witnessed what they'd done. It got me to thinking that our son, Dick, was somewhere in the North Atlantic on the cutter *Hamilton*. I wondered if he missed us and the Cape surf as much as we missed him.

JUNE 1977, PROVINCETOWN, MASSACHUSETTS: A BEACH SEASON BEGINS It was not a good weekend for the travel magazine writers to see Cape Cod the way it often was—an east wind, fog, intermittent rain. Worse, it was the kind of bone-chilling cold where you wore a tight-knit polyester turtleneck under a wool sweater so that any surf that found its way into your collar had minimal effect. Everything seemed wrong, because there were a lot of surfcasters moving around on a night when the fishing was not likely to be any good. We seldom, if ever, got fish anywhere from Truro north on an east wind. The truth is, I was disappointed because the errant wind had prepared me for sleep. Still, Swede had gone past heading toward the light; PWB was speeding in the same direction; George stopped long enough at another buggy for a brief exchange and then went west as well. You didn't have to be a rocket scientist to know that there were big doings in the surf, and it couldn't be too far away because you could only go west for about a mile before you went driving right into Cape Cod Bay. Joyce begged off as the girls had not eaten and the buggy was a wreck.

Whipping the chase vehicle west, I felt the familiar exhilaration of another season beginning. I kept running the notion over and over in my mind that an entire summer was ahead of us. It was a feeling that could not be experienced in any other way: I was with my high school sweetheart, and we were looking forward to eighty nights of fishing. We would be making more money, some nights at least, than I could ever earn in a day job. But most of all, I basked in an overwhelming sense of euphoria, of having health, survival, and adventure. There was nowhere on earth I would have preferred to be.

Rounding the curvature of the shore, I could see casters spread on the high beach looking like characters in some mystical play. Everyone who was in the water was fighting fish, and for each of them there was another bent over a large white belly on the sand, some using pliers while others carved away at removing hooks with knives. I could see George making a cast; I dropped right over to his right shoulder, where there was space that the others had not known how to find.

"Hi, George, what's going on?" I asked.

"Frankie, I've been fishing this beach since 1948 and I ain't never seen it like this. Crissakes, people who don't even know how to fish are here catching stuff that most people have never seen."

"George, you're kidding me."

"Even the townies are out here every night," George added excitedly.

He set up on a fish, and it started snapping line off of his reel against the drag just as I felt the solid take of a good striper.

"Townies? Buck, Conrad? Those guys are no surprise," I mused, trying to put on line against the fish.

"There are so many fish at the dock that they can't ship fast enough. People are coming out to get in on the money. Townies we don't know, who don't know how to fish, are coming out every night. Some have quit their jobs. You have to go clear to Hyannis to get a used four-wheeler. It's the money."

"There goes the price," I responded. "You know how it is, George. It does no good to catch a ton if they're going to pay twelve cents."

"Frankie, that's the thing, they're not getting bass anywhere but here and packers are paying top dollar."

George's fish slid in the foam just before he put his wader foot down on it. He looked at me. "There hasn't been a fifty-pounder on this beach in five years. I can't remember when. There have been three," he continued incredulously, "and we've only been fishing three weeks!"

Fifty-pounders. The notion of such monsters coursed through my mind.

Each of us dragged his fish up to his respective buggy, hit it on the head, and tossed it inside. Both were roughly in the high-twenty-pound class. It was a thing we did whenever we fished in a crowd or strange disappearances ensued; you might know you had four on the beach but later could only find three. When we both met again in the sweeping surf that gathered from the east and roared around the corner into Cape Cod Bay, George sidestepped over: "Here's the part you're gonna love—the boats can't get them!"

"Certainly not tonight, George."

"No, I mean even when the weather is good, even during the day. The boats ain't touchin' 'um. Half these guys are fishing in short boots and the other half is townies who don't know how to fish. It's a surfcaster's nightmare. You wait all your life for good fishin' and these buggers come out of the woodwork."

"Well, George, at least you have the satisfaction of seeing boat fishermen learn how to cast."

"It still gets your ass. Oops, I'm on!"

With the storm over, the winds had gone around to the sou'west, pushing over the dunes and driving our casts seaward. With the weather change, it was a certainty that fishing would be different than it had been the night before when we had had them at the Race. It wasn't that we weren't able to find fish again. The question was, where? The way so many buggies were passing and heading for the Race, most of them had to be expecting it to be there again. Still, this wasn't a group of accomplished surfcasters; it was a herd of townies and boat fishermen who knew little or nothing about fishing the beach. I told Joyce we would head for the Back Beach, east of the Coast Guard Station and clear of the mob. With a lowering sun, we found all points devoid of anglers. By full dark, however, a steady drone of vehicles went by us, all with lights on in the search for fish either under your buggy or on the end of your line. Then something funny happened.

Both of us hooked up at the same time with one of those routine thirty-pound fish. We put them away so that no one passing would know there was anything doing. Then we hooked up again and while fighting the fish I noticed that any buggies coming on had stopped west of us but had not moved again. Moreover, the rigs to the east were neither coming back toward us nor moving farther east. It was as though all movement had been banned. Why would everybody suddenly freeze? It had to be striped bass. Certainly, if we had them every cast, that was the reason why others weren't moving. It got me thinking: *Here we are catching twenty-dollar bass every cast and for the mile that we can see in either direction, not one out of a hundred buggies is moving. Can there be that many linesides? Is it possible?*

Not only was it possible, but it was evident that everyone was taking bass because we could see lights flashing periodically near the buggies. Keep in mind that these were novice anglers who had not yet felt the sting of their inexperience when using lights. They didn't know that putting a light on was a clear signal to anyone who was looking that you had just taken a fish. Of course in this case it didn't matter; there was no point in being secretive with every surfcaster east of the Canal taking fish. I guess it was more a case of resentment on my part over the reality that these local pilgrims had found fishing on a beach that for them had been there for so long, they'd forgotten about it. You get possessive.

Around midnight we saw a buggy turn around and head off the beach. A few minutes later another rig passed us, then turned onto the exit road. Then it hit me. Unlike the beach crowd, who came to stay whether for weekends or for vacations, these people were heading home to bed because they had to go to work tomorrow. The slowdown in the action was the excuse they needed to leave. In contrast, I knew that the stripers hadn't left. They had simply moved. We chose east, downtide, because people above us had left in greater numbers than those below. Sliding east in parking lights, we saw a pair of surfcasters casting feverishly but not fighting fish. A mile later we stopped at a point, and I felt a fish turn on my plug without taking it—clear evidence that there were some around. Two casts later I saw Joyce go into a knee bend punctuated by her bending backward at the waist—clear evidence she was on. We had them. My next striper weighed forty-two pounds.

The methods utilized in our family had evolved. For Cape surfmen, the ticket had for years been big plugs, usually Atoms, some wooden Stan Gibbs plugs, and a plethora of wooden creations usually out of small garage operations in New Jersey and Long Island. Their commonality was in size—say, ten inches and around three ounces. For us, plug choices were largely what was known as the "girl thing" among these hard-core traditionalists. Girl plugs were Rapalas, Rebels, or Red-fins designed with spinning tackle in mind. They could be bought in sinking models, which helped you cast them, but if catching fish was more important—and you have to know how we felt about that—then floating types offered the best fishing. Besides, with Joyce and three daughters fishing, it seemed to me that a "girl thing" in lure choice would work out fine. A further refinement was that Dick and I had been fishing with conventional tackle and much heavier lines; we'd become proficient in throwing one-ounce models on squidders. Some nights, and this was one of them, a floater Rebel could make a seasoned surfcaster with a big blue Atom plug look bad enough for him to want to pick a fight with you. Our other choice was one we had learned from the New Yorkers—the rigged eel.

Almost everyone knows that the eel and striper are natural enemies. Some say that a bass will take an eel when it's not feeding because of its devotion to killing eels. The way the fairy lore of relationships in marine life goes, bass and eels share the same estuarine environment while traveling in opposite directions. One, the striper, is anadromous—a saltwater fish spawning in fresh; the other, the eel, is catadromous—a freshwater fish spawning in salt. They have to be acquainted, which gives rise to the notion that they are far from cooperative in their efforts at survival. Most of all, the notion that there is substantial hate between them fuels the lore that keeps the fires of surfcasting well stoked and the arms of its casters energized. When a New York surfcaster who has spent a good part of his development slugging it out for space in the Montauk surf believes something, there has to be something to it. They ritualistically kill an eel without body damage; they run a line from vent to front hook; and they bend the body of the little beast back and forth, listening for the snapping sound of cracking vertebrae. As a religious experience, rigged-eel fishermen have all learned that a dead one rigged is far better than a live one retrieved. Rigged eels raise no fears about having your baits die—that's already happened. Ours were on ice in the buggy.

A few nights later, a Friday night, we saw one of the townies we knew. He had apparently gone into the business of taking tourists out on the beach to enjoy the sensational fishing. I had noticed him a couple of times because I had occasionally sold him bluefish; he had a distinctive manner that wasn't easy to miss. Most of all, I knew that beach fishing wasn't a thing about which he knew a whole lot. Now that he was a "guide," he might have swaggered a little more, but he was not any more knowledgeable about the situation. Anyway, Joyce and I had a moderate pick going on the Back Beach and we were all by ourselves. I knew that I had to keep putting the bass away to keep from drawing any others. The problem was that these were all big fish and beaching them required a short drag in the wet sand—which left an easy-to-see furrow that appeared dark on the sand in headlights. Worse, we had made so many trips from the water to the buggy that all the sets of tracks were a clear sign of activity. This guy wasn't that dumb. In they drove with all the rods on the front bumper spikes, sinkers bouncing all over the gear, clear evidence of having been bait fishing at Wood End. High beams were on us to make sure that they had a picture of our activities—and the picture was clear. The first guy ran down to the water and laid into the cast so hard that the force lifted his left leg off the sand. Rule one in the *Pilgrim Identification Manual* is that you have to stay on the ground with both feet or you could end up casting yourself. However, he forgot to open the bail on his reel, and the line parted with the snap report of a small-caliber rifle. The other two guys, untangling the sinkers hanging from the rods and swinging around each other from every bump of the miles of beach trails, worked to get things operational. It occurred to me, *Oh, Christ we're going to catch more than they and they're going to get mad about it.* It's something that seems to go with beach fishing, and it's one of the reasons I dislike fishing in a crowd. I might not be the best fisherman in the bunch, but I'm not the worst either, and as long as I'm catching more than someone else is, I run the possibility of collecting a poke in the nose. Worse, the girl to whom I'd been married for twenty years had just set up on a large striped bass, further raising the prospect.

"She's got one!" one of them yelled, as the guide feverishly cut away at the tangled lines.

"It's plugs. It's plugs," the guide hollered.

One of them ran to the back of the buggy to start the classic tackle rummage listed in the index of the *Pilgrim Identification Manual.* With dome lights on in the buggy and flashlights on at the gear, another ran down into the surf "to help the little lady" by flashing his five-cell light on the surf, purportedly to find the fish. In reality he was hoping to learn what *kind* of plug she was using. There was no point in taking a swing at one of these guys because (a) there were five of them and (b) it's very hard to catch fish with sand in your eyes and mouth while your nose is bleeding. Let's say that I momentarily forgot why we were there.

When she landed the lineside, all five of them were standing in the wash shining lights on it—a thirty-eight-pounder. Within seconds one of them shouted, "It's Rebels. It's Rebels!" We left.

Of course there is more to fishing a Rebel than just casting and cranking it in. Also, our driving away must have raised some confusion among them as to why someone catching bass would leave. I can only speculate about what happened, but no doubt the universal malaise in uninformed plug fishing is that "smart" surfcasters have a wire leader for protection from bluefish. The guide had probably rigged all the Rebels with wire leaders, strong ones, with big enough snap-swivels to breed with a brook trout, and the plugs didn't work correctly, looked unnatural, and crashed and burned as a result. Because they weren't catching, they assumed we had left because the fish had moved and that we had some extra sense on striper behavior. Before long they came bounding down the beach behind us just as we were hooking up on a pair on the next point. In the glow of their headlights, they could see us on to fish and I could hear the addition of fuel in the guide's carburetor at the sight.

Keep in mind that none of them had yet caught anything, and the greater the disparity in our catches, the more convincing it was for them that we had some sort of mystical hold upon the striper surf. Now—and everybody gets this idea one time or another—their minds were smoking with the possibilities: *We aren't reaching them; change to a sinker Rebel. Are these people, this man and woman, deliberately being mean to us?* Of course it had never occurred to them that they had followed and inundated us twice. It went beyond them that they had cast between us, over us, around us, and had shone their lights on the water we fished, on the fish we caught, even in our eyes so that when and if we ever returned to darkness, we would remain blinded for an hour. After a few empty casts, I whistled Joyce in and we moved—back to the point we had been fishing ten minutes before.

Sliding to the place in darkness, we got out and began casting—only this time there was nothing taking. It almost felt good to retrieve without fighting a fish while mulling what our poundage might be and wondering what the market price would yield. Then headlights shone down the beach from the west—our friends were coming. We kept fishing until they pulled up, scattering on all sides of Joyce and me. After everyone had cast, I whistled her in again and we went back to where they had just left. Instead of using the same stick, I lifted the rod with the rigged eel off the bumper. Side by side, we started—she with a "girl thing" of a plug and me with a New York rigged eel. I was on right away and sidestepped to her with the update: "Use a rigged eel."

Using an eel, she was on to a lineside on her first cast. It's something we'd seen before, what I call the law of propensity. Often, when into a group of fish, all the ones that are interested in a certain kind of offer, in this case a Rebel, will either be stuck or taken, leaving a large, perhaps more selective group comprised of those that are not interested in the plug. When you change your offer, you begin to draw from the second group, often with a renewed level of success.

By switching over to rigged eels, our fishing had been revitalized. Then it hit me. These guys down the beach, now seemingly tired of chasing us, would never have rigged eels.

"What are you doing?" Joyce shouted, as I spread our catch of moby stripers all over the sand around our buggy.

"Sons a bitches want to play games? We'll play some games."

When Joyce slid her fish up, I removed her eel and deliberately used my flashlight on the side of our buggy where the boys below could see us. A few minutes later, although we had none to remove, I "removed" another with my flashlight on, then checked the carnage of our stripers strewn all over the beach. Brake lights ignited, followed by headlights, and the vehicle started back. Then, just as their headlights began to show on Joyce, I started hurrying among the bass as though I sought to hide them from view. They switched to high beams. For five guys who had yet to take a fish, it was enough to make them puke.

As Joyce landed another, I maneuvered over to her to help her bring it up—all these bass were over thirty pounds. One of them approached us, asking, "Are they bass or blue?"—really just a ploy to determine what we were using. He knew it was a bass because the first P-Town bluefish for that year was easily five weeks away.

"What's that?" the fellow asked.

"Bass."

"No, that," he said, apparently pointing to the rigged eel.

"Sir, that is a striped bass."

"No, no, no. That!"

"Didn't you just ask me striper or blue?"

Anyone who thinks he can tell you how a season is going to go in a particular area has not been with stripers long enough to understand the complexities of fishing for them.

Bass fishing is the quintessence of conjectural junk science. Angling theorists will say that bait determines the arrival and acquired residence of a great number of linesides when, in fact, they have no clue about either what's there or what might cause it to be there. I've been a striper observer all of my life and I'm sure of one thing: Nothing is absolute. You could marry a beach, as Beaumont and I had with Charlestown, Rhode Island, then miss it seriously when the crush of reality—fish gone or fish somewhere else—set in.

Still, what was happening in P-Town, night-after-night blitzes of big stripers, had not been seen in twenty years. To further heighten the bewilderment, the coastwide striper drought had gotten so bad that many magazines were no longer accepting material on the species, feeling that stripers were no longer a likely target for sport fishers. The 1977 Rhode Island Striper Tournament did not produce a single fish despite hundreds of fishermen trying for an entire holiday weekend. States were discussing the imposition of controls on them with endless debates over no-sell laws and various regulatory alternatives. Sure, we had stripers, but there were so few small fish, you could draw a crowd with a ten-pounder. Never forget that any species' future, even humans, begins with young. For every point in the debate over striper management, there was a viable counterpoint. In 1970 the newly formed bass conservation group, Stripers Unlimited, desperately sought to attract to sport fishermen to the cause of more restrictive regulation, saying that linesides had lost their viability. Yet 1970 was the single most successful reproductive year ever recorded at the time. People blamed those of us who sold stripers, despite the fact that we took them with rod and reel. Meanwhile, haul-seiners encircled fish with nets along the beaches of Long Island and many other areas while trap boats, manned by professional commercial fishermen from the Maritimes, took everything that tried to swim by the Rhode Island coast. Pogy boats, like the one Squid Beaumont ended up working for when he could no longer make a living bass fishing, would make a set around a school of menhaden. He told me that in addition to the bunker in those nets there were also great numbers of huge linesides that had been feeding upon the bunker. These would be taken ashore with a small boat in a different port, and the proceeds used for "shack money" to be split by the crew. In addition, where the menhaden were offloaded, there was no incidental catch to explain or for which to take heat. As for all those six-pounders from 1970 that were now seven years old and should have been all over the Striper Coast, where were they? Gone.

Back to what would be later recognized as the "Provincetown Blitz": Nobody knows why the fish settled in our waters that year. No one can tell you where the bass were during the day or why they came in at night. One evening, with a moderate onshore wind at Race Point, you could see them swimming through three-foot waves taking something. If you threw a seven-inch Rebel or Rapala, you hooked up right away. One fish, a twenty-eight-pounder or so that Susan had beached, regurgitated a small weakfish around eight inches. As I walked away from her—the sun on the horizon sagging like an illusion in the way it often seems to do, as though in some melt over Plymouth—a school of eight-inch weakfish beached themselves in the foam. That night, when the tide was beginning to rise, one of the girls landed a nice bass—but her teaser was gone, so I added another with no further thought. A little later her sister had a fish on a teaser and her plug was gone, clear evidence that something was missing or she would never have been able to cast. When I strengthened their leaders, they began beaching *pairs* of big stripers—one on the plug and one on the teaser.

Anglers who were there those years will tell you that we caught a lot of stripers because there were five of us. That's true. Still, we knew how to look for them—which is something that newcomers could not do and something that few with genuine experience had ever completely mastered. For example, how is it that a young couple from Nauset Beach with a pack of small children could locate stripers at Race Point nightly when people in their fifties who were born there didn't even know enough to fish the most prominent current-collision location in the Northwest Atlantic? We used to see a buggy stop at a point on the beach, and all the dyed-in-the-wool surfcasters within would get out and stand there and cast nonstop for hours. Had they spread along a beach and passed one another moving the buggy with the last man to the head, they could have covered miles of beach in that same number of hours. We did it all the time, calling it the Russian Trawler System. That's another thing about how we operated: We fished places that had no names, so we named them. We ate food that resisted customary dining protocols, then named the option after those who had done it first like Castro and Guevara. We had, out of necessity, developed an esoteric family jargon for choices and successes that no one would ever decipher. Moreover, we had the one greatest possible advantage over any group of similar size and experience: the boundless trust that can only come within the most traditionally important social unit, the family.

Students of behavior can tell you that whenever you change a part of a culture, it influences other facets of that culture. There had to be some reason why disputes began to arise on the beach that

seemed part territorial and part accident and presumably were related to the sheer numbers of surfcasters. Certainly, if there are more
of us, there is bound to be more conflict. To us, if space became a
problem, it was much easier to move than to roll on the sand with
somebody you didn't know and would probably never meet again.
Besides, whenever I was looking for a place to fish, I had to plan it
for more than one caster and, at times, up to six; as a result, we were
pretty much alone.

One dawn the boys were standing around after a night of fishing
and talking about "Spike," who had coldcocked a drunk surfcaster at
the bottom of the Second Rip when the bluefish were going by.
Apparently, there had been two of these guys. When one of them had
gotten pushy Spike had warned him—and ended up taking on both
of them. Spike had come out of it okay, but it made some of us wonder why anybody would want to fight over fishing. There was also a
rumor about a couple of guys who had been going around starting
fights and had apparently done so at Chatham Inlet that summer.
PWB said that fighting sprang from fishing for money. He claimed
that in a lifetime of fishing for trout in the Catskills, he had never
heard of such a thing as anglers thumping each other over fishing. It
didn't seem like a big deal to me at the time.

No gold rush is over going to go unnoticed. Every weekend new
people showed up on the beach from inland while more came on
from town. Moreover, even the regulars from Nauset Beach, who
were doing little in the way of fishing there, had come north to join
the blitz. So many regulars, so many newbies, so many townies,
made you wonder if there was a saturation point, if all of it could get
so big that either the fishers ran out of energy or the sea its fish. Still,
it just kept chugging along. There were so many fish in our daily
morning drops at the pier that there was no point in hiding our takes
or worrying about what could be conjectured from our slips lying
there in full view. The difference between an amateur and a professional was numbers; and the difference between them and us was the
number of rods in our operation. What a job we did!

One night, after fifty buggies with a hundred surfcasters (including us) had hit them really hard the night before, the whole world
showed up expecting another blitz. It took only a few minutes to
realize that it was not going to happen again the way it had previously. You could see that no lights were going on in either direction.

An occasional buggy went by, cruising slowly, high beams on—the big checkout. Could all of them have been caught? I didn't think so. Joyce was sagging in her seat, rapid eye movement imminent. I was listening to Boston talk radio, Larry King, kind of enjoying the slowness. Buggies, one by one, were driving off in defeat, when it hit me. *We've had a wind shift! The sweeps are coming down the beach from nor'west rather than from over the dunes.* Whipping the family chase around south by east, I tried to estimate how much water pushing harder left to right, rather than from behind, would change the bait and thus the bass. We drove one mile, then a second, with no headlights and a quarter moon. *Let's try it here.*

I staggered out at a nice point with no one around, only the occasional taillight glowing but getting smaller. That night it was a Giant Pikie, a four-ounce, thirteen-inch wooden monster. It drummed in the current, swung hard, then went down. While line left the spool, I banged on the rig to wake Joyce and I have to say that when it comes to fishing for money this is a girl who can really move her butt. Casting above me, her plug was eaten as soon as it hit the water. After beaching mine, I pulled a pair of rods off the roof and spiked them on the front bumper so that we would each have another stick to work with, then made a cast with my spare. It was like taking candy from a baby. With four fish bouncing on the beach, Joyce pulled another rod down from the roof for herself along with Dickie's little kid stick, which had not yet seen a cast this season. The reel gave off an awful, dry bearing screech on the cast, but it could still catch striped bass. Anyway, after a session of cutting plugs off everything, Joyce hooked up again and we started the process of filling up the rods once more. It's important—because you don't know when a blitz will end—to continue to fish until it's over. You shouldn't waste time removing a fish from a lure when they're still hitting. This went on from around 11 P.M. to 3 A.M., and we were loaded with close to nine hundred pounds. Usually we stowed the fish in coolers that kept the salt water and slime off the interior, but we had long since overloaded everything, and the bass virtually leveled our brand-new four-wheeler right to the windows. Heading back nor'west, toward Race City, we ran into Joe Crow, a fellow whom, unaccountably—and I hate to admit this—we both trusted and liked. Everybody gets to know everybody else through the buggy, and we recognized one another right off.

"The bass really screwed them tonight, " Joe said, laughing.

Then Joe looked into the back of our buggy from the opening of Joyce's window and gasped. "Oh, my God! And I thought *I* did good."

He had hit them farther east with pretty much the same situation that we had, the bass having dropped down as a consequence of the wind shift. When you take into account that Joe was alone, he had just about matched us. Before he left, he pointed out that this nor'west wind had potential at the Traps, which are just east of Race Light. This was a well-known set of conditions with some of the regulars, but not widely known by those all over the beach. We told him we would catch up with him.

Joe had about an hour's head start before we decided to join him there. When we rounded the mild bend of the beach, we could make him out fighting fish; a mix of bass and blues was strewn around his buggy. Because these were the first bluefish of the season, I had a bad feeling that their arrival could spell the end of what had been the best striper fishing any of us had ever seen. Nevertheless, there was no time here for ruling on it. The three of us tonged with the resulting mix roughly half jumbo blues running from fifteen to eighteen pounds and the rest stripers between twenty-eight and forty pounds. The defeat came in the numbers. At twelve cents per pound, the bluefish tore up equipment and exhausted a caster by the time he had a hundred pounds; in contrast, that number in bass brought six or eight times as much money. You just had to keep fishing. On one cast, a new day's fire lighting off in the east, I could make out the forms sliding through the waves as I snubbed a monster down, trying to determine its species. Then I noticed that Joyce and Joe were sitting on his tailgate, grinning widely. They broke into simultaneous applause once they were sure that I could see them. Joe's buggy was in complete disarray, loaded to the windows with mostly bass. His wooden roof box was level with bluefish so that it was clear he couldn't carry any more of anything. He easily had another hundred pounds strewn around his rig.

On the next hook-up, Joe called, "Let's give him the clap." And the realization that I was killing myself for no purpose sank in enough for me to quit. Sitting with Joe and Joyce on his tailgate, the three of us exhausted, we pondered the limits of a blitz happening in the face of certain coastwide striper crash. Nobody had them but us.

In the meantime, if history was any teacher, the arrival of bluefish was a bad sign for the striper blitz.

The transition was slow but tied directly to the arrival we had witnessed. Bluefish don't always move into an area a hundred at a time; they often come in a hundred *acres* at a time. Within three days you could not buy a striper, let alone sell one. During the night tides you could drive the beach clear to Highland Light without seeing a caster. The handful who had come from Nauset Beach, townies, even the boatmen, were soon gone. The Provincetown Blitz of 1977 was finished by late July.

10

MIDWATCH HUNTS FOR STRIPERS

AUGUST 1977, THE BACK BEACH   Anytime from late morning on, you could look out the window at a passing chase vehicle heading to town with a load of bluefish. At night we would pull up to a point and take turns. The one whose turn it was would cast short, allowing the plug to drift until it went down hard from a bluefish take. If the call came, "Not here!" we'd move on in the hope of finding bass. The first few nights, this routine was almost welcome; neither of us could have held up to more of what we had been doing night after night. Still, the absence of fish checks began to work on me because we had two daughters who would soon be facing college. It was time to try a wild shot.

With my Cape Cod map, I found that Jeremy Point was surprisingly close to Billingsgate Shoals, where some of the boating highliners had been taking an occasional haul. At the end of one night, around dawn, I watched Jack Townsend pass the race heading home; the next day I observed that he had dropped the only landing of bass the dock had seen all week. Nonetheless, Jeremy Point was a low-tide run under some cliffs at the start, and law enforcement, with the location closed, had been watching the place for buggies. In addition, it was a certainty that any crossings made at low tide would leave us stranded on some island until daylight, when we would surely be arrested. We wanted the money of a good hit of fish, but we were just too spooked by the pressures that came with fishing the place, so we dismissed the idea.

A year before, however, we had heard about a hit of linesides "way east"—wherever the hell that was. As a result, we had started driving east with a full tank of gas. We drove so far east, in fact, that after a while we were going south. Talk about being spooked. South of Highland Light the surf washed right to the dune base and, while you stood there, big chunks of clay fell and slid into the water. If you wanted to go past, you had to wait until a wave slid back, carefully timing a few before you moved on the situation to gun the vehicle through. Then, when you were on the other side of this scary place, you didn't know if you were about to take on worse or if that was the end of it. Why would someone take a chance with a situation like that? Striped bass was why.

Joyce had a hit on her rigged eel and there were no cuts on it, proving that it was *not* a bluefish. The thought of August prices on a Striper Coast without stripers was wild. Wouldn't that be nice! Moreover, what excited me most was that this was like fishing on some yet unknown planet. There were dunes that were two hundred feet high and nearly vertical. Some of the narrow spots would scare even a dyed-in-the-wool P-Town regular and, as a result, ensured a greater privacy. At low tide you could read the bars, which, unlike those at Nauset, stretched perpendicular to the dry beach. Where the bars met that beach, there were deep little corners that consistently held a small mixed pod of sperling and sand eels. There was so much structure, so many places that had to appeal to stripers, that you could not possibly fish it all in one night. Even when I had a fish on, I found myself rushing it in so as to see a greater part of the shore. That first night we boxed three hundred pounds, which did nothing to alleviate my excitement. What had me in high-altitude supersonic flight was what we had learned.

The following evening we brought Susan and Sandra. The plan was to arrive just after sunset at low tide, when we could begin casting with a firm view of beach structure. As I pulled up to a hole, I dropped one of them off until we had all spread about a mile. They were each instructed to flash once if they made contact, with the understanding that I would answer with one flash. The whole time I was driving south, I had my eyes in the rearview mirror except for a few seconds when I was turning around. Then, with three of them casting to the north, the first flash appeared before I could even get out of the buggy. Whipping the family chase vehicle back toward them, I spotted a second flash closer—both needed help. All of a sudden there was another flash. *Do all three have fish, or has someone flashed a second time?* I thought. As it turned out, all three of them had bass on the beach, and they were all monsters. When I pulled up on Sandra, she ran to the front bumper spike of the buggy, lifted a surf rod, and hurried back down to the water for a cast. Before I could cut her plug free from the first rod, I heard the groan of her second. Another flash from the north reminded me that there was more work to do. I put a clean ready rod in Sandra's hat, which was lying on the beach, and drove to her twin who was backing in half-light. "Mom needs help," she said.

Joyce's cow was flailing wildly in the shallows while she backed away from the water. She knew better, but it was more tactical to back up than to try to pump and reel properly. Expediency took the place of form and sport fishing. Susan was waiting, and I already knew Sandra was on again. Cutting plugs from both of their fish, I urged them to get into the buggy. I was trying to pull them all together, to consolidate activity, so that the four of us were not spread for a mile of beach with me driving back and forth. Because each of them was convinced that she was into a school of big stripers, they did not want to move. The truth is that they were.

"Saddle up," I said.

"But."

"Get in. Sandra needs help!"

We ended up fishing where I was confronted with the most resistance to leaving, though I suppose that it didn't matter, as they were all on once they got down to the surf. That night ended with Joyce and the twins having hauled about nine hundred pounds from a Cape Cod surf that was supposed to be devoid of stripers. If anybody saw those fish anywhere, on the beach, at the dock, at the gas station, the revelation would have transformed us into hunted meat. Once someone knew you had hit fish, all he had to do was find you, and that was easy.

The next morning we went to the dock, filled a washtub with ice, dumped it on top of the fish, and drove away. People were unloading bluefish all around us, and no one saw our catch. There were no bass on the floor. That afternoon, when there was no activity, we went back and unloaded our fish, weighed them, wrote them up, and I danced up the stairs to the office to speak to the accountant, Kenny.

"Hi, Kenny, how ya been doin'? Got another undercover favor to ask."

"It's okay, Frankie, I understand. Your business with us is none of theirs."

On the desk all the slips sat in full view of anyone who wanted to read them. They listed thousands of pounds of bluefish—from Swede, George, PWB, and the Long Island crowd. No one knew about us.

Late that afternoon, all four of us were dead-to-the-world asleep during a time when everybody else in Race City was splashing in the surf. Around five o'clock there was the classic pandemonium of an entire community running to their rods and casting, in some cases twenty-five feet from the water in a dead run. The plugs hit the water, got popped once, and got eaten—bluefish. It must have occurred to a few to wonder what was wrong with us that we did not run out to get in on the fun. That night, after a candlelight dinner, we all slipped out right after sunset and drove east for another go at Cape Cod's hidden stripers.

We beached poundage similar to the previous night, although slightly less. This time we were all together and I was able to keep a better handle on things, but not so well that I could have made a cast. We had no fifty-pounders—but on the other hand, there was nothing under thirty pounds either.

Once, during a short lull in the action, one of the girls started to complain about this being neither fun or of any value and I admonished her, "Dear, I have never forgotten that I am your father. However, I am also your coach, so keep casting."

The girls surfcast like professionals because they had been at it in a serious manner for more than ten years. For instance, they wore baseball caps, not because they were in the habit, but because the cap could be used to cradle a reel should laying a rig on the sand become a necessity. They knew that sand in the drag could hang the spool up on a running fish and stop everything designed to work against the escape of a moby lineside. Most of all, they knew that sand in the equipment offended me greatly, and they probably worried more about what I would say about the sand than what havoc it might cause in the fight.

At one stop, during a slow period, Susan wanted to check one of her pet bars in the shadow of Highland Light. She was so confident she was going to do something that she lifted one rod from the bumper spike and dutifully put it in her cap on the sand. Then she lifted a *second,* signaled to me to move on, and walked down to the water to cast. Of course we all know that the most productive thing the kids could have done was to cut and remove the fish themselves. Then their father could have joined them in the blitz. However, removing a plug with nine barbs from a thrashing forty-pounder on the end is one of the most dangerous things a surfcaster can do. If you don't know what you're doing, the excitement of battle can make you forget the little things you're supposed to remember. One bad experience could turn any of these youngsters away from fishing forever. It's one thing to love fishing, but part of that love is sharing the experience with those whom you most want to be with. Besides, how many bass are you going to beach if you're bleeding in an emergency room fifty miles from the blitz? Nevertheless, my greatest sense of satisfaction came from seeing their accomplished, disciplined dedication to the cause.

One night we had the bass cornering bait where the bar met the beach. It wasn't like some of the bluefish blitzes you see where casters are on for every throw. You had to hurl your plug ten times before a forty-pounder ate it. Of the five of us that particular night, because Carol was there, there was always someone backing on a wildly thrashing striped bass; I was really the busiest one of all. Walking among them like a high school coach, I urged them on: "Keep casting. Carol, slow down; you're retrieving too quickly. Sandra, fish the whole cast. They can be in the first wave. You have it. It doesn't have you. Mind your equipment. Let's avoid break-offs."

Then, at a point in the tide when all the bass seemed to be making one last effort to overwhelm us, I looked south and four women, their feminine forms silhouetted in the filtering light of an impending sunrise, were engaged with hundred-dollar stripers. Maybe you have to be reminded that keeping the lid on this was as much of a challenge as catching the bass. Having tasted the action, pleasure, and easy money of beach fishing, a million people were starting to miss it. They asked a lot of questions and would smell the upholstery of your buggy for any evidence that you might be doing it without them. They were, and I hate to admit this, a lot like me.

One late afternoon at the dock, I almost had what our daughter Carol used to call a "conniption fit." Then, as now, there were few women in the striper surf. There was, however, a character from New York named Sylvia who always seemed to look disheveled—and are you surprised by this?—like she had been up all night. She never wore a bra, dyed her hair blond—it was usually hell west and crooked—seemed as old as stone, probably fifty, and had a raspy, three-pack-a-day voice. Her forward, almost aggressive manner, which sometimes bordered on vulgar, was the most inexorable part of her charm. I had just finished rinsing off the previous night's load when she walked over to me.

"Holy shit, Dayno, where the hell did you get them?"

"These aren't mine," I said, trying to seem irritated. "I just had these," pointing to a small pile of bluefish.

Then Sylvia started climbing among the cows that we had taken, examining them like the FBI. Beginning to worry somewhat, I said, "That load is probably from a Billingsgate boat."

Knowledgeably, she ran her hand along the edge of where the gill cover makes a seal on the outside of the body, trapping a pinch of sand that she fingered and sought to identify.

"These are beach fish—Highland . . . Balston, maybe Nauset."

"Don't know," I said, trying to seem casual. I walked into the office, made out a slip for thirty-six pounds of bluefish and put it on top of the pile in the hope she would notice it, retaining a blank slip in my pocket for upstairs. Tidying up around the buggy outside the dock, moving coolers full of ice over again to kill time so that no one would see me go upstairs, I heard her talking to the man she was with:

"I don't trust that sonovabitch. I got a bad feeling about him," she said, "that f—— Dayno."

The tires on Sylvia's buggy were hard, which meant that she was not going back on the beach—thus any suspicion that she had was not an issue. Still, I had a bad feeling about her. That gnawing notion that we would be caught catching never left me. I would lie in my bunk for an afternoon sleep, thinking about the fish sitting in the coolers, hoping there was enough ice on them.

One day, a fitful dream came upon me. In the nightmare, the six of us were on a great plain with rifles, and I could clearly smell the burned cordite of our muskets. Carol was handing me a new rifle much in the way she so dutifully would fetch a surf rod. Everyone was shooting, and everyone was taking care of business, just like they had the other night—only, in the dream, we were on some unrecognizable shore and from another time. The children were dirty and their teeth needed attention. Joyce and I were old and homely in some bizarre personification of evil that I could not then understand or today explain. A great buffalo cow stepped into my sights with a pair of calves at her side and I mechanically shot my rifle. The ball struck her with a *wump* and she fell to one knee and died; the little ones looked at her in astonishment, and then they looked at me, causing me to think of those young ones as our young ones. I felt an overwhelming guilt, this gnawing inability to separate buffalo, striped bass, and humans. Though I knew I was dreaming, there seemed to be no way to escape what was happening. I kept going from the buffalo to the linesides that we had hounded for most of our lives. The more I shifted between them, the more I sweated. Conscious arguments that ours was a noble cause because we used no nets were being trampled by the dream, which characterized us as killers. I awakened wishing that the terror and apprehension of the dream would go away. Then I drifted off and was revisited by a different form of guilt; I rubbed my hands in the pulverized gravel that took millions of years getting out into the North Atlantic in order to wash off the blood. Even so, no matter how hard I scrubbed, my only relief came in being awake.

The best week we had was twenty-three hundred pounds, for which we were compensated a dollar per pound. For the season we had beached 11,500 pounds of striped bass. It's a strange thing about money. All your life you read about people who have it and before too long you learn that the management of that money is a body of knowledge within itself. Still, that is all you know at first. You don't know what the knowledge is—only that accountants and millionaires are acquainted with it. It's abstract for anyone who is broke. I used to ponder all of this some mornings on the way to work. That summer we had earned—and Dad had managed to catch a few of them—seventy-five hundred dollars. Our showroom-new SUV with air, FM radio, full-time four-wheel drive—options that in those days many could not afford—had cost sixty-one hundred dollars. It got me to thinking that if I cashed all those checks at once, someone might start asking questions about how a pair of schoolteachers—

and we all know that teachers are always bitching about money—could come up with so much of it all at once. Might they have found a bale of marijuana washed up on the beach? If so, it might be legal to find it but not to sell it. The checks were piled under a lace doily on my bureau, and every couple of weeks I would cash one, saving the twenty-three-hundred-dollar check for last. I used to really get off looking at it, because it represented the capability to spend the summer fishing and still feed a family. It got me to thinking that going back to work was for suckers when I could stay on the beach smoking cigarettes, bounding down the waterline trails, and chasing stripers full time. I felt I could match a summer's haul in the late season before hunting and half a summer's haul in the spring. The numbers came out better than they did on a top-step teacher's paycheck, and you didn't need a master's degree to fish for striped bass.

One night over dinner in a favorite restaurant, I advanced to Joyce my proposal that I give up my teaching job for the striper surf. I told her that we only go this way once, then I gave her a chance to express her opinion.

"Let me see if I have this right, Frank. Now that you are tenured in the top step in teaching, have a master's degree in education—which you have held for six months and which you spent eleven years acquiring—you've decided to become a full-time commercial fisherman. Let me finish. You're going to fish for a species that most people believe is becoming defunct, a species for which they are considering closing the season in most states. Don't answer! Have I got that right? You're going to play with the boys on Cape Cod while I wipe the noses of his, hers, and theirs here at home. Have I got that right? Be quiet and don't answer. And whom are you going to be married to while engaged in this romantic profession? You will have a wonderful life. You can fish with Swede and hunt deer with PWB. They have a lot of deer in Pennsylvania. *And you can stay there.*"

"It was just a thought," I said, sheepishly, trying to hide the emotion and regret that I just knew had to be coming through, the whole time thinking it probably wasn't a good idea in the first place.

11

CHANGING FORTUNES

THE EXCITEMENT of another summer never subsided, even after twelve such beginnings. What was changing was that the crew was shrinking. Dick had been transferred from the cutter *Hamilton* to Alaska after a stint in Aviation Electrician Mate School in Memphis, Tennessee. His secondary job on a C-130 was as dropmaster for resupply flights to Coast Guard facilities over the Aleutians. He liked pushing stuff out the door of the cargo plane, saying that the timing was kind of fun. Carol had run off with a boy from school and hadn't come home. We hadn't known if she was even alive for a while, but when we learned that she was all right we adjusted. Susan and her twin, Sandra, had agreed to go separate routes in college. Susan applied to the Coast Guard Academy in Connecticut. It was the only one of the military academies that didn't require a congressional appointment. Her acceptance was based on leadership qualities, academic distinction, and athletic talent. Sandra's "separate route"— with equal qualifications—was to the Massachusetts Maritime Academy. With one year of high school remaining, each had committed to summer programs and local jobs. When Joyce and I learned about both of their decisions, we could only laugh at how nature always seemed to have them on the same wavelet.

MID-JUNE 1978, PROVINCETOWN, CAPE COD, MASSACHUSETTS There wasn't any real hurry. We were confident that the bass were going to be in all their standard haunts—it was just a case of determining which game they were playing. George always said that big bass were hard to catch because they were all females; they had difficulty making up their minds when they saw your plug. After a good sleep the first evening, I got up before midnight for the Second Rip. The crowd was small: Swede, George, Buck, and a couple of guys who weren't familiar to me, all fishing halfheartedly. Nothing was caught and the gang began leaving, heading toward the west to fish the Race, where a moderate onshore wind was blowing and a few linesides were subsequently taken. At the turn of the tide, rising water was pushing us away from the rip where the fish lay; it took longer and longer casts to reach them. I was really busting a gut to get out there with a good plug and a better dropper when a big guy started getting pushy. Being taller than I was, his position was in front of me. The Race Bar drop-off was very gentle, so a two-inch rise in water could push you backward twenty feet. I could feel stripers on every cast but always at the beginning of the drift—if you didn't hook up right away, there was no point in finishing the retrieve. Every time I was pushed back by the rising water, I had fewer of those telltale rubs, hits, takes, and body turns that tell you you're over fish, and that big tall bugger whom I didn't know was in my way. I had what the fish would take and his location was keeping me from reaching them; his methods, on the other hand, might have put him in the strike zone, but he was still fishing wrong. Finally, out of sheer frustration and concern that if I cast over his head he might come after me, I decided to move deeper. Once I felt the cold water coming into my waders, I was further reminded that my bladder was screaming for relief, so the warmth of my kidneys and the cold sea battled for control of my waders. The big guy seemed to be watching me, and I was very uneasy. Worse, I had a solid take and began fighting a decent lineside. Wet and apprehensive, I realized that this was a perfect time for him to make his move on me—while I fought a striped bass!

"Frank," he said, "is that you? Are you the guy that writes the articles for *Salt Water Sportsman* magazine?"

Sheepishly, I replied, "Yes."

"Man, this is great," he said. "I come to the Cape for the first time and I meet the guy who inspired me to come here and he's next to me fightin' a fish."

Water pouring into my waders, I was greatly relieved that there was not going to be a problem with the big guy. I could feel the ever-increasing pull of the current hurrying into Cape Cod Bay. The bass was taking line, and this stranger was holding out his hand to shake mine.

"I'm Jim Corson, detective, New York City Police Department. It's a real pleasure to meet you," he said.

By the time I beached the lineside, with him following me, I had so much water in my waders that the weight was making it difficult for me to exit the surf. I all but crawled ashore with my fish. After that he followed me to my buggy and we talked about the fishing.

"Do you fish Nauset Beach?" he asked.

"Yes, from time to time," I told him, "although we had so many bass here last season that we didn't go."

"They've been blitzing them for a couple of weeks," he said. "I'm surprised you're not there."

I didn't respond to this remark because I didn't want to raise the issues of the insight—or lack thereof—that I would be exhibiting by admitting to not knowing what was going on. The truth was, I didn't.

The next morning, while dropping three bass at the dock, I gasped at the sight of stripers piled high on the cement floor. Because they had been rinsed, a major deposit of sand had collected in a worn indentation near one of the scuppers for a drain system designed to allow water to go back into the harbor. The sand was very fine, talcumlike, its grit like none you'd ever find in P-Town. On one of the drier fish, I found more of the small-grained sand. It could come from only one place—Nauset Beach.

That night, a quiet Sunday evening, we cruised along the waterline at Nauset where we spotted a lineside just below the surface; Joyce took it. After dark we proceeded to beach roughly three hundred pounds in a slow all-night pick that was better fishing than we had seen to date that season. Leaving the beach at sunrise, we were surprised to see a collection of New York buggies spread on the beach. This was a revelation for a number of reasons: First, Nauset had always been frequented by a clutch of surfcasters from Massachusetts, none of whom were townies. New York surfcasters fished in P-Town and didn't even seem to know about Nauset. It was a first for us to see the New York plates—and we were not thrilled about the added interest.

Dropping Joyce at the store for groceries, I left the fish at the dock, then put our slip under the door of the office. It wasn't neighborhood fishing, but at least we were in business.

That night we worked Nauset Beach with only a few other buggies. A cat-and-mouse game developed, however, with many of the vehicles moving south passing one another. At first whoever was fishing a point stayed put, but once another rig passed him, he got into his own vehicle and passed the ones who'd just gone by. You had the distinct feeling that some sort of competition was developing to see who could get to the inlet at the end of the beach first. It had always been an unwritten law—it seemed to us—that if somebody was working a point, you left it alone; the area was his, albeit temporarily. At one stop, though, we had four guys pull up with their lights all over the water. They checked all around our buggy to see if anything had been beached, then spread around us and between us, crowding us on a point that was along an eleven-mile beach. Because they could've gone anywhere, it made no sense to me that they would be so pushy. We left for another spot to the north, one that was out of the loop of these clearly aggressive surfcasters.

While doing so, I noticed a section of beach that everyone had been driving by. Officials had closed it to vehicular traffic supposedly because of erosion. Some pallets had been erected with arrows that funneled traffic to the back trail away from the water. It occurred to us that there was no visible "erosion," so we dropped below the track onto the wet sand to investigate. Once inside, we could see that nothing about the terrain appeared to be different from the rest of the beach—absolutely nothing. The detour seemed to be just a convenience for a local cottage owner who didn't want to see or hear any beach traffic. What was different here was that, with everybody bypassing a full mile of the outer beach, there could be no lights on the water. If we chose a place to fish in that locale, it was unlikely that anyone would even see us to crowd us. Most significant, if we did come upon some fish, it would not be necessary to lose time putting them away. We were alone and it was private.

The first viewable chunk of structure that appealed to us was an outer bar a hundred yards off the shoreline. It had shallower flanking bars roughly a tenth of a mile apart. In the rough center of the outer bar was a deep opening that periodically fed the hole with a rhythmic rise from a good wave sweeping over the bars to drain out the opening. On the beach, a break in the dunes had been widened by repeated foot traffic from the cottages to the front beach for bathing and other recreational use. A couple of pallets had been erected there on either side of an old icebox, the material having been placed to ward off erosion. We referred to it as the refrigerator, and for us this surfcasting location became known as the "Refrigerator Hole." It was memorable because one night we took twenty fish of better than thirty-five pounds, with one that weighed fifty-three. At dawn, the light changed enough for us to look seaward and see more clearly. We were, at the time, convinced that we had caught or pricked every lineside on Nauset Beach, but instead we saw acres and miles of nothing but breaking stripers. It was like a dream.

On an ensuing night in early August, I remember clearly, we had been in there for only about an hour. We had a couple of fish strewn out in the open when a buggy, an *illegal* buggy, came upon us. At first I thought it was the Chatham patrol. Then I saw spinning outfits lined up on the front bumper. I was relieved and yet at the same time distressed because they were fishermen. Keep in mind that we were on an eleven-mile beach with a mile of it closed, and among all the holes they could have chosen, these two guys parked twenty feet from our buggy and walked down to join us. They saw Joyce hook up and me gaff it, a bass over forty, while they didn't take a thing. After we beached another pair, they began crowding her, so she went on the other side of me. One guy with long hair hooked one and dropped it, while the other guy set but missed. When Long Hair finally beached a fish a while later, we had seven. They then crowded me because I had caught the last one. After I went around them again to Joyce's other side the four of us hooked up. The score: 9 to 3. Frenzied with their success, they didn't notice that we had moved south to a bar corner to land two apiece. Score: 13 to 3. Distracted and busy at their buggy, one of them prompted me to think he might have broken off. Joyce had another. When things slowed I went up to the vehicle and put rigged eels on two rods. The next time Joyce beached one I told her to use "Plan B," the rigged eels. The score, now that we were casting something the bass had not seen, was 14 to 4. Then it began to get light, and if you had thrown a switch it could not have ended any sooner; the fish were suddenly gone.

One of the other two, the one who had not caught much, was still in the water when Joyce and I began picking up. Stripers were scattered all around us, most with plugs or eels still hanging from their jaws. Pulling a knife from my kit, I began cutting out plugs, after which Joyce dragged each bass to the tailgate. The guy with long hair came over to me while I worked and asked, "Are you the famous guy who writes the stories in the magazines?"

"Sort of," I answered. "I write the stories and my wife thinks I'm famous."

"How much do they pay you for them?"

"It depends," I replied, feeling rather flattered that he cared to ask. "Anywhere, magazine depending, from fifty to five hundred."

"Listen," said the fellow, "the next time you have one, sell it to me. It would be worth three hundred dollars not to see it in print. We have enough assholes out here, don't you think?"

Led perfectly into the suckering, all I could think of while I carved a Rebel from the maw of a forty-pound striper was one word—*screw*. And that is what I told him.

It was an awful experience to have been approached by someone I didn't know and blamed for the demise of what many believed was the last stronghold of striper surf, of the Cape. Then I remembered a warning that had been muttered on the Second Rip: *The people who make all the trouble are the ones who were outfished.* It kept running around in my head, the way songs do sometimes. We had done a job on these guys, especially the quiet one who had hardly taken anything. Could they have been the bullies we had heard about?

The next day, late morning at the Flying A, getting gas, the fellow who runs the place asked, "Been to Nauset, Frank?"

"Some," I said, not wanting anyone to know where we were fishing on the chance that we had been seen unloading at the dock.

"Heard you pulled a knife on a guy down there."

I didn't answer because at first I couldn't figure out what he was talking about. Then, after remembering those two guys at the Refrigerator Hole, I was able to connect what Long Hair had said to me while I was removing plugs from bass and what the guy pumping gas had remarked. I blew it off, although I must say that it made me think about how fast news travels and how it gets distorted.

We continued fishing Nauset because it was about all that the Cape had in stripers. For all that Provincetown had been the year before, this summer it was devoid of bass. The August bluefish run came on time, reviving interest in angling there, especially among the boats. The hard-cores, the Long Island bunch, said they were striper fishermen and pooh-poohed the bluefish until they began to get desperate for action. Many knew about the good fishing at Nauset, but only a minority went after it. Some of the gang was saying that the fights at Chatham were too much, but we hadn't seen any of it. On a night off when we stayed in P-Town, PWB, the only one standing in his waders, started busting chops when I joined a bunch chewing the fat in Race City.

"Hey, mister," he said, grinning and looking for validation from the others. "If you want to fish here, you can have the spot. Just don't pull a knife."

Tipping my head both in disbelief and because I didn't think it was funny, I was puzzled when Buck, George, and the others all laughed. Then I looked at Buck and reminded him, "There are too many people around packing heat under the front seat for us knife fighters to be taken very seriously."

While the others giggled, Buck unconsciously looked over at his buggy as if checking to see whether anyone was picking up that he kept a pistol under the seat; I was sure that everybody got it, along with his reflexive response. They all had to be thinking that a false knife fighter is a lot safer person to have around than a person with a real gun under the seat. Which meant the joke was over.

The enticement of good beach fishing manifested itself in a number of ways. The start of it had been in P-Town in 1977, so the Provincetown crowd knew little of Nauset because there had been no reason for them to go there. Keep in mind that 1977 was the first year we didn't go. When the fish showed at Nauset in 1978 and failed to show in P-Town, those drawn to Nauset viewed the P-Town surfcasters as interlopers, which was probably why Long Hair had suckered me. Of course, knowing that I was a writer, his concern—because he viewed me as new at Nauset when it was *he* who was new—was that I would blow the lid off the place. A consequence was that three groups emerged: the ones from each of the two beaches and those who fished both. One night we met a fellow way south in Truro, almost at Lecount, who was frantic to get out of the area. He practically ran up to me, asking if I knew the way off. He was driving a Wagoneer with four-wheel drive, so I asked him if he had mechanical problems. "No," he said, "I just want to get the hell out of here and not come back."

Susan and Sandra fished barefoot during our best striper season. All big fish and no small ones—a bad sign.

Surfmen lined the beach in P-Town during a season when none had ever seen it so good.

That season the big bass showed at Nauset with nothing in P-Town. You just can't figure them.

Pointing north, I said, "Just go about half a mile and follow the buggy tracks off."

"No, please," he begged, "you know the way. I'll follow you. Please."

We saddled up, wasting all of five minutes with the Wagoneer right on our tail, and showed him the way. Once we were on the hardtop road he got out, greatly relieved, and began pumping my hand and thanking me, while Joyce and I wondered why the heck he had been so afraid. We didn't think too much about it, though, because we had gotten used to meeting people who were new to the beach and driving it. My only concern was that I didn't want any more friends—that can happen when you're nice to people—but we hated to see someone suffering like that. Also, by getting rid of the guy the beach would be a lot quieter.

A few weeks later at Nauset, working the holes off, we spotted the same Wagoneer somewhere between the Refrigerator Hole and Pochet. We killed our lights as we passed with no intention of fishing where somebody else was. He gave us a big flash, though—a frantic one, as if there were either trouble or fish. It was the scared guy from Truro whom we had led off, and he even knew my name.

"Frank," he said, "I got some bass here."

Joyce was up and moving toward the front bumper and her spinning rod while I thought, *Is this guy nuts or what? Nobody stops people in the track to report fish. What have I done by helping this guy? Is this something like when you help an Indian and the sonovabitch follows you around for the rest of your life trying to return the favor?*

Going down into the spot, Joyce was on right away, and the three of us proceeded to take maybe four apiece in the low thirties. It wasn't a major blitz, but when your boxes are empty and the price is over two dollars, four fish is like eight. At dawn, the fish were gone and the three of us were really dragging. He told me his name was Danny and that he was a physical education teacher in upstate New York. I didn't want for us to be friends. Then he asked me how I liked my coffee. Now, when you've been up all night and you use coffee like a drug, it is pretty hard to say no to it.

"Hope you like regular," Danny said, motioning me to his tailgate.

Then he hoisted and began shaking a large glass jar that contained a mix of different-colored powders and proceeded to explain.

"If you put four spoons of this stuff in your cup, you should end up with one coffee, one sugar, and two spoons of powdered milk. Hope you like regular," he said again, reaching for a thermos of plain hot water.

I looked at Joyce, but she had walked around to the other side of Danny's buggy.

"Want a coffee, Joyce? Regular only."

"I'll pass," she replied, as politely as she could so as not to hurt Danny's feelings. "It might keep me awake."

As we sat on his tailgate, the soft light of a new day beginning to light off the seascape of the Cape's Nauset Beach, I small-talked Danny with an obvious question: "What time do you think they'll come tonight, Dan?"

"Don't know. They were here when I got here at two."

"Well," I said, "this being your spot, I don't want to get here ahead of you. They're bound to pack in here again tonight."

"I can't come tonight," Danny told me.

"Dan, you have to come tonight. You're good for at least a couple of hundred bucks," I said, all the while thinking that if he didn't it meant more bass for us.

"Not Monday nights. Disco lessons."

Looking at Joyce incredulously, I noticed that she had turned away to hide her face. *Disco lessons? Is this guy freaking nuts?*

"We always go to disco lessons on Monday nights. My wife likes that. It's a chance to get out, get away from the kids. I have to go to disco lessons."

Then, as we prepared to leave, I began thinking about the long drive back to P-Town and how I needed to dump the coffee that was too sweet, too weak, and had too much milk. I poured the stuff under the back wheel of his buggy where the track would cover it and returned the cup before we headed north off the beach.

I was laughing and Joyce knew why. "Disco lessons, I can't believe that. Here we are, an out-for-blood bunch of rod-and-reel commercials, some say are killing each other for the chance to slay the *last* striper on the planet, and this guy calls time-out so that he can go to disco lessons."

Then Joyce launched into a big-time fourth-grade sermon on how all people are different, and perhaps dancing was Danny's way of making life better for his wife similar to the way in which Joyce made life better for me by fishing the surf. And I, because I caught the dig, blurted out, "Look, Disco Danny probably gets to have his way with her if he takes her to disco lessons just like when I take *you* surf fishing."

Then we started talking at the same time, in feigned disagreement. Joyce said there was a big difference on the romance scale between fishing the striper surf and discoing and it hit us both between the eyes: "Disco Dan!"

"Is that his name?" Joyce asked. "Where did you get that?"

"No, that's what we should call him."

"Does he mind?"

"It doesn't matter if he minds. Listen to me. Some townie sheldrake comes up to me to bust chops while I'm carving plugs out of bass and I become Mack-the-Knife. It's the way it is."

By August we had handled roughly half the bass we had caught the season before, but the market-price money, averaging $2.50 per pound most of the time, had our fishing income at about the same level. Nevertheless, the things that were beginning to bother me were all related. Everybody was noticing the shortage of small bass, and now there was even a shortage of big ones. Bluefish were everywhere, having been reported even in Maine, where they had not been seen in a hundred years. All of us were fishing harder for fewer stripers, and competitive pressures were building among an increasing number of factions on the beach . . . who seemed always to be looking for someone to blame for more surfcasters looking for fewer fish. There was more talk of fights between anglers at places where crowds often formed. It made even the ones who had not been involved edgy. For the better part of the summer, Joyce and I had been repeatedly crowded by groups of men who would pull up and encircle us in order to determine whether we were catching bass. Even so, the word that I had pulled a knife on a guy had yielded an interesting change in behavior.

On one particular night, just before we reached Long Bar, we had been casting a point when a buggy went by us only to stop a quarter mile farther south. A few minutes later another rig passed, but it, too, kept going. Joyce was sitting in the cab listening to the radio and, because it was slow, I went over to talk to her.

"I'm a little surprised that nobody has stopped to check us out, aren't you?" I asked.

"Frank, haven't you figured it out yet?"

"Figured what? They're probably just being polite, giving us a little slack."

"Word has more than likely spread that you, ah, pulled a knife on somebody. You know how they talk out here."

Another indication of the depths of our desperation came in our decision to fish live eels the way we had in Charlestown ten years before. Any striper regular can tell you that the value of live bait is irrefutable. Until then, we had been using rigged eels because live ones had not been available on the Cape. When we heard that a shop had opened up in Truro—another product of the newfound beach-fishing industry—we checked it out. We discovered that they had some typically overpriced tourist items for surf fishing and, to our astonishment, *live eels*. I don't know if one reason the eels were better was that they represented a change in method and pumped our enthusiasm as a result. Nonetheless, we did notice a slight improvement in our landings, and would often take a bass on a live eel after having cast for a while with plugs to no avail.

We were making a combined eel- and plug-caught drop at Seafood Packers when we ran into a pair of brothers who came from inland. We had come to know them over the years since we had started fishing P-Town. One of them was eating a piece of cold chicken. They were picking up ice and perusing the fish slips on the desk the way everyone did. They never saw our slip, because it was upstairs with Kenny, but they saw us with the bass, which erased all doubt. Let me remind you about how things worked. The brothers knew that whatever we had was not merely a statement of what we had done the night before; rather, it was an overview of what opportunity existed in sixty miles of the Cape, because we were watching all of it. Sure, there was a chance that we had inadvertently missed a blitz and that they were wrong—that latching onto whatever we were doing was a mistake. Still, with nothing else to go on, they could have done worse. There had never been a problem between the two brothers and us, other than a nagging sense of resentment that they seemed to hold toward both of us spending the summers fishing and retaining our identity as a fishing family.

The following night we went to the shop in North Truro as we now did regularly and bought our eels, not thinking a thing about the brothers. I no longer remember how we did that specific night, but if it had been a big deal I would have remembered the numbers. The second night after meeting them, we went into the shop; the lady there didn't have any eels. I looked at her with a combination of betrayal and disappointment, speechless. She explained that she had had enough eels for us earlier but two fellows, one of them eating a piece of chicken, had bought everything she had in stock—more than they would ever need.

On Nauset Beach that night, we could see a buggy to the south working the points. Just before moving I put the light on at our tailgate and noticed a fresh chicken bone on the sand. On closer examination of the shore, I also found a dead eel. It was still wet, so I rinsed it and placed it in our cooler with the drinks, thinking that if stripers ever started taking chicken bones we could have picked up plenty of them as well. On the next point there were two furrowed drag marks made when big linesides had been dragged to a tailgate; also, there were three dead eels that I collected. At the next stop Joyce beached a thirty-eight-pounder while I rigged a pair of eels using the ones they had left behind, figuring that if we couldn't fish live ones we could at least go back to using the rigged ones.

That night at the inlet, there had to be at least twenty surfcasters working the rounded end of the beach. No one was sitting around in a buggy—a clear sign that fishing was at least decent. Two guys, who were approximately in the middle of the bunch, seemed to be doing better than the others when, all of a sudden, an awful lot of yelling and swearing erupted with lights going on all over the place. Silhouettes gathered and moved apart, more yelling followed, more lights appeared, and a few buggies began moving without regard for headlights. It was kind of messy, out of character; presumably, there had been trouble. At slack tide, when only about a quarter of those who had been there remained, we had a decent time, catching perhaps three stripers apiece with the rigged eels that I was thankful I had picked up on the way in. Doing my usual investigation of the inlet to find out what we might have missed, I found a bunch of chicken bones and a twenty-five-pounder that had been left behind, which I promptly stowed. PWB was fishing a hundred yards to the west and seemed glad to see me. He told me that there had been an awful fight between one of the brothers and another guy.

"You know, Frank," PWB offered, "these guys are fighting, they're on edge, and it's not just because of the money. They have responsibilities during the day when they should be sleeping if they're going to fish at night, too."

Not understanding, I thought that the Pennsylvania Wonder Boy was trying to say something that he wasn't saying. I could only go by what he actually said, and he by what I said. The discussion made me feel something must be going by me. Then PWB let fly.

"It's drugs, Frank. Nobody can work a day job and fish out here all night without help. Fine, you bitch mightily about boatmen running motors out of the water while you're trying to sleep but you drop right off afterward. These guys, *some* of these guys, have to be speeding their brains out or they wouldn't be able to burn the candle at both ends. As a teacher, I'm sure you know that amphetamines can make a person awfully edgy."

Edgy, I thought, *I've seen a 230-pound high school junior on the wrestling team who had bulked up on steroids nearly kill a 110-pound freshman.*

"Some quiet night," he counseled, "notice the dubies glowing from inside the buggies. They're brighter when drawn on than ordinary cigarettes. Those who have that stuff have access to all of it."

"What's a dubie?" I inquired.

Thus ended a summer that had been vastly different for us. For the first time, we had fished a season without children. We had felt more of the sting of social disharmony in one season than we had witnessed in all of the fifteen years before it. True, we had made some friends despite my concerns that friends could end up being more an encumbrance than an asset. There are times, however, when nothing can be done about that. Occasionally people are drawn together because they simply forget to be aloof or maybe because their guard is down. Take the call I got from a boatman that autumn. He was a guy who could barely muster a wave on the way to the dock. And I was just as glad that he didn't, because in a world where having a sister in a whorehouse is better than having a brother in a boat, I would just as soon have the sons a bitches go right on by.

Then, the phone rang: "Frank, this is Tom Rodericks. You know, from the race—big white Whaler—Tom Rodericks?"

"Ya, P-Town," I said, really distracted, because I had probably talked to this guy three times at the dock in nine years.

"Stay with me on this because I want you to know. You're a pretty straight guy and never bothered anybody."

What does this guy want? I was thinking.

"I was in the midst of negotiating with an auditor for the IRS over my company's return when he sprang another thing on me. It seems that the dock in P-Town got into some s— with illegal swordfish from a Canadian trawler and they came down on their books with the IRS. The auditor grabbed me on a *second* issue and while he was in the can I looked at his desk. They have a list of the whole beach crowd. Your name was on it."

"For what?" I asked, because I couldn't make any sense of it.

"Frank, all those fish you caught. Did you ever pay taxes on the income from those fish?"

"Taxes?" *Huh?* "Taxes on the fish money?"

12

WOLF AT THE DOOR

Unlike civilian colleges, where people file through a "chow line," meals at the Coast Guard Academy are "dining" with a distinct set of protocols. After opening announcements by the cadet duty officer of the day at the head table, followed by grace, cadets at the dining hall are brought their food on large platters. A "firstie" or senior sits at the head of each table with fourth-class cadets (4/c) along the left side and upperclassmen on the right. Platters are placed in front of the first 4/c nearest to the head of the table, who hands one to the first-class cadet to begin the meal. Food goes down the upper-class side first, where it is quite depleted before it gets to the "swabs." The fourth class waits in silence, using no more than the front four inches of their chairs and speaking only when spoken to, with four seconds to chew and swallow their food when addressed. They sit "braced," "eyes in the boat," for up to fifteen minutes during dinner until the head table grants "leave at will"; then those of the upper class can depart. Fourth class are permitted to rise at least a minute later after requesting, "Sir/ma'am, permission to shove off." After "leave at will" is granted, 4/c are permitted to scrounge for more food with permission from the 1/c head of the table. This is usually for desserts, but where steak, lobster, or some other favorite is concerned, the dining hall can become a madhouse of 4/c running around scrounging for their entire table. Returning with a full platter of the best can be very good for a 4/c cadet's day.

Letter from the U.S. Coast Guard Academy, New London:

Dear Mom and older-than-a-chief Dad,
Life here has settled into a dismal, scary period. I know that I
will graduate someday, perhaps in another life, but I still worry
if this is the kind of existence that I can both do and want to live
with. It is a little bit like getting married in that it is such a total
commitment. It seems as though we are being prepared for some
sort of metamorphosis wherein I will be placed into a mold that
I am unsure is what I am or what I want to be. I sense that it is
happening to me, that I want to protect myself from being lost to
it. Yet there is a part of me that becomes more committed each
day. There is a kind of relentless transition finding its way into
my soul where each day that passes I am becoming more com-
mitted to the mission of someday being a worthy officer. There are
times, maybe when at colors, that I am so proud; during others I
am afraid that I will fall through the cracks.

Today we had etiquette training in the dining hall, and we were
all braced and serious with upperclassmen doing their thing. I was
in total control, and a form of creamed chicken was being served.
Seeing it brought me back to the Cape Cod beach like a time
machine. The cadet opposite me at the dining table was staring
because he apparently saw my lips move as I thought, Chicken
a La King. *The serving took me back to when we had all been*
together, and the wind blew through the buggy, and Mom always
looked for a fresh apology when she served it. My eyes welled up
in tears when I thought about how much we had then, and how
simple life had really been. As the cadet stared, I am sure he
thought I was disappointed with dinner. If the truth were known,
what I would give to be eating Chicken a La King again at
Nauset Beach. It was but one of many lonely thoughts that seem
to visit my mind without warning. If you get the chance, spread
some Cape sand into the blustery sou'west with me in mind.

We are being given liberty this weekend, which will give us a good
chance to "splice up the main," as they say in nautical lingo.

Love and miss you, Mom and Dad,
Cadet Sue

Later during that summer Joyce and I saw Susan braced for her preliberty inspection in the academy courtyard; she had on dress blues that now hung limp over her tiny frame from the weight she'd lost, and we both fought tears. Over dinner in New London, wondering what they had done to our baby, we tried to endure the second cutting of the umbilical cord, and Susan could tell that we were both concerned about her new career. Dick was in Alaska, Carol had fallen off the planet to parts unknown, and Sandra was sweating out her last summer in an inland pizza joint, by choice, saving money for college. Acknowledging that they were scattered like leaves in the wind, we knew with a certainty that we would never get our commercial-fishing bunch back to where it had been.

BACK TO CAPE COD   When you examine the lifestyle that had evolved for us and for many others on Cape Cod, two elements were critical: a population of striped bass and access to those shores from which they could be fished. Take either away and commercial fishing was pointless. In the twenty-eight years of commercial activity before this period, coastwide commercial striper landings fell from 15 million to 3.5 million pounds per year, and annual juvenile production was devastated. Not only were there no fish, but none were being born; the dim future wafted over the Striper Coast like a dark cloud. In 1979, with striper stocks in virtual collapse, an amendment to the Anadromous Fish Conservation Act created the Emergency Striped Bass Study. Researchers learned that excessive fishing mortality from both sport and commercial sources was the primary reason for collapse of the striper population. Over the span of these twenty-eight years, 74 percent of the total commercial catch had been harvested by the "producer" states of North Carolina, Virginia, Maryland, and Delaware. Most, but not necessarily all, were eleven- to thirteen-inch "pan rocks." And while the typical Massachusetts rod-and-reel commercials carried on a clean fishery—none of the disgusting "by-catch" that netting produced to bloat and float with the tides—they also selectively killed the most fecund, most productive members of the fishery: the cows. Any ten of this species' matrons could, in the right river under the right conditions, have saved the entire Striper Coast.

It just gets worse. When the national seashore park arrived on Cape Cod in the 1960s they told the towns, the beach-buggy association, and anyone else whom they thought they could befriend for purposes of milking the Washington Cash Cow that they wanted only to "retain the local color and customs" of the Cape. Here is how they kept their promise to do it.

The government people established "self-contained areas" so they could herd everybody into a few areas where they could be watched. Then they abolished these areas, because they were too comfortable. They took Herring Cove, then Race Point, then made a squeeze on the other side by closing High Head. They closed the dune roads for environmental reasons but kept them open to beach taxis. They buried live clams on the flats, drove over them, and determined that it was bad for them so they could outlaw driving on the flats. (Rule one in Frank's Book on governing: Go in equipped with a study.) Then they banned driving in the dune grass, which implied that people had been driving in the grass. They closed off huge sections of beach as nesting areas for terns and plovers with the notion that over-sand vehicles ran down the chicks, but they refused to shoot the foxes that ate the nesting birds' eggs or, later, what survived long enough to become chicks. In the seashore park you need an environmental impact statement to shoot a fox, while you can hunt them for twelve months elsewhere in Massachusetts. They closed vehicular use of Wood End, a spot that hundreds had been utilizing for shore fishing, then bitched mightily when Race Point grew "too crowded" with all the surfcasters they had displaced through their own regulation. They closed the beach south and east of High Head, when few fishers had any interest in going there. When you look at what was done to keep Americans off of America's beaches, you can't help but realize that if they'd spent a like amount on the actual striped bass, we might not have lost them.

Once lines are drawn, the idea in any dispute is to win over the larger group of unconcerned citizens, those who neither know nor ever cared about the issues. Within this group, superficialities govern people's decisions. It made no difference that surfcasters had never sought to catch their stripers and blues in the dunes. I doubt that anyone professing to be concerned about shorebirds—terns, plovers—really looked beyond the consideration that the species were endangered, except to say that the beach buggies were running them over. The idea was to build a case of innuendo and emotionalize it by emphasizing the death of *babies,* the chicks, while blaming every conceivable ill in the shore environment on the fishermen. The cry over much of Cape Cod was that the beach buggies had to go.

That area from the base of the dune to the crest of the beach is the only part of the Cape Cod National Seashore that is of interest to the beach fisherman. But a "dune buggy" is a joyriding device—usually a Volkswagen with a fancy-shmancy body—used mostly by those interested in vehicle performance. The more these folks can use the dunes, the bigger the challenge—and the fun. The dunes, however, are environmentally fragile. When vehicles are misused, bearch erosion accelerates. Critics know these things, but it's more convenient to avoid any clear separation between the bad and the harmless. Users of what soon became known, through a deliberate mixing of terms, as "dune buggies" further degraded any shred of respect that surf fishermen might have garnered. Once we could see it happening, some of us began to curse and decry every irresponsible salesman who sought to sweeten his sales commissions by use of the term *dune buggies* followed by a list of where they were allowed, and the seashore park was on that list. While entirely different, dune buggies and beach buggies became thought of as the same. Guilt by association was inevitable after that.

The Cape Cod surfcaster was further victimized by poor regulation, which led him to sin. When most of the users of the beach got there in the late 1960s, beach trails wound like a maze through the dunes. You could hear the water breaking on the beach and still ended up driving miles before seeing it. The winding trails, largely created by dune tour operators who took tourists out to see the beach, served no purpose except to invite irresponsible destruction of the fragile dunes from those who didn't even have an interest in going on the beach. When the park service took over in the 1960s, one of the first things they did was to close a straight track leading two-tenths of a mile down to the water, known then as "Joe Drew's Hill," then created four miles of tracks in the dunes. Later they complained when people didn't stay on those tracks, fortifying their efforts to banish beach vehicles with more botany and marine biology studies. Where went the sensitivities that should have taken into account the guy who works all his life to raise a family or winds a fishing rod all winter to rekindle the dream of just one good night in the striper surf? You have to love hearing, feeling the heightening contempt in your gut, buzzwords like *multiple use, local customs, recre-*

ational opportunity, which park managers used to dignify their positions. The frightening part was the growth of the we/they atmosphere on the Cape among cause-oriented socialites who—rather than trying to solve the discord—viewed every environmental conflict as a reason for coming together over wine and cheese.

The beach from which we cast into a fishless sea was shrinking while the so-called producer states hauled the last of the 1978 year-class—which could have, if only wisdom had prevailed, saved our Striper Coast from itself. During midwatch hunts for stripers, we listened to oldies on the radio while taking turns on some lonely point that was lacking both fish and fishermen. At times we told each other the same stories of days when the world had been both young and productive, of when the kids were with us. How Carol had always tried to be the mom and Dickie the dad. Joyce used to fall silent, often not answering me when I brought up a time that stirred her memory. How could she do this when, in those same stories, she had so often finished my sentences? There is no preparation for something like that. We all know that distress lurks in the deaths of our loved ones; we know that there is risk in everything that engages us, or in which we choose to engage. But to me it seemed as though the departures had taken place in concert with some conspiracy for which there was neither training nor warning. The despair was heightened by the experience of once having been so good at what we did. Just when I thought that it could get no worse, it got freaking awful.

A form letter from the IRS arrived late that summer, almost a year after Tom Rodericks had called to tell me my name was on a list. They had the seventy-five hundred dollars in fish money from 1977 listed as "unreported income." Then came an identical form for 1978 for about the same amount—again, "unreported income." I called my insurance man who was a law student; he said he didn't know what I should do, but maybe I should get a tax accountant. As I began to perspire, he added, "I guess they put people in jail for that. You'd better get some help."

The prominent local attorney who ended up representing me, whose specialty was real estate, met with me for an hour in his office. Gasping at the figures on the IRS forms, he pointed out that there were people working in local factories who didn't earn that kind of money in a year.

"All we can do is plead ignorance. That you didn't know that taxes were required on, as you say, fooling around fishing."

"Am I going to jail?" I asked.

"I would doubt that, but you are supposed to pay taxes. It is income."

"Everyone at the beach always said that fish money is part of the underground economy. If they start taxing fish money, every sport fisherman in the country will begin writing off his pleasure boat."

He began to laugh. "Frank, don't even bring up the notion of an underground economy. You had the income and you have to pay the taxes, plus penalties, plus interest. And be glad to get out of this with your freedom so that you can go fishing again."

I had always kept a log of our activities. Along with the obvious fishing nuances—time, tide, wind direction and intensity—I had records of poundage and dates. My counselor asked that I bring it to any meetings with the IRS.

"Let's ditch the freaking logbook. Why make it easier for them to screw me?"

"Frank, that logbook is evidence and I'm an officer of the court."

"Aren't you working for me?"

The lawyer made a funny noise as though he was trying to say that I was being difficult. Then he took a deep breath and said, "Just bring the log. If the auditor asks to see it, show it to him."

By the time we got to the stone office building that housed the IRS, I was about soiling myself with fear. When we got inside, we went to the office number listed on our notice. The auditor was not a *he* but a disarmingly attractive *she*. When I rolled my eyes, my lawyer pretended not to notice either her or my noticing her. After introductions, she left the room to fetch my folder. He stuck his finger in my chest and whispered: "This woman is an official auditor for the Internal Revenue Service. If you so much as look at her again like that, or look cross-eyed, you are going to be screwed beyond your wildest dream. Do you understand that, Frank?"

Then she came back, sat at her desk, opened the folder, and looked directly at me.

"Mr. Daignault, our records show that for 1977 you were paid about seventy-five hundred dollars by a fish packer in Provincetown for fish that you landed there. Do you contest this?"

"Mr. Daignault admits to having unreported income for that year and does not wish to contest the IRS's findings on this matter," said my attorney.

"Mr. Daignault, are you aware that failure to report such income, this income from fishing, is a federal offense punishable with a fine or prison?"

Just as I was about to answer, my lawyer put his hand on my knee and said, "Ma'am, Mr. Daignault is in agreement with the Revenue Service's findings on this matter and willingly intends to pay any and all taxes, penalties, and interest that the IRS deems to be appropriate."

She settled back into her chair, put her pen down, and looked at me as though she sought to reduce the formality that had begun to stiffen the proceedings.

"I am willing to adjust your fishing income so as to take into account any normal and incidental expenses."

Then she paused—waiting, it seemed, for one of us to say something about what it cost for the catching of these fish. Translating, my look, she then told me more plainly that I could list deductions related to the cost of fishing. But I really didn't get it, and they could see it on my face.

"For instance, Mr. Daignault, we will permit you to deduct your boat and the cost of its operation from your taxable income."

"We don't use a boat. We're surfcasters."

"Well," the auditor added, "you can amortize the cost of your nets."

"We're surfcasters, ma'am, we don't use nets."

Her impatience rising, the auditor slid farther back in her chair, the squeak of its rollers breaking the silence in the office.

"There has to be something about this operation of yours, Mr. Daignault, that I don't understand. How does one take just under four tons of fish to the dock with neither a boat nor nets?"

The lawyer looked at me, waiting for me to answer. By now, however, I had learned that the drill was not to answer whenever I was spoken to. Still, neither of them had any clue what we did, so when he nodded the okay, I explained.

"There were five of us, but there used to be six, but Dickie grew up and is in the Coast Guard. What we do is go down the beach and spread out and cast plugs, and sometimes flies, into the surf until we find the stripers. Once beached, we hit them on the head with a bat and throw them into the buggy. You have to know how to fish and hurry when the fishing is good. Your success is very dependent upon knowledge of the natural world, a willingness to work hard, and observation of the conditions that the fish like—that make the fishing good. When the girls, our daughters Carol, Susan, and Sandra, and my wife, Joyce, do really well, we have a better load to take to the dock for sale."

"Ah," the auditor said, "a buggy? What is a buggy? Is this a vehicle utilized in your fishing?"

"Yes, ma'am, I guess you could say that it's like a boat."

"Do you use this, this buggy, every night in your fishing?"

"It's a must."

"How much gas does it take to run this vehicle?"

"About eight dollars per night on average."

"How many nights?"

"Eighty or ninety."

"We'll use eighty-five . . . How long would a vehicle like this one last?"

Thinking *ten years,* I started to speak when I was nudged under the table.

"Three years."

"We'll depreciate for three years. Let's discuss equipment. Surely there is equipment involved in this, this commercial-fishing endeavor." Her eyes rolled as though she had never been involved in anything quite like this.

"We buy about one surf rod per season, and what I do is sell a pint of blood—I'm a professional donor—to the hospital for twenty-five dollars. Then we buy a Penn 704 reel, which costs about twenty-five dollars with what we call the blood money."

"I would just as soon not get into that. Let's call that one a wash," said the auditor.

"I also have the girls—well, not my wife—on bonus, which acts as incentive when they get tired."

"Bonus? Incentive?"

"Yes," I pointed out, "nights when the fishing is good and I want to keep them in the surf, I put them on bonus so that they get credit for everything they catch. The first hours I give them 20 percent of the fish money. Later, when they begin to sag from the hour and the work, I put them on double bonus. By the end of the summer, the girls have a pretty good nest egg, close to a thousand."

"Do you have any record of this?"

Leafing through the log, I stopped at a back page where there were a bunch of entries listing the twins' names with amounts of about $690 each. I pushed it across the desk for the auditor to examine. After seeing the figures, she wrote something and looked up at me.

"That's not your income. It's theirs."

"Yes, ma'am, you're right."

"Let me have a minute with this," the auditor said.

She asked me to leave the office and apparently put her head together with my attorney. Later, he told me that bonus money paid to the girls would be deducted from the original amount, and that we were getting gas money and 33 percent depreciation on the buggy, a 1977 Blazer, which had cost six thousand dollars new. The twenty-five I got for selling my blood to the hospital was income but that never went any farther. We agreed to the same setup for 1978, and the figures came out largely the same. Here is what I received a few weeks later:

Explanation of Adjustments—Tax Year 1977
Income fishing—$6121
   Expenses—$3188
   Adjustments—$2933
   Increase in tax because of adjustments—$1164
   Self-Employment Tax—$220
   Penalty*—$58
   Interest—$210
Amount owed—$1652
*Since the underpayment of tax is due to negligence or intentional disregard of rules and regulations, a penalty of 5 percent of the underpayment is added to the tax.

At the time the going rate for most attorneys was fifty dollars per hour, and some of the better ones even got seventy-five dollars. My lawyer had spent an hour in his office with me, studied my situation for an hour, and accompanied me to the audit for three hours. As a result I was braced for the hefty fee that I figured would amount to enough choke-a-horse folding green to leave no change from five hundred dollars. I was wrong. His bill was fifteen hundred dollars.

Of course the social ramifications of the "Big IRS Roundup" had all the surfcasters and surfcaster wannabes pushing and checking each other to brag that they were on the IRS hit list. It was a little like being a war hero. The ones who bragged the most about being "rounded up" by the Internal Revenue Service had really been bypassed as unworthy of attention. (Less delicately, they didn't catch enough for the IRS to bother with.) Nearly all the Cape fishermen who were actually brought in were boat fishers, because it has always been accepted that they were the ones who hauled the lion's share of stripers. Between the P-Town wire jiggers and the Billingsgate murderers, it was really never a list of surfcasters. For that reason those of us who had *really* been through it could spot the phonies at rifle range. Even when Tom Rodericks had called me that time, he had said that the list of Cape fishermen were all boat except for me and some guy from Pennsylvania whose name they had put a line through, apparently because he was passed on to another IRS region for pursuit. *Pennsylvania, Pennsylvania,* I was thinking. *PWB? That freaking nerd? The IRS got PWB, the whaler?* Naw, I thought, then began to laugh.

Anyway, that next year on the beach—and you could spot him a mile away due to his funny walk—I approached Allan and asked if he knew anything about the big IRS roundup. He began to blush like a hillbilly. One look at him and you could tell that nobody ever suspected that *he* was a highliner. Then, in my best Swede inflection, I said, "You fooking murderer." We laughed together. All the while I was thinking that PWB was a piece of work, and—much as I hate to say this—I was beginning to like him.

Whenever a situation is in decline, you will notice how everybody digs back into the past. More and more, those few of us who were on the beach would stand around in circles, smoking and reminiscing. Townies, except for Conrad and Buck, were gone. We had fish in 1977, Nauset had them in '78, and no one had them in '79. Freaking bluefish. Many of the regulars had stopped calling them blues and had gone to disparaging references such as "a school of scumbags." Surfcasters began to skip weekends, and there were fewer vacationers from New York. We used to say that if we could hit them somewhere it would be so nice to have them to ourselves. Yet it was also bigger news when stripers were found.

One night in late July, a local guy fishing near Joyce and me at Chatham Inlet took a fish, and he saw us with a few. It would not have been a big deal in the old days—yes, old days, three years before. The following night it was old-home week. All I could think of was that movie *The Longest Day*, where the beachmaster is standing on the beach with his dog, tanks and armor off-loading the LSTs in Normandy. Keep moving. Get on with it. Everybody was there. Around ten there was some sudden movement in the moonlight, perhaps a hundred feet over from us. One of the casters had thrown a punch at another, which apparently had missed its mark. When the guy who'd started it tried to run away, the other fellow speared him with the butt of his surf rod at the small of his back; the runner went down like a stone, crawling off into the darkness. I could tell that it was Disco Danny who was still standing but I couldn't tell who had started it. Within a minute the first guy, the puncher, came back all apologetic and, holding his hand out, said, "Listen, this is crazy. If we can't fish here together, what good is it all?"

Danny, glad to see an end to it, stepped from the water to shake hands with him. From where I was, from what I could see, they seemed to be ready to hug each other, and I was relieved that it was ending well. Suddenly the guy butted Disco Danny with his forehead, causing him to fall to his knees with both hands on his face, the blood pouring from his nose like a fountain and running down between his fingers.

As I went over to help Danny, the guy who had told anyone on the Cape who would listen that I was a knife fighter brandished a hand gaff because he thought I was going to enter the fray. Two men, one with a weapon, who had no issues facing them at the threshold of eternity, stood side by side and watched while Disco Danny bled and writhed in the storied Cape Cod surf. I thought, *What the hell are we doing?* Here we were pounding and suckering one another for the privilege of being the one who could kill the very last striped bass. Joyce, having heard the commotion to her left, came over. She gasped when she saw the amount of blood mixed with the tears forced by the blow of a broken nose. She began to cry, and because she was crying I began to cry, and I knew that these "men" must have thought it humorous that we could care so much about one another when we were, after all, hardly acquainted. I didn't understand. Still don't.

The desperation of our efforts to find linesides may best be illus-
trated by a night when we had put more bass into our buggy than
we'd seen all season. We had five, all better than twenty-five pounds,
all at the inlet in a span of a few minutes. Given the way the rods had
gone down in sequence, I was convinced that the fish were moving
left to right, coming with the tide toward Pleasant Bay. The best way
to get ahead of them was to move the buggy west toward the end of
the beach, so I whistled Joyce in and we moved without benefit of
headlights. It was new moon, foggy, high at midnight; the tide was
full so that the whole seascape was level—water and sand. Driving
around the rear of the buggies lined up at the inlet without lights, I
felt a lurch on the right side of the vehicle that was foreign to me.
Before I could figure out what had happened, we were drifting and
sinking in eleven feet of water. Joyce and I went out the windows,
with water starting in at the bottoms of them, seconds before the
buggy sank and that leaden feeling of having nearly gotten killed hit
me. Most of all, it was just one more experience that made me ask,
What are we doing here? Why are we doing this?

The next day, after having been given a ride back to P-Town to
our big camper rig, Joyce and I feasted on a lobster that Joe Crow
had brought to us from one of his pots. We drank too much wine,
made love, and stopped surfcasting long enough to think about
where we were going—and to be thankful for where we had been,
and having each other. At one point, late at night, in the candlelight
of our camper—remember, we had been in the habit of fishing all
night—I raised my glass, thankful that we had used that last year of
depreciation allowed by the IRS.

In Provincetown Joe Crow had heard that the rangers were planning a raid on the over-sand self-contained vehicles the next day.
Ours had not moved in weeks, and I had doubts about the battery.
We had stayed on so long with a bunch of fake passes that the sand
had built up on one side of the wheels—the sou'west side. With all
the days we had left on the books, there was no point in taking a
chance on getting caught with a fake pass. The rangers are like the
IRS in that once they catch you, they have reason to watch you more
closely afterward. So the day Joe warned us we jump-started the old
corn binder with cables off Joe's chase and went through the motions
of going to the dump—watering and gassing up, putting the rig

through its paces. We renewed our pass with that disgusting, pompous, in-triplicate chief boatswain mate and started out onto the beach. About two hundred feet down the back dune road, the whole side of the exhaust manifold blew out, the noise resembling the sound a bunch of hawg Harleys. When you don't know where a sudden loud noise comes from, it can really startle you. Once I realized what had happened, I decided not to take the rig out on the beach, so we started backing up. Once I saw the sand across the road, I knew that it was time for me to swing the steering wheel and brake. When I did that, the brake lines on the back burst from corrosion and the pedal went to the floor. To use a line from one of the boatmen coming back from town and doing the same thing we'd been doing before the big raid: "Frank, that truck has had it."

That day we nursed the camper off the beach, exhaust fumes in the cab with no brakes, double clutching and downshifting into low, low, then shutting off the key. We made it into the backyard of a friend in town, parked it behind the barn, and set it there for good. While the big raid was being executed on the beach, we walked to the Provincetown Ford dealer, looked around the showroom, and bought a brand-new Bronco, a red one. What the hell, we could depreciate it over three years now that the IRS had put us in business as commercial fishermen.

We ended the season with roughly three thousand dollars worth of fish, and our poundage was awful. I used to stare at the logbook, wondering what I could conclude from the declining numbers, wondering how many times something could be cut in half before we could actually fish for nothing the entire season. At tax time, I used all the numbers that I had learned in the audit. There was $3,100 of depreciation on the Bronco, ninety-three nights at $8 per night, $150 worth of tackle, the annual beach permits for both Nauset and P-Town . . . which all added up to a *loss* of over $1,000. I would have asked my lawyer if he thought I could assess the government for penalties and interest because they owed us money, but I feared he might soak me another fifteen hundred to answer. Why look for trouble?

13

THE LAST HURRAH

During the summer prior to the start of their third year (2/c), Coast
Guard cadets are sent to five two-week training programs, one of
which is flight school. Even cadets who do not aspire to flight operations attend. Many of them are turned on to flying as a result of the
experience, while others hate it and rule it out. While it is mostly
classroom training, the trainees do get up with a qualified pilot, jump
from helos into water to simulate rescues, and experience the
"dunker," the most feared part of school, having heard all about it
long before getting there.

A shell of the main compartment of a helo is used—no rotors or
extras—to simulate the inside of a helicopter with seats. Held on a
slide, it's dropped into the water with four cadets or so strapped in
and wearing flight suits and helmets. Dive instructors are not present in the helo; rather, they are in the pool awaiting the drop, when
the shell goes down with a splash and the compartment fills with
water. Naturally, cadets have been instructed in advance on how to
get out safely—but it still scares the daylights out of most of them.
They have to let the compartment fill up first, all the while holding
their breath and allowing the water to go over their heads before
releasing the safety straps. If cadets release the straps too early, the
rushing water pushes loose bodies about within the compartment,
often causing injury to others or bringing about a loss of orientation.
An added vertigo complication is that they often spin or flip the unit

so that the passengers are no longer straight up when they go under—a real-world situation.

Cadets have been instructed on the location of escape hatches as well as other nuances of the situation, but fear itself is the lion that needs taming. Once they find the escape hatch—and *if* they've managed to keep from puking and know which way is up—out they go to the surface, where they are greeted by the applause of fellow cadets yelling their support while dreading their own turn.

Commonly, one or two of the cadets will really freak, and the divers have to come and pull them out. Small wonder—these are men and women aged nineteen to twenty-one, hearts pounding, scared half to death. Volunteers go first, but they all have to do it eventually. They are allowed to go again, and many do. Even if they're labeled "crazies," by now they have learned that experience can ease their fears. Susan went twice.

SUMMER 1981, ON THE BEACH   That season a hard-core could average one striper, weighing well over thirty pounds, per week. Anyone who caught two such fish from shore was in for some ribbing for taking more than his share. Keep in mind that anybody in this discussion was fishing every night. There were frequently a few small fish—in the two- to or three-pound range, from the 1978 year-class—in places like the Pamet River, but most of us, having gotten used to cows, left them alone. In September, after Joyce and I had gone back to work, there was a pre-autumn blitz at Nauset Inlet.

Nauset Inlet is the outflow that flanks the north end of Nauset Beach and allows the exchange of water in Orleans Town Cove. Twenty years earlier, locals had managed to have the big campers thrown out of there because these so-called squatters spoiled the residents' view of the Atlantic. Beach people like us had less of a habit of fishing there because, in addition to being unwanted, the longer ride to Chatham Inlet at the south end of Nauset proved more productive. Townies, on the other hand, could drop in for an evening without running the entire beach. A consequence of this traditional use separation was that townies got very possessive about Nauset Inlet. It became "theirs," and the less desirable Chatham Inlet, which was a long way down the beach, was relegated to those of us considered outsiders. Eventually, as locals increasingly became interested in the fishing, they pressured selectmen to elevate the popular spot to a town beach, which changed its designation from "public right-of-way" to a new "super public right-of-way" for residents only. Signs warning of the restrictions were placed partway down the hill—anyone who didn't know how to get there was not going to find it easily. My old friend Edward "Moose" Dobwado, who fished there out of a camper and was one of the people ejected from the area as a nonresident, used to like going in there with a short vehicle. He would often say, "It was all right for me to go to Korea, though. I wonder how many of us would have been willing to go to Korea had we known that back home they were developing two kinds of public for their rights-of-way. I'll just give them one of my Bronze Stars if they give me trouble and I'll still have a few left for the rest of the week." There were complaints about nonresidents breaking the rules by going in there, but, as you might expect, if the striped bass called, we could hear them too.

When the small blitz hit Nauset Inlet, the locals, seeing outsiders in on the fishing, went crying to the Orleans police about the out-of-towners taking their fish out of their private town beach. One result—in addition to tarnishing my memory of what a garland of Striper Coast jewelry Cape Cod had been—was that the police patrolled the spot for the rest of the season, busting outsiders. I doubt that even a Congressional Medal of Honor would have helped.

OCTOBER 1981, NAUSET BEACH   The Friday night when we got there, four-wheelers were spread the full length of the beach and the surfcasters were all in the water—strong indication that things were in full-scale blitz. It was still light, and birds hovered all along the outside, changing positions quickly, then suspending themselves again. From what some of the people there said, this was the third night that big stripers had slid in over the foam-laced outer bar to hammer eight-inch sand eels. As daylight subsided, great fish moved along the dark sloughs in small pods, six here, ten there, chancing the foam-capped emerald shallows to ingest the bait. They were big fish—forty, fifty, sixty pounds—and one of them took a live eel as it swam. Then, immediately sensing something wrong, it blew the eel out into the suds—and a caster on the beach set on a surf rod into the wind. Within seconds another bass seized the same eel firmly, and this time when the rod came back it arced hard over, forcing the reel's drag to give up line. It was the stuff of stripermen's dreams, with some fishers landing two or more over fifty pounds—after waiting a lifetime in whispered prayer for *one*.

In the dim light of sunset, I saw a fish lost and another landed, beaching a forty-six- and a thirty-three-pounder myself; the latter was to be the smallest fish that I would see all weekend. A stranger passed me while fighting a lineside, which was later weighed in the low fifties, and he said that the night before he had one fifty-nine. Later, PWB, who was fishing with Buck (who as far as I knew had never fished Nauset before), told me that fifty-pounders had been taken steadily all week, with even a few sixty-pounders thrown in. *I don't think so,* I thought. Fifty pounds is a magic mark, a hallowed ground of striperdom, the point at which you run to the taxidermist before breaking out a vintage celebration. When you take a fifty-pounder you have satisfied a dream, something you never really thought would happen. Now this gilt-edged mark of excellence was being tossed around as though it were an everyday affair. It was hard to believe—and of course there were many exaggerations. After all, the fishing was good, but the people doing the fishing were the same ones I had known for a long time; there was no reason to trust or believe them completely. There were no forty-eight- and forty-nine-pounders, despite there being every number below and above those. One vehicle with fish, which I was asked to look at, was purported to have *five* fifty-pounders and had none. In contrast, confirmation for fifty-pounders was less important for surfcasters who had multiple numbers of them, making it more difficult to actually measure what had been caught. I know that two linesides over sixty pounds were beached by others—I weighed one of them. The local taxidermist Wally Brown, was commissioned to mount four bass over sixty that week. A wild guess at the number of fifty-pounders—still more than from any situation ever known in sport fishing—would be sixty or more such fish. Still, it was quality, not quantity. Some experienced fishless weekends that October on Nauset Beach. I had one ten-hour period without a hit and averaged only a single contact for each four-hour period.

The notion of *contingents,* a family or river-of-origin group of outrageously big stripers, has gained credence in scientific circles. Ten days before the Nauset Beach event, Wally Brown had received a similar number of inquiries for taxidermy from Martha's Vineyard, and I also had a charter skipper there tell me that at least fifty bass of more than fifty pounds had been taken from both shore and boat—a full ten days earlier than what had happened at Nauset. It's highly unlikely that these migrating stripers would have ventured *north* in autumn. It would follow, then, that we could safely postulate the existence of two such groups of memorable stripers. Sometime in the late 1980s—we weren't there—there was a similar November blitz on Block Island. Huge, really outrageous, linesides were never again seen in numbers—only in Joyce's dreams and in mine; only during Buck's final fitful nights before he died of AIDS five years later; only in the tall stories that PWB would someday tell his grandchildren.

That winter letters addressed to both Susan and Sandra arrived from the Internal Revenue Service. Identical to the form letter we had received a couple of years before, they complained about the fact that both had failed to file for and disclose 1978 "Fishing Income"—the bonus money on which the auditor said I didn't have to pay taxes. Included with the material was an investigator's phone number; I called him that day because that IRS return address puts a knot in your stomach when you find it in your mailbox and it doesn't go away until you either pay up or leave the country. I couldn't call my lawyer for obvious reasons, but a teacher at work had told me that kids earning under a certain amount didn't even have to file. So I took a chance that if I pretended to know what I was talking about, maybe I could hornswoggle the investigator into believing I knew the rule. Why shouldn't I? Those people had already proven that if they could come down on your side, they would. I told the investigator that as twin seventeen-year-old schoolgirls earning less than a thousand dollars, they didn't have to file. The investigator paused for a moment, then asked their ages again. After that he excused himself and told me that he would take care of it, that I was right—they did not have to file.

The prospects of starting the following season in a buggy that lay dead in a friend's backyard in P-Town were less than exciting. The future of striper fishing was gloomy; few fish had been born since the one, hopeful young-of-the-year index of 1978—and that had been cleaned out before any of them had a chance to migrate so that we Yankees could kill them.

Having always wanted to fish for Atlantic salmon, we fished in Maine on the Penobscot for a couple of weeks. Having spent my life fishing at night, I didn't even know what sunscreen was and picked up an awful burn. Joyce had a salmon come up in slow motion and take her fly, pulling line off the reel in a smoking run. Once in the shallows she said slyly of the nine-pounder, "How much can we get for it?"

And I, trying not to offend, and desperate to either retain or, at the very least, restore her sensitivities about salmon fishing, sought to point out gently that salmon were never meant to be killed nor marketed by sport fishermen.

"Then what's the point?" she continued, enjoying my discomfort.

Now came the price for what we had done. Now came the pain of having always had a place in the scheme of things. Now came the void of having been striper fishers without stripers. Who but the buffalo hunter misses the buffalo most? We were not alone. Along the full length of the Striper Coast, the winds of change affected those among us who had cared the most and who, at the same time, were admittedly most responsible for the dilemma.

CHICKAHOMINY RIVER, MARYLAND, AFTER DARK, LATE APRIL 1982

They came against the current in water so shallow that their movements made the surface of the river bulge as they sought a suitable place where soon the water would boil with their mating. The females, heavy with eggs, were pressed by the noses of the smaller males below, causing a pale ribbon of pearls to emerge and mix with milt in the darkened gloss of a sweet-water river miles from tidewater. Later, tiny striped bass would emerge from the eggs into the river, where they would grow and make their way downstream past decaying docks, under bridges, past eelgrass-laden tidal marshes to the Chesapeake. The process, with varying degrees of success, was repeated in the Choptank, Nanticoke, Mattaponi, and Rappahannock, each yielding its offering to the largest estuary in North America, the third largest in the world.

In order to predict the future of striper fishing, the Maryland DNR conducts annual young-of-the-year seining surveys to count the little striped wonders born that season. Figures were only average that year, but it was a better count than had been seen in the previous four. Once data were digested by the scientific community and made known to sport fishers, we all wondered if we were getting another chance after having failed to protect the moderate results of 1978. Here time was of the essence, because two years from hatch-out these pan rocks would suffer the same fate that Chesapeake watermen had been and were still imposing upon those born four years earlier. First-time migrants would suffer a similar fate to the north. Call it "sustainable yield" or "traditional use"—when they're all that's left, they need care.

The 1984 Atlantic States Marine Fisheries Commission (ASMFC) Interstate Striped Bass Management Plan, after its Amendment 2 in late '84, required a 55 percent reduction in harvest by striper states. Under the federal ban, soon to be known as the moratorium, states that did not conform would not striper fish—sport or commercial—at all. This touched off various efforts at conformity. Massachusetts limited sport fishing to two fish, each a twenty-four-inch minimum. Rhode Island closed sport fishing entirely but, once they saw their neighbors still fishing, they reopened in July. Maryland, and later Delaware, declared stripers a threatened species and moved to impose a ban on the "taking, possession and sale of Chesapeake Bay stripers effective January 1, 1985." This was a far cry from Maryland's initial efforts to *raise* their size limit to fourteen inches a year before. Nevertheless, fifty thousand pounds of stripers were harvested by Virginia, a "producer" state drawing from the 1982 year-class, during the first three months of 1985. Such events, in addition to being highly distressing, also serve as a reminder that striper protection was a new endeavor.

Under Amendment 3 it was clear that the efforts to protect the 1982 year-class females needed teeth so that those fish could spawn at least once. The benchmark for declaring Chesapeake Bay stocks "restored" was a three-year running average in the young-of-the-year index of 8. After that striper states continually raised size limits intended to keep the minimum larger than the ever-larger females of 1982. It wasn't long before people were catching linesides of nearly eighteen pounds that weren't large enough to keep—a phenomenon that gave rise to a new term on the Striper Coast, *keeper*. At that time you needed two hands to throw the fish back.

By the mid-1980s people were arrested in Connecticut for marketing stripers while surfcasters slashed one another's tires on Block

Island for the privilege of shipping the same stripers to market. One year before, linesides had been sold on Cape Cod with a single restriction—a sixteen-inch size limit. My, how things can change.

In the fall of 1985 tributaries of the Chesapeake Bay began receiving stocked juvenile stripers through a cooperative program of the Maryland DNR and the U.S. Fish and Wildlife Service. Designed to supplement natural reproduction, the five-year program was intended to release four- to six-inch fingerlings. By the end of the second year, however, 1.4 million linesides had already been liberated. So many federal hatcheries were involved in the plan that the 8.5 million fry (between nine and eighteen days old) that were needed to start the project had to be airlifted to hatcheries in Alabama, Georgia, North Carolina, Ohio, Virginia, and West Virginia.

In 1989 the Maryland young-of-the-year index skyrocketed, more than likely as the result of the seven-year-old females having spawned successfully in Chesapeake rivers. Nonetheless, when the index was determined, most of the juveniles had come from one site known as Hambrook Bar. The baby stripers for that location alone numbered 97—a whopping three times the largest overall index ever seen in their history of measurement. Clearly everyone involved had concerns over the validity of this count as a suitable measure when other locations in the survey had no juveniles at all. This best-in-nineteen-years survey—the second largest count ever recorded—touched off remarks by Maryland officials about lifting striper harvest bans; after all, they'd met the federal mandates of a three-year running average of at least 8. True, 1987 and 1988 had been lean, but the height of the 1989 index—set at 25—was enough to lift the average to management benchmarks for the relaxation of regulations. The cries of foul could be heard from Florida to the St. Lawrence. Commercial interests viewed it as a signal that fishing could resume; sport-fishing interests saw it as a return to overfishing based upon bad data. The event became known as "the anomaly at Hambrook Bar," which discredited the index as a sham sprung upon sport fishing by the Maryland DNR in order to get their watermen back into fishing. Sport-fishing interests sought to have the juvenile stripers seined at Hambrook removed from the survey. With that site discounted, the index would have dropped to 12—lowering the average to *below* the number required to relax the moratorium. Clearly sport-fishers wanted to retain protection and not relax the moratorium while there was still something left. Watermen wanted us to live up to the deal we had previously agreed to—an average of 8 as restored. Yet anyone who had not already been polarized in this situation could see the rules were changed after the fact. Years later, all that's really clear is that an awful lot of stripers came back.

Many of us, and who can say how many of us fish the striper surf, were very glad to see the stripers return. For those of us who remembered how to fish them, it was a chance to cover the old haunts, even run into the old friends we had known on the shore. Of course we try not to think about it, but as a result of the moratorium many regulars didn't come back—their age precluded participation in a young man's game. Others just died. A few of us had unaccountably been elevated to near-sacred status as veterans of the Cape Cod glory days. At sport shows I gave seminars that taught surfcasting for stripers, and people would walk up to me and say things like, "Uncle George from Nauset says hi." And I, who had no clue about whom they were speaking, would say something like, "And how is your aunt."

For me, though, the most important thing to return was the privilege of writing about surfcasting for stripers. All through the moratorium, editors had taken on a policy of not accepting any material about a fish—striped bass—for which it was not legal to fish. I kept my hand in scribbling by talking about trout and dropping in the occasional Latin nomenclature—*Hexagenia limbata*—that those guys like so much.

Slowly the stripers came back, and there were still enough bluefish to provide sport. The magazines began publishing articles about fishing for them all again and many surfcasters, a lot of them new to it, returned to the shore. A new crop of neophytes were, like their fathers and uncles before them, up to here in the striper surf. Do tell!

14

THE HAMMER BLOWS OF TIME

HALF A LIFETIME PASSED since our truck camper had begun its decay in Provincetown. With chipmunks and field mice nesting safely in the manifold of a very dead truck camper, Joyce and I had switched to trapshooting, skeet shooting, downhill skiing, steelhead, trout, and salmon fishing, as well as hunting. If you try to analyze it all, it's clear that these were all feeble acts of desperation after losing a life of high adventure in the striper surf. We were members of gun clubs, one of which cost more than most people earn in a month and where we also fished for trout that were as big as bluefish. In addition to the drastic change in our hair color—mine gray to white, and Joyce's from brown to salt and pepper—the passage of time had altered everything about us to which we could lay claim. Dick had come back from his hitch in the Coast Guard after hunting and fishing on Kodiak Island as a civilian for a year. There anglers took turns fishing while one of the others stood watch with a high-powered rifle against brown bears weighing half a ton. Carol, who had divorced and earned her RN nights at no small sacrifice, had two teenage daughters. The twins, who vowed to go separate ways to break that sameness from which twins so often suffer, had both been commissioned ensigns of the U.S. Coast Guard—Sandra from the Massachusetts Maritime Academy and Susan from the Coast Guard Academy. For us the beach was nothing more than a distant memory as we looked for other adventures.

Late in June, Joyce and I would drive north to Bangor to fish for Atlantic salmon on the Penobscot. Among others, I became one of the founding members of the Eddington Salmon Club by loaning them money so they could buy a clubhouse on the river. Think about it: Here I was fronting a salmon club with money earned through the sale of striped bass.

In this part of the salmon world, this particular river is considered to be a spring river, which means that the run takes place during the freshet, the snowmelt. Two factors draw the salmon from the Atlantic to the gravel of their birth: flow and water of a suitable temperature. Alone among the world's salmon rivers, the Penobscot draws them in spring. On May 1, opening day, everybody in the area, along with a few from as far away as Maryland and Pennsylvania, lines up his fly rod on racks in the order of their arrival and hopes to be the first to take a salmon from the river. The person who happens to experience the honor—providing that he's a Maine native—has caught the "presidential fish" and has the privilege of taking it to Washington and presenting it to the president. It is a distinction for which Mainers fish feverishly. However, I recall one spring when a Republican refused to take his salmon to a president who was a Democrat—or was it the other way around?—and the presidential fish had to be caught all over again, which, salmon being what they are, was not easy.

In Maine the therapists' waiting rooms are filled with salmon fishermen. The reason for this is that salmon are not at all like striped bass. Salmon don't eat, because their reason for being in the river is to party. Thus, there is continual frustration over seeing so many beautiful fish—and salmon, in my opinion, are the most magnificent creatures in nature—without being able to engage them in the combat to which anglers are accustomed. Gathering in "pools," which are places the salmon like, customarily stopping there to rest, the salmon will often lie for days before moving on to the next suitable spot. Pools are known so well to the salmon fishers that they have constructed racks for the rods and benches for the butts while each waits his turn to fish through, the rule being to make one cast and take one step. Those failing to keep track of their casts and their steps are known as "lead-footers." Most salmoneers are pretty honest about pacing their steps and casts equally. Still, when that big blue-and-silver salmon either rolls or leaps clear in the pool, it can sometimes be cast and cast instead of cast and step—a clear sign that, in addition to being a serious adversary, the salmon has corrupted many otherwise honest folks.

To any of us, most of the river—and the Penobscot is particularly perplexing because of its size—looks the same, so the salmon
pools would be hard to locate were it not for the established knowledge. At first, the pitfall is that many "folks from away" take one look
at those crowded benches that represent a two-hour first-cast wait
(while those who are fortunate enough to be fishing are being
encouraged to hurry) and say to themselves, *I'm not going to do that.
I'll just fish beyond the pool.* True, you can then just walk out of the
pool down to the river while the locals who are sitting on the bench
whisper about you derisively as being a "striper fisherman," but the
worst thing is that you're unlikely to catch a salmon.

With all the waiting inherent to fishing pools in rotation—and to
offering a fish that does not eat food in the form of a fly—someone
is bound to ask you about your background. If you say that you're a
striper fisherman, you may as well confess to your parents having
failed to marry prior to your conception. Still, whatever salmon fishers are, and they can be a lot of things, they are at least polite about
the revelation and, given enough hours warming a bench for one's
turn, there is a certain bonding. It's the salmon that are the bastards.

The Maine Sea-Run Salmon Commission was then stocking out
one million genetically superior native-strain salmon. These were
salmon with the advantage of thousands, if not millions, of years of
natural selection. Each race of salmon is different. For instance,
Norwegian fish, which can climb steep mountains and survive in
cold water, would more than likely not survive in Maine's warm
water. A true Maine native salmon has a better chance in rivers that
more closely resemble those of its ancestors. Now, for all these qualities, Maine celebrates only a one-half of one percent (0.005 percent)
return. One million are stocked out, and five thousand come back.
The cost is placed conservatively at two hundred dollars per salmon
returned to the river, and the salmon fishers catch only about a third
of them. Consequently, imagine having one in the shallows with your
fly in its mouth. While its gills are opening and closing, you're trying
to decide whether or not to keep it, and you are probably not conscious of the fact that it cost the Salmon Commission six hundred
dollars to get it there. Remember that it is the one in two hundred
survivor of Icelandic nets, seals, drought, freshet, lamprey, and cor-
morant. This is not a dumb fish rolling in the pool, raising your

blood pressure, keeping you awake at night (and which my wife suggested we sell to some local fishmonger for twenty bucks) that you are going to release—and that some might not believe you caught. Not one salmon on the planet can claim predictability. They will roll to tell you where they are; they will leap to look at the next obstructing dam long before they seek to mount it. One might stalk your fly, coming up to look at it repeatedly while never taking it. Then, once perfect celestial alignment has taken place, one will suddenly rush to the take and chase your offer. Meanwhile, you prepare another cast with the fly swishing on the surface in unplanned disarray, until the beast bumps your waders, driving you hell west and crooked toward the safety of the riverbank. Now let's talk about the most distressing part.

At least once per day on any Penobscot salmon pool, a caster will come tight from a take, heading from wader depth to the shore, shouting "fish on" as he goes. This is a signal to the others to crank in, go ashore, and get clear for the fellow's long-awaited fight. Ah, but there is something wrong. This "salmon" doesn't happen to exhibit the usual salmon behavior, and the caster is soon back to his spot in the rotation, disgustedly kicking stones the whole way, mumbling, "F—— striper."

For us this is an ever-present reminder of where we have been, what we have lived, and that to which we can never hope to return. As I try to forget what I have just heard, I cannot shake the memory of the then and how it relates to the now. I believe that part of the pain and disappointment is directly related to the measure of what we had once known. The greater it was then, the greater the loss is now. The contempt most salmon fishers exhibit toward stripers is particularly distressing for people like us. Any of Squid Beaumont's Rhody stripers could eat a salmon. With linesides coming back, it was never again necessary to salmon fish. Besides, it was strange to fish in daylight.

AUGUST 1991, CHARLESTOWN, RHODE ISLAND My high school sweetheart and I walked the beach with live eels exactly the way Butch and Norman had done more than twenty years before. Only for her the live-eel fishing here was abstract, because back then she had the responsibility of the kids and never had the luxury of fishing. A classic victim of the lackluster shore that Rhody uses to hide her striped bass, she was a Cape Cod surfcaster who'd been spoiled by the rips and fanciful bars of the well-structured striper surf. Joyce had never experienced good fishing on this beach and typically wondered about its potential. I instructed her in how we would "farm" this dismal shore.

"Go around and pass me after your retrieve, just like we did on the Cape," I urged.

But she was slow in her turn to retrieve the live eel, causing a break in our rhythm. Once, I looked over and she was dreaming of something else; the crank of her reel had stopped for the thought of who-knows-what. It was as though the world had forgotten striper fishing and some inscrutable power wanted me to taste it once more the way God had meant it. At sea, out toward Block Island, a commercial vessel fought the wind-tossed water, headed home perhaps with a load of hake or swordfish to the warmth of hearth and scent of new babies. I felt the cold of reality that I had become older, while reflecting upon the incessant feeling that I was walking in someone else's boots.

"Keep casting," I urged like an athletic coach. "You have it. It doesn't have you."

And she, getting the hint of a time when we had been young enough, vibrant enough, when life was simple and forever, laughed at my poking fun at who we were and where we had been, and got into the swing of it.

Just west of Split Rock the first take came to her. Not wanting to alarm me prematurely, she never told me of the contact. I found out when I saw her knees bent in classic Joyce style, her spinning rod groaning and line snapping off the spool. The curious thing was that now that I could do my coach routine, I didn't want to. The excitement of having a decent lineside on the go was the kind of excitement that tourists experience—what we had become.

Later I released a striper of roughly the same size, in the low twenties like hers. Around three, once certain that we had enough fishing, I killed what would end up being the last forty-pounder for a long time, going home with one fish, which was way more than we could use. Of course, the thought of taking a load to market to stow some folding green came over me before remembering that the moratorium had stopped all that. It was hard to adjust to the new thinking that once you have one to eat, the fishing, or the reasons for it, fades.

As victims of the moratorium, we sought other things to fill the void left by the striper drought.

We still fish the beach with more stripers than we have ever seen, but we have never been able to find the thing we once had.

That dawn we had cocktails at home after our first postmoratorium striper blitz. Four hours later, we were at the gun club shooting sporting clays, but our minds were not on shooting pairs of forty-mile-per-hour targets passing at once. Rather, all we could think about was the return of the striped bass. Waiting our turn at a station, we found it difficult to study the targets. Our conversation kept returning to the stripers on the beach while clay pairs flew past among the treetops in the ninety-five-degree heat. As each shooter took his turn and yelled "pull," the action of a launch mechanism sent them this way or that; the twelve-gauge would bark and recoil, smoking a target most, but never all, of the time.

After sporting clays there were the ritualistic bar drinks and dinner, the banter over a bad shot or a good one with people whom we had come to know in this new life. That night late, at home, just before bed, a crushing force developed across my shoulders as though a steel rod had suddenly been inserted while I fought to retain consciousness. When we arrived at the emergency room, a nurse, looking at me, called out for help as I lost consciousness.

While I lay on a table one of the nurses said, "Think of your pain as one to ten. What is your pain?"

Trying to say nine, I could not speak. I wanted to save my chance to use ten for dying.

"I am a nurse practitioner. Take this," she directed, as she put an aspirin in my mouth.

Then someone called, "TPA, stat!"

Whatever it was, they shot it into an IV and the practitioner asked me again, "One to ten. What is your pain?"

"Three. Three, Jesus Christ, three!"

Never have I ever wanted a cigarette more in the forty-two years that I smoked. That week in intensive care I awoke one day with one of my granddaughters calling out softly to me:

"Poppa? Poppa? How ya doin' Poppa?"

Sonovabitch, I thought, *I'm going to die.*

The guy in the next bed had. He'd been a big vaquero when they brought him in. He'd said that it was all a mistake, and he'd been misdiagnosed. He had reminded me of the cowboys we had spent our lives with on the Cape. A couple of days later they took him for a treadmill test and he came back white as a sheet. Just before I was released, he had disappeared. Nobody wanted me to know what happened, but I knew. The poor bastard had died. That really blows your sense of wellness. I would lie there thinking, *Son of a gun, we get the fish back at Charlestown and before I can call Beaumont to tell him that they stocked the pond I get a freaking heart attack.* Then there were the cigarette plans. We have all seen the butts standing in the white sand in those large ashtrays at the doors of the hospitals. It seemed to me that I could grab one on the way out, and—providing I had preacquired some matches—I could light it, a longer one without a filter, a Pall Mall or a Lucky.

Later that week they took me by ambulance to another hospital for what they called "catheterization," where they put a rigging needle in a place I didn't even know I had. While it was harmless, it was scary; I kept thinking of all the eels I had rigged over the years and that maybe it was payback time. Of all the things that were new to me, the realization that I had been in touch with my mortality probably bothered me the most. In an interview, my cardiologist asked what we had done leading up to the event and, tipping his head facetiously, said, "Let me see if I have this right. You fished all night and had cocktails at dawn. Then you slept four hours before going to the gun club to shoot all day in the ninety-five-degree heat *before* stopping at a gin mill for cocktails and greasy fish-and-chips and beer, smoking the whole time. Do I have that right? Don't answer. That was rhetorical. What I want to know is, why didn't you stop at a bordello between the beach and the gun club?"

Because I couldn't figure out if he was kidding or really miffed with me, I didn't answer.

The last morning at the hospital, as a male nurse wheeled me outside, I couldn't help but notice that there was no tall ashtray. I had asked him to forget the wheelchair but there was something in their protocols that required the process, and it was easier to go along than to make a stink. While Joyce went to get the car, a soft rain like the ones we had spent so many nights in, both on the Cape and the in Rhody surf, angled from a gray sky. It was one of those symbolic rains, the kind that make you think more than you should, the kind that remind you of the heightened tragedy of a heart attack when it is yours. We just waited there protected when it came to me that maybe I was being given another chance like the bass had been given. I was as scared as I had been when she had brought me in the week before.

"Wheel me out. Wheel me out from under this."

"Sir, it's raining."

"I know. Please."

In the parking lot, I tilted my head back to savor the cool moisture of a sky under which I had spent a lifetime to feel the release from the fear. I would not and did not ever smoke again.

Forget Charlestown and all the moby stripers that we had. All that stuff was replaced with a life without any real fishing. The cardiologist was opposed to all-nighters, saying that sleep was the heart's rest. About a week later, I received a greeting card that had followed me past two hospitals, always with a new forwarding address, full circle back to home.

> Dear Frank,
>
> It has been rumored on the beach that you've been sick. The old crowd from the Second Rip was particularly distressed by the news, until I told them that your ailments were caused at the hands of a jealous husband. Somehow, they seem to feel that it is more fitting that it be the case rather than any heart attack.
>
> Many of us from the old gang are still around except for Buck who died a couple of years ago. Carlezon was real sick for a while but he's back and very much the same, as are Swede, Froggie, Conrad, and the New Yorkers. We all go through the motions, and there are nights when we find a few, but it could never again be like it was when you and Joyce used to work Race Bar and the points. Some of the guys talk about what has changed, and the talk always goes the same way, and Conrad shuts down like he doesn't want to talk about it. Ah, but life, I'm sure you know, goes on and we can't go back.
>
> I am aware that being in a hospital with a heart attack or husband bruises (just kiddin') is a major bummer, especially for a guy like you, but you just have to ride this one out. I know. During my little fishing trip to 'Nam, there was a whole lot of s— coming at us all the time. There was the time when I felt a sting and then numbness, and the whole lower part of my leg was gone, and I kept looking at it and wondering, Jeeze, man, where did my leg go? They gave me something at the LZ and

I woke up at "D" Med at Dong Ha, and I was really bummed as I kept thinking about my leg. Then I realized that just about all the other guys in my ward were also from Con Thien where I had been hit. The nurse told me how many of them had lost both legs. I think she told me that so I would feel better because I at least had one leg, and it did make me feel better. Later, when I was being shipped home, there were caskets and body bags on the tarmac and I felt even more accepting of my situation. I tell you this because maybe in some small way I can make you feel a little better, like the nurse—and even seeing those caskets—did for me. I've been there, Frankie, and I know that when things go bad and you are in a hospital you think that the world is never going to get straight. But it will. You just have to wait. Write back something for the guys or I'll have to make up something. We'll be pullin' for you.

Semper, ma man,
Allan, aka "PWB" (Pennsylvania Wonder Boy)

Everything happening to us was scripted by a past of which we had been both benefactor and victim. Inspired by a life of adventure, we had remained connected to old times, as well as to one another, by our mutual experience. Our forty-five-year love affair had been spiced with an angel's gift of companionship. Even the hammer blows of time could not drive the characters of life's play from the set. Striped bass were coming back in numbers that no one had ever seen. There was always a way to fish the beaches, and we had been renewed by the return of the linesides. While forging our steps, every adventure had affected us in some way. Though few were acquainted with one another, somehow the people we had known were undeniably connected to each other through us. Indeed, if there is any detectable bond, it is the striped bass and the beaches that they ply. There is no better example of this inscrutable connection, this commonality that bound us all, than from the words spoken by a man who had been plucked from a storm-ravaged North Atlantic twenty years before when he had been rescued by mere boys. Those who saved him were following a tradition and keeping a promise that they had made when they took an oath in the Coast Guard. We had almost forgotten them all.

FROM THE PULPIT, UNION (CONNECTICUT) CONGRE-
GATIONAL CHURCH, OCTOBER 1995

I Believe in Miracles

I am very happy to be here today and to see all of you. For those
of you who don't know me, please allow me to introduce myself.
My name is Arno Groot, and I normally sit in the west corner of
the balcony with my wife, Janice. I was born in Den Helder,
Holland. In 1950, my father, with twenty-five dollars in his pocket, after missing the boat to Africa, decided to bring his family to
this land of opportunity.

I remember seeing the Statue of Liberty from the frigid deck
of our ship in New York Harbor. My journey in a new land was
starting. Our first home was a twenty-foot trailer down in Vernon
Circle. On my first day of school I came home crying. I told my
parents in Dutch, which was all I spoke, that no one understood
me, a problem my wife says I still have.

After college and the army, Janice and I were married here
in Union Church. We bought a house and had two beautiful
daughters, Rachel and Jennifer. I had a great job and our future
looked bright . . .

On August 8, 1975, a Friday, at the end of work, my father-
in-law, Dave Luginbuhl, and I went down to the company plane
to fly to Cape Cod to be with our vacationing family. The weather was marginal, but my instrument training qualified us to make
this trip that we had made so many times before. When we
departed Ellington at sunset, the weather over Rhode Island was
beautiful. But ahead to the east, the sky was dark and ominous.
Calling approach control, I set about the task of going to my initial approach marker for Provincetown Airport on the tip of Cape
Cod. Cleared to land, I started my final approach to the field.
Upon reaching the point where I should have seen the field, I did
not. So I executed a missed-approach procedure. I went back to
the initial approach point to try again, now having a better radio
fix, with an additional instrument. Again I came to the missed-
approach point to try again and looked out; nothing. Then I saw
the field and flew over and looked out my side window. After
bringing my attention back into the cockpit, I became disoriented.

I was out of control. My mind could not focus on the task at hand. I struggled. Before I could think, *Pull up*, there was a loud crash.

I felt at peace with myself, all was warm and quiet. Janice was there. "I love you, good-bye." Jenny was there. She told me she loved me. "Don't go. Don't go."

I popped up in the ocean and gasped for air. I felt my head, all gashed, my teeth and lips hanging, and I could not see out of one eye. My foot was dangling beneath me in the water.

Oh my God! I thought. A green aura came around me in the blackness of the raging storm-driven sea. Suddenly, right in front of me, up popped a section of the landing gear with the tire on it. *No, no, this can't be happening.* Pushing the tire away, I wanted to die. The tire came back. I grabbed it and held on. *Oh my God*, and seeing a lighthouse in the distance, I cried out. "Help, help. Help."

On the beach, fishermen heard my cries for help. Driving to the Coast Guard Station, they burst in and told the duty officer that an airplane had gone down near the lighthouse and that there were cries for help. The three lowest-ranking seamen there— David Kelley, Ned Rogean, and William Beard—were sent with a new and experimental piece of equipment, a thirteen-foot outboard-equipped rubber boat.

With beach fishermen showing the way, they dragged the new boat behind them to the beach where others had gathered, hearing my cries over the wind and roar of the ocean. They tried to launch the boat, but the surf washed them up onto the beach. Again they tried and again the sea washed them to the shore, wet and covered with tangled line and sand. Rogean said that there was only room for two in the boat, so Beard stayed and Kelley went. Again, they were washed up. The exhausted Coast Guardsmen were making a hopeless effort until a man named Frank, one of the surf fishermen helping with the launching, called, "Wait for the sea! Wait for the calm between the swells." Then Rogean and Kelley in the now half-deflated boat got the motor started, waiting for the word, when the surfcaster yelled, *"Now."* Everyone ran carrying the boat with the running motor, and they made it through the surf.

More than an hour had passed. I was locked onto the tire but could no longer cry out. I was not able to see the light anymore, and the storm was getting worse. And I thought, *I can't hold on anymore. I'm so cold. Oh, I'm so cold. I can't hold on.* I saw a light just before a black object suddenly came upon me. Then a hand reached out and pulled me up saying, "We've got you."

"Please find my father-in-law," I said.

"We have to get you back!" they exclaimed.

"Please find my father-in-law," I repeated.

"We have to go now," one of them said.

Suddenly the seascape was bathed in light, as all the buggies lit their headlights and one of the men holding on to me said, "Hold on, we're going to crash."

I felt the surf crashing around me, and many hands carried me out of the water while I still clung to the tire.

My wife and mother-in-law got the news at the Coast Guard Station that only one person was being brought off the beach. Janice said to her mother, "I hope that it's Dad." Her mother said to her, "I hope that it's Arnie." Dave's body was recovered the next day.

I spent the next several days waking up from one operation after another almost always seeing faces of friends and family. Was this a dream? No, my friends were really here every time I woke up. Some doctors wanted to amputate my foot while others struggled to save me at Rockville General. When, after forty days of recuperation from more surgery, I was told, "Okay, Arno, let's go for a walk," I said, "How will I start?" And the answer was, "One step at a time."

During the rest of my recovery at home, I had a hard time dealing with what had happened, causing me to turn to alcohol. With little regard for the well-being of those around me, I was at my lowest, testing God, seeing if He would let go. New Year's Eve I woke up out of a drunken sleep—sober! God was talking to me and I got the help I needed. With my life turned around, I have learned that "one step at a time" is how I try to live my life today. My personal tragedy brought about the reality of what it's really all about.

By sharing with you today, I hope the miracles in your life can happen without the tragedy. I ask that you think about the miracles that happened to me. How did I get out of the airplane? I believe that my father-in-law did it. Why didn't the sharks eat me? The tire that kept me afloat sank when thrown in fresh water. Why did the Coast Guard buy a new boat? It was destroyed and never used again. In the blackness of the ocean, how did they find me? The burning bush was not consumed. The Red Sea parted and the Israelites were saved. Jesus Christ was resurrected. I believe in miracles and most of all, I believe in you. Amen.

Arno Groot, Rhode Island Mobile Sportfishermen
(RIMS #33) aka "Short Cast"

The night that plane crashed in Provincetown, it never occurred to me that its pilot was a beach fisherman and that we had no doubt spent many nights in the Charlestown, Rhode Island, surf side by side without knowing it. He was just another person known as "Short Cast"—another faceless character of the striper surf with whom we might have shared a beer or a striper hot spot. A greater guilt came from the sudden insight that while we were having a good time, blitzing bluefish and carting stripers off to market, people like PWB were leaving their legs in obscure places—like Chu Lai or Pleiku—remembered only by those who had bled there. Every time that I recalled, yet always failed at the time to question, about Allan's funny, gimpy walk, the flush of overpowering guilt took hold of me. What would one of them have given for a night on the beach with us during that horrible time? Was it the realization that so many of us had forgotten about Vietnam that caused us to latch on to the catch-phrase, "Welcome home"?

MAINE, SUMMER 2001   It is as though someone else is fishing in Frank Daignault's boots while he thinks about all the time, all the people, and all the midwatch hunts for stripers. The man, fishing a greater autumn than the one in his cast, knows that having tasted youthful adventure, once youth is gone, so goes the adventure. We had a life on the Striper Coast, but we don't have it anymore. I choke up and chill with the realization that I have become, like every person from every generation, an anachronism. As I indulge in the joys of contemplation, I strain to establish who I was. Am I the man in my boots enriched with the sensitivities of age or the one thirty years younger who has seemed always to urge me on, pushing a four-wheeler along waterline trails or dragging his spoon through the cornflakes at variable speeds and depths? Yet, for all that I've learned about both myself and the striper surf we had come to love from years of ritualistic pursuit, I'm not yet able to define the still-blurred separation between compulsion and sport. A lifetime ago, when I told them to keep casting because we had the fish, I was wrong. We didn't have them; they had us.

HARPSWELL SOUND   Dedicated to the mission of having found stripers, we are bounding and skimming on our Susan's seventeen-foot center console. Checking the clip on my granddaughter's life jacket, I tell her that "Aunt Sue" is satisfied with herself, much as I am with the passing of a family torch. Our lovely granddaughter, who is nine, listens politely and grins when I tell her that we can hose her auntie Sue and her mama down, but we can't cleanse the stripers from their blood. As we head for our mooring under a lowering sun, and the piney fjordlike rock-studded shore of Harpswell Sound, I can't help but wonder how surprised the old gang would be if they could see me. As cultists of the striper surf, the squid stink and salt spray coursing through their veins, what would they think if they could see me fishing from a boat? I understand that the use of a boat is functional for some, but the surfcaster in me is alive and well. I know that no matter where I have gone, whether it was a river, a bay, or a beach over the horizon, no matter where I look, I cannot relive that fleeting time we once knew. Meanwhile, the sand and the salt drift in perpetuity from the wind and eastern tide, imposing minute decay upon the porcelain and galvanized steel of an old refrigerator in a dune break on Cape Cod that we had once thought would last forever.